SUPERHEROES

The Heroic Visions of
BORIS VALLEJO and
JULIE BELL

Text by Nigel Suckling

THUNDER'S
MOUTH
PRESS

Published in the United States by

Thunder's Mouth Press

An Imprint of Avalon Publishing Group Incorporated.

161 Williams Street, 16th Floor

New York, NY 10038

First published in Great Britain in 2000

by Paper Tiger

An Imprint of Collins & Brown Limited

London House

Great Eastern Wharf

Parkgate Road

London SW11 4NQ

Previously published as *Titans*

1 3 5 7 9 8 6 4 2

Library of Congress Card Number: 00-104003

ISBN 1-56025-273-1 [cloth]

ISBN 1-56025-339-8 [pbk.]

Editor: Emma Baxter

Designer: Paul Wood

Reproduction by Global Colour Ltd, Malaysia

Printed and bound in Italy by New Interlitho Spa

Distributed by Publishers Group West

Contents

Introduction 6

Spiderman 8

Marvellous Universes 26

Marvel Knights and DC Days 66

Avengers 82

X–Men 100

X–Women 128

X–Marauders 152

Introduction

(below)

BEAST

1995, Boris

Trading Card. Fleer Publishing Co.

TM & © 1995 Marvel Characters, Inc.

All rights reserved.

(right)

LADY DEATH

1995, Julie

Cover. Chaos!Comics

TM & © 1995 Lady Death

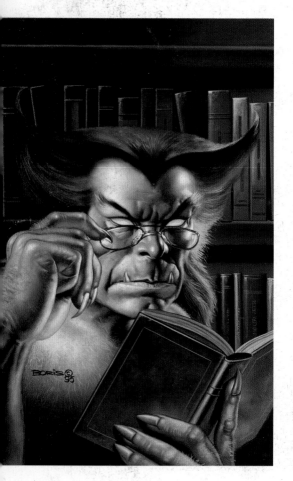

This is the definitive collection of Boris Vallejo and Julie Bell's comic book superheroes. There are a few other paintings that could easily have been included, but too few to matter. To Julie and Boris this feels like a complete set so far.

My first encounter with this dynamic painting duo came through being asked to write something for a portfolio of Boris' pictures. This was a slightly odd commission because I was no expert on either his work or this area of fantasy, but it was an interesting challenge so I said OK.

I was a bit nervous. From the gusto with which Boris wields a battleaxe in many paintings, I was expecting some prickliness from him at having a complete stranger being invited to introduce his pictures. In fact I was a little relieved to be doing it from 3,000 miles away. To my pleasant surprise, however, Boris seemed to like what I wrote.

I then got to know him slightly, and Julie much better, through interviews for *Hard Curves* and *Soft as Steel*, her first two Paper Tiger books. Due to various complications these were the first ventures I tried doing by phone rather than interviewing the artist in the flesh. It should have created big problems, but Julie is such a natural interviewee – friendly, vivacious, charming – that it was great fun. Later it was much the same with Boris' book *Dreams*.

Both artists like to work in many different areas, but the field of comic superheroes is particularly suited to their talents. The figures are costumed, but only barely, so Boris and Julie can exercise their love of the human form honed beyond perfection. The characters are then set loose in worlds of wild magic where imagination is almost the only limit to what can happen.

The mythologies of these characters are often as complex and fascinating in their own way as any ancient epic. The superheroes act out their dramas on a grand scale, one which I'm sure the gods of Asgard found immediately familiar when Stan Lee imported them wholesale into his Marvel universe. Step into the world of comic superheroes brought to life by the combined talents of Boris Vallejo and Julie Bell and prepare to be dazzled!

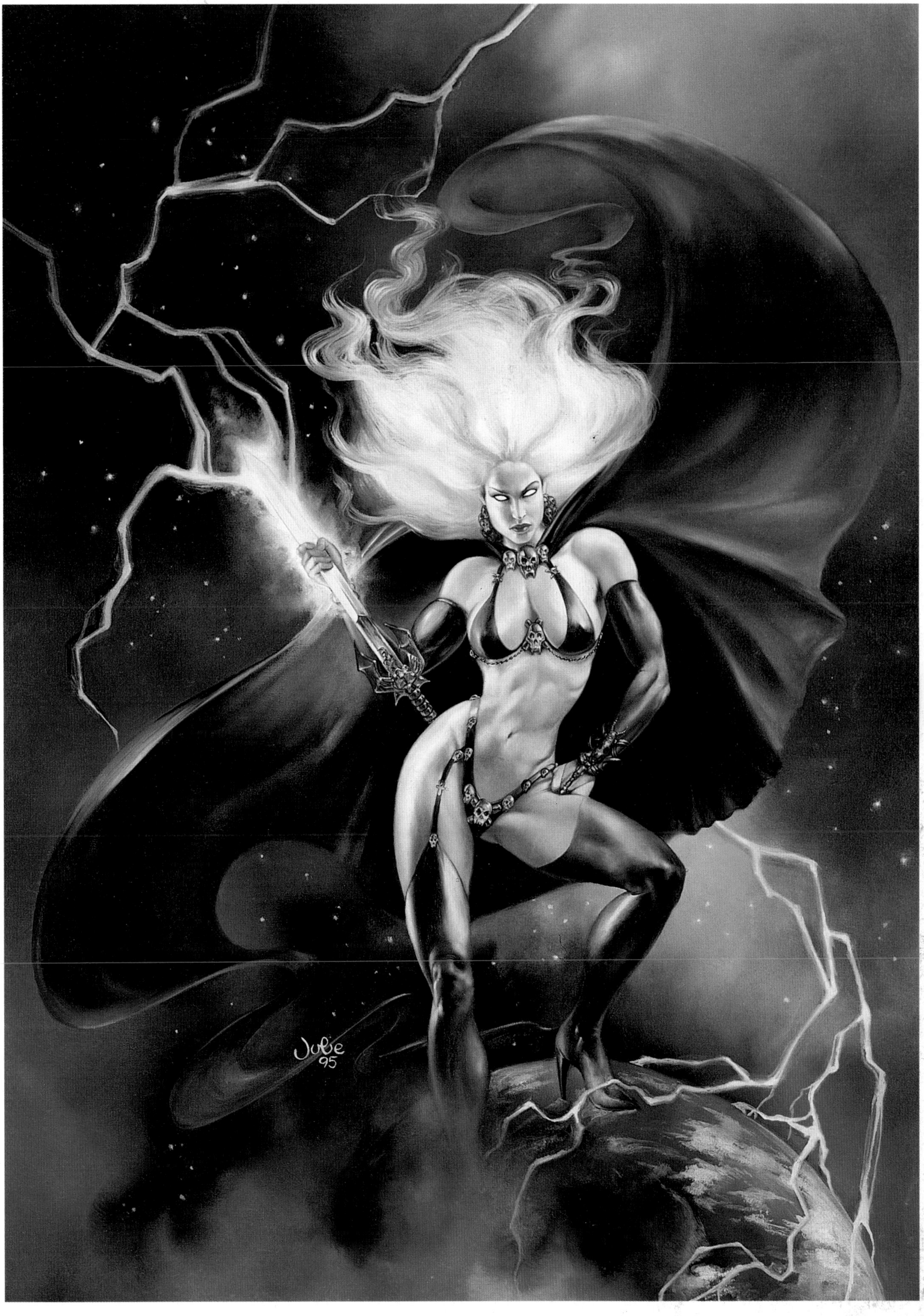
Julie
95

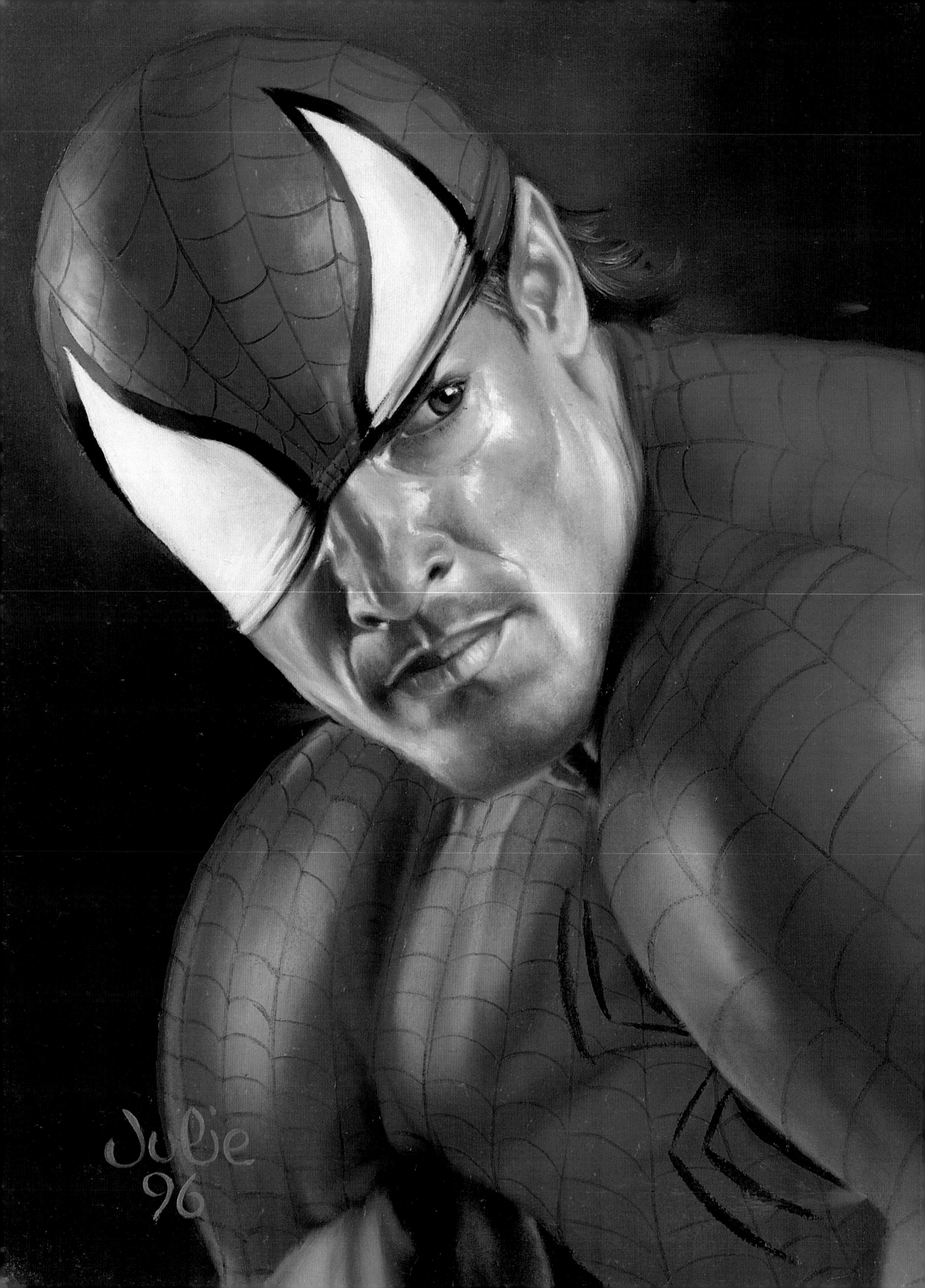
Julie
96

Spiderman

Besides a few book and comic covers that were included because they seemed appropriate, most of the pictures in this collection were painted for trading cards. Why did Marvel and the other publishers not simply use cells or covers from their own comics? Well it's one of those publishing phenomena that everyone would love to predict but never can. At one time the only real trading card activity in the States was in sporting heroes. Then Boris did a set based on his fantasy paintings and they just caught like fire, setting off the whole fantasy trading card scene. Spotting this, comic publishers' eyes suddenly lit up, though it was Julie they actually managed to book first, commissioning her for a set of four trial paintings which, to everyone's delight, were just perfect.

Boris soon followed and between them they have gone on to produce the collection presented here. A few publishers have tried making cards straight from the comics but for some reason they just haven't caught on in the same way. People look for the high degree of realism and heightened drama of works like Boris and Julie's. Fantasy trading cards have become an art form in themselves.

The cards are rarely exact scenes from a particular story. Beyond being pointed towards the right characters and occasional storylines, Boris and Julie are left very much to follow their own inclinations. Very occasionally they do get asked to change their rough sketches, but they do have a lot of freedom which allows them to really throw themselves into the work.

As a result they were thrilled when Marvel commissioned a whole set of about 120. There was a wonderful security in knowing the months stretched ahead with a steady flow of canvases and cheques. But Boris also says he would not want that to last forever, he likes the uncertainty of never quite knowing where the next commission will come from. Life tends to be more full of surprises that way.

(left)

**SPIDERMAN/
PETER PARKER**

1996, Julie
Trading Card. Fleer Publishing Co.
TM & © 1996 Marvel Characters, Inc.
All rights reserved.

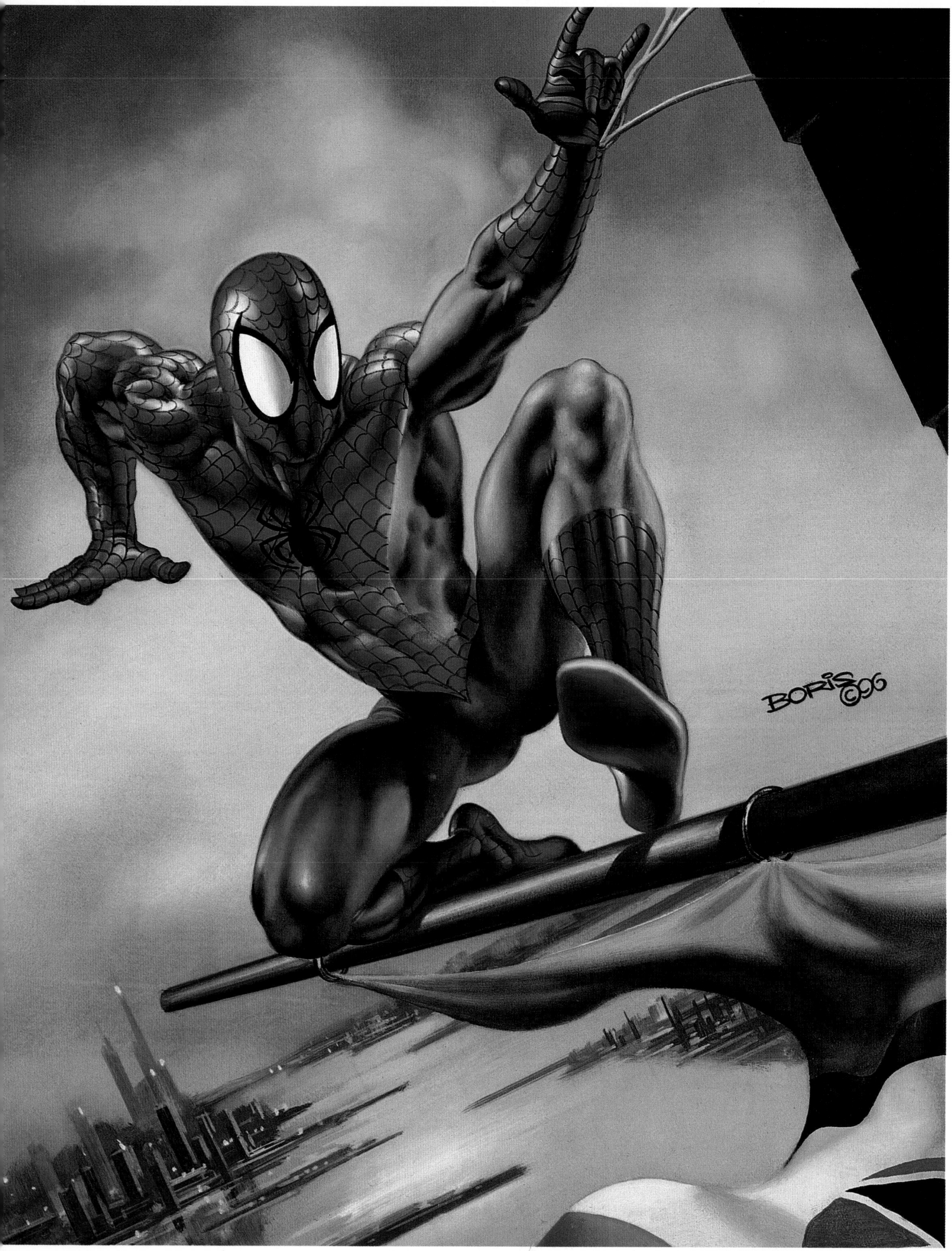
BORIS ©96

(left)

FLAG OF CONVENIENCE

1996, Boris

Trading Card. Fleer Publishing Co.
TM & © 1996 Marvel Characters, Inc.
All rights reserved.

The great thing about Spiderman is that
he is one of the few comic superheroes
who is also often, unintentionally, a
clown. He often slips up and it is his
mistakes that make him more loveable
than many other characters. We can
all relate to him.

(right)

SPIDERWOMAN

1995, Boris

Trading Card. Fleer Publishing Co.
TM & © 1995 Marvel Characters, Inc.
All rights reserved.

Like many other Marvel heroines,
Spiderwoman has a long and tangled
relationship with Wolverine, who is a bit
of a lady-killer on the side. She has
similar attributes to Spiderman but
acquired them in a totally different way.
Peter Parker became Spiderman when
he was bitten by a radioactive arachnid,
whereas she (at least in her Jessica Drew
incarnation) was evolved from a spider
into humanoid form by some genetic
wizardry.

Among her many other attributes,
Spiderwoman occasionally exudes
clouds of pheromones which cause men
to fall suddenly and passionately in love
with her. Attempts to suppress the
pheromones led to the loss of her other
powers, so being irresistably sexy is
something she has just had to learn
to live with. Some people have it hard.

(left)

SPIDEY IN THE RAIN

1995, Julie

Trading Card. Fleer Publishing Co.
TM & © 1995 Marvel Characters, Inc.
All rights reserved.

One of the attractions of painting
superheroes is that the action is so much
more exaggerated than on normal
fantasy or SF book covers. A new
approach has to be taken to human
anatomy, but the figures still have to
remain credible.

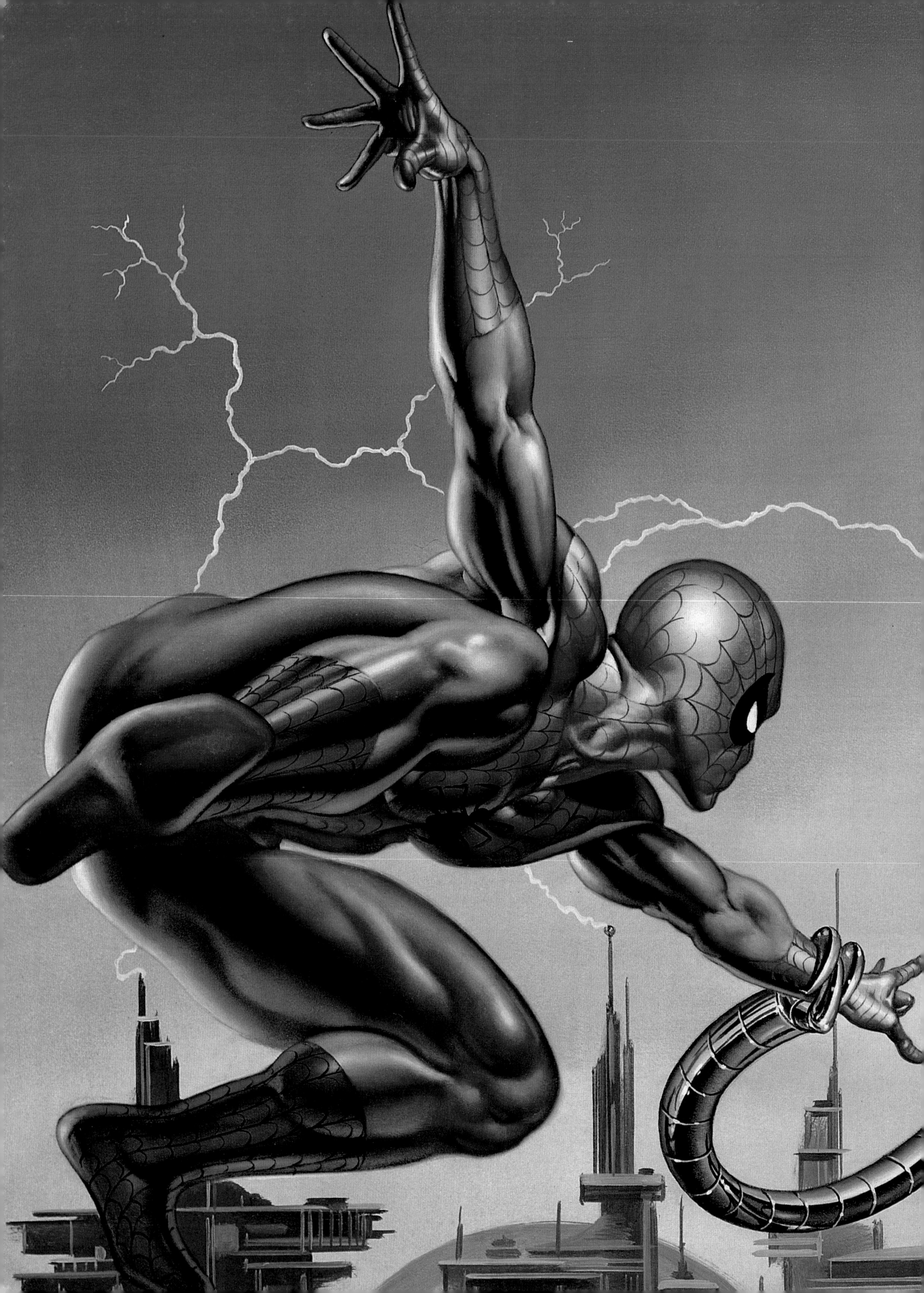

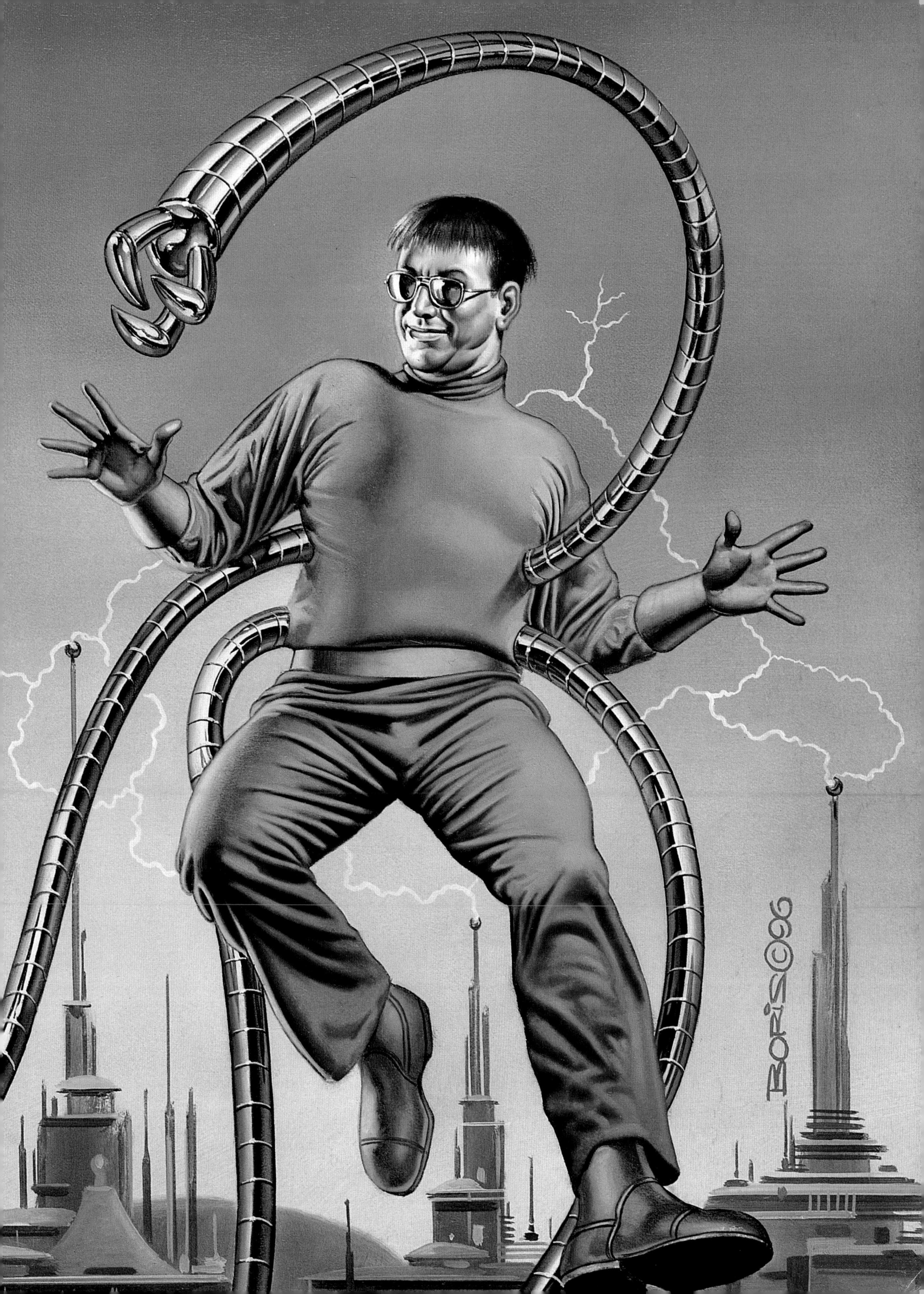
BORIS©96

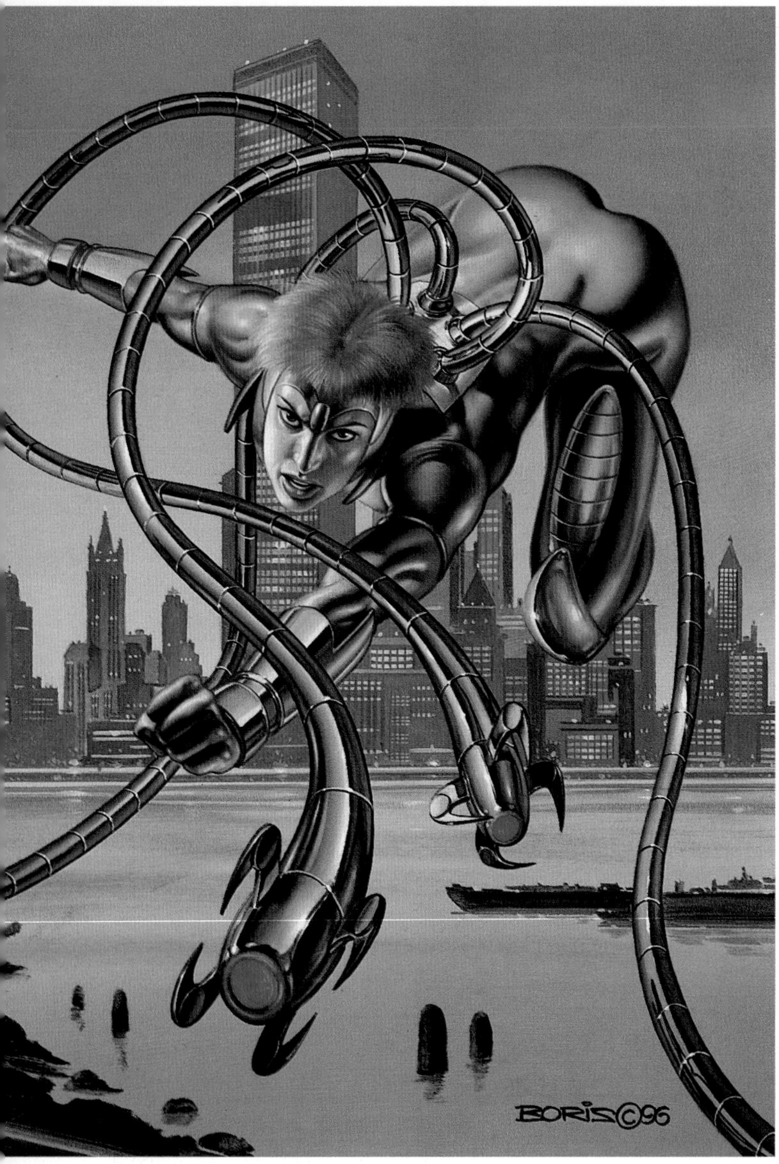
BORIS©96

(previous page)

SPIDERMAN VS DR OCTOPUS

1996, Boris

Trading Card. Fleer Publishing Co.

(above)

DR OCTOPUS

1995, Boris

Trading Card. Fleer Publishing Co.

At one point in their conflicts, Dr Octopus blasts Spidey with the Nullifier weapon that induces amnesia. He then convinces him that he's really an arch criminal and takes him off on a crime spree. Luckily, of course, Spiderman comes to his senses in time to foil the evil doctor.

(below)

SPIDERMAN VS CARNAGE

1995, Julie

Cover. Byron Preiss Multimedia.

(right)

CARNAGE

1996, Boris

Trading Card. Fleer Publishing Co.

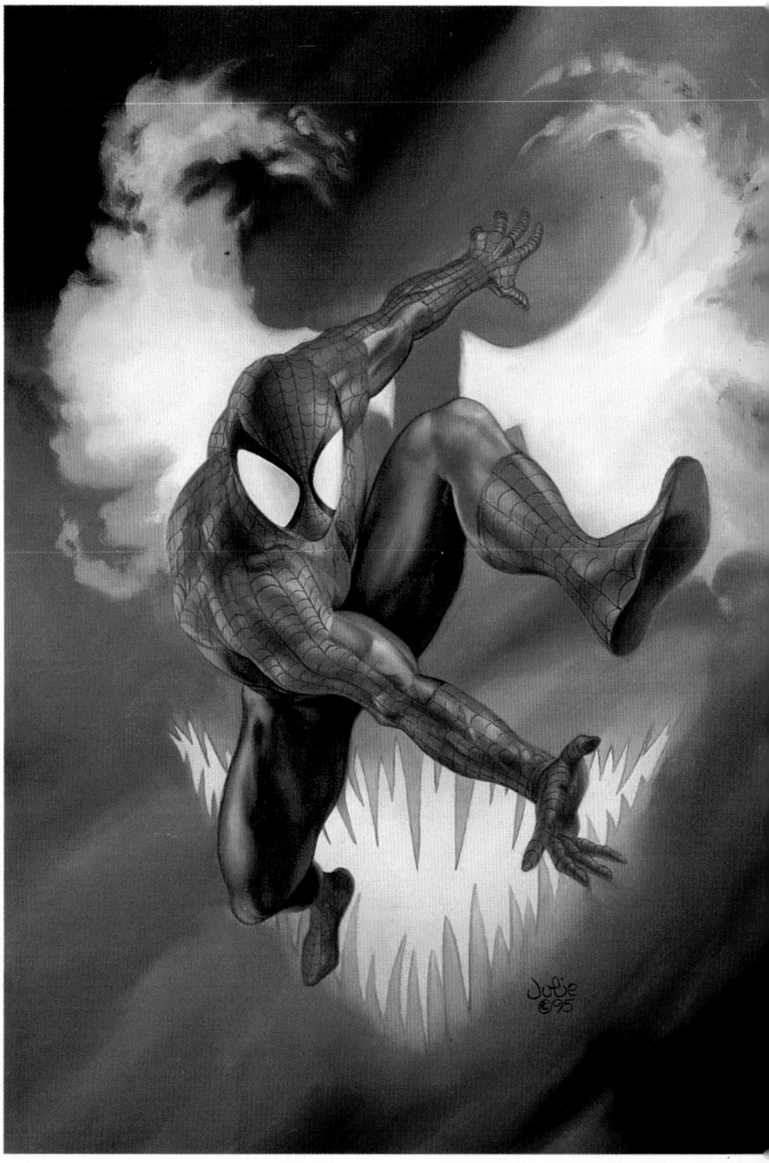
Julie ©95

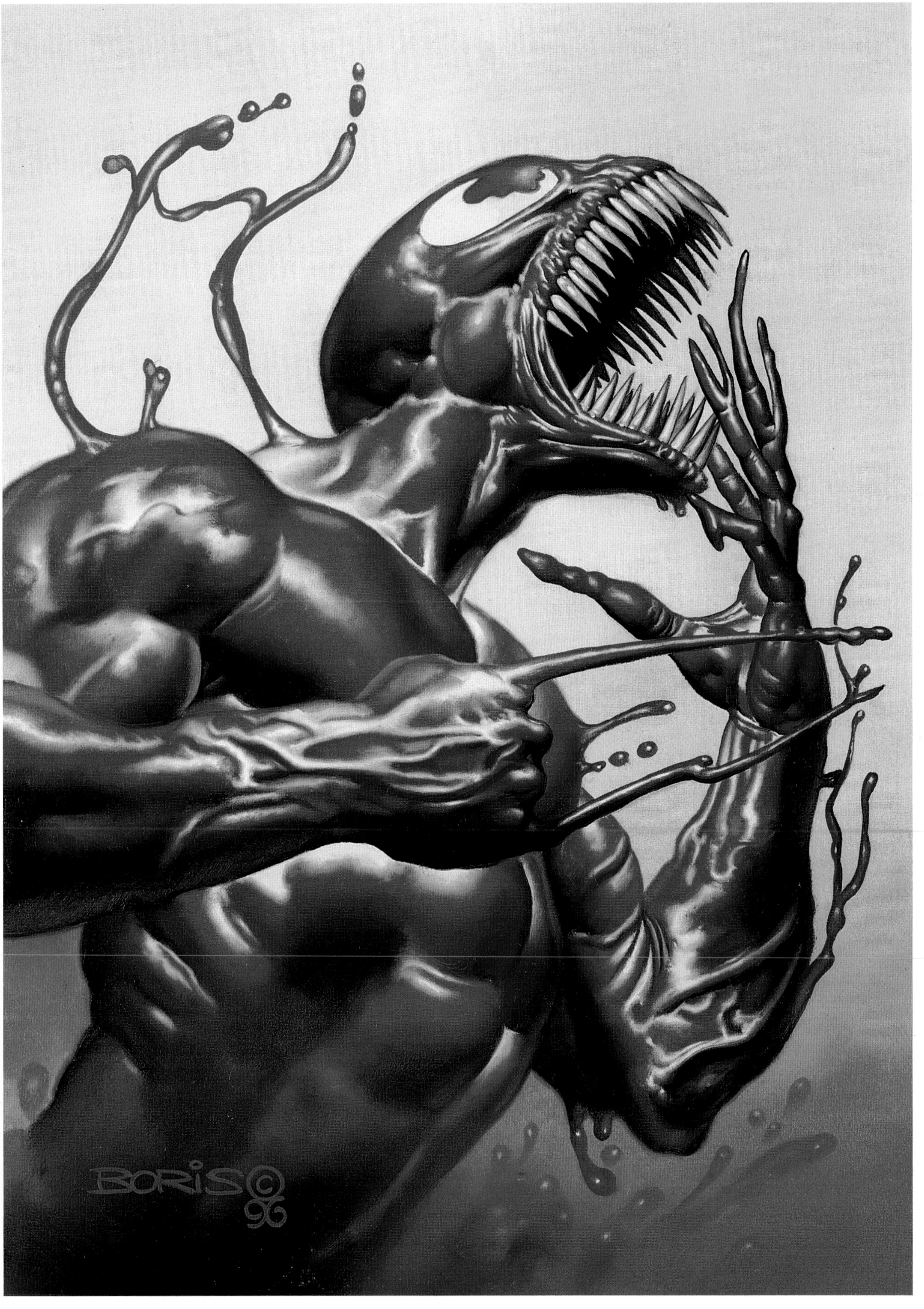
BORIS©
96

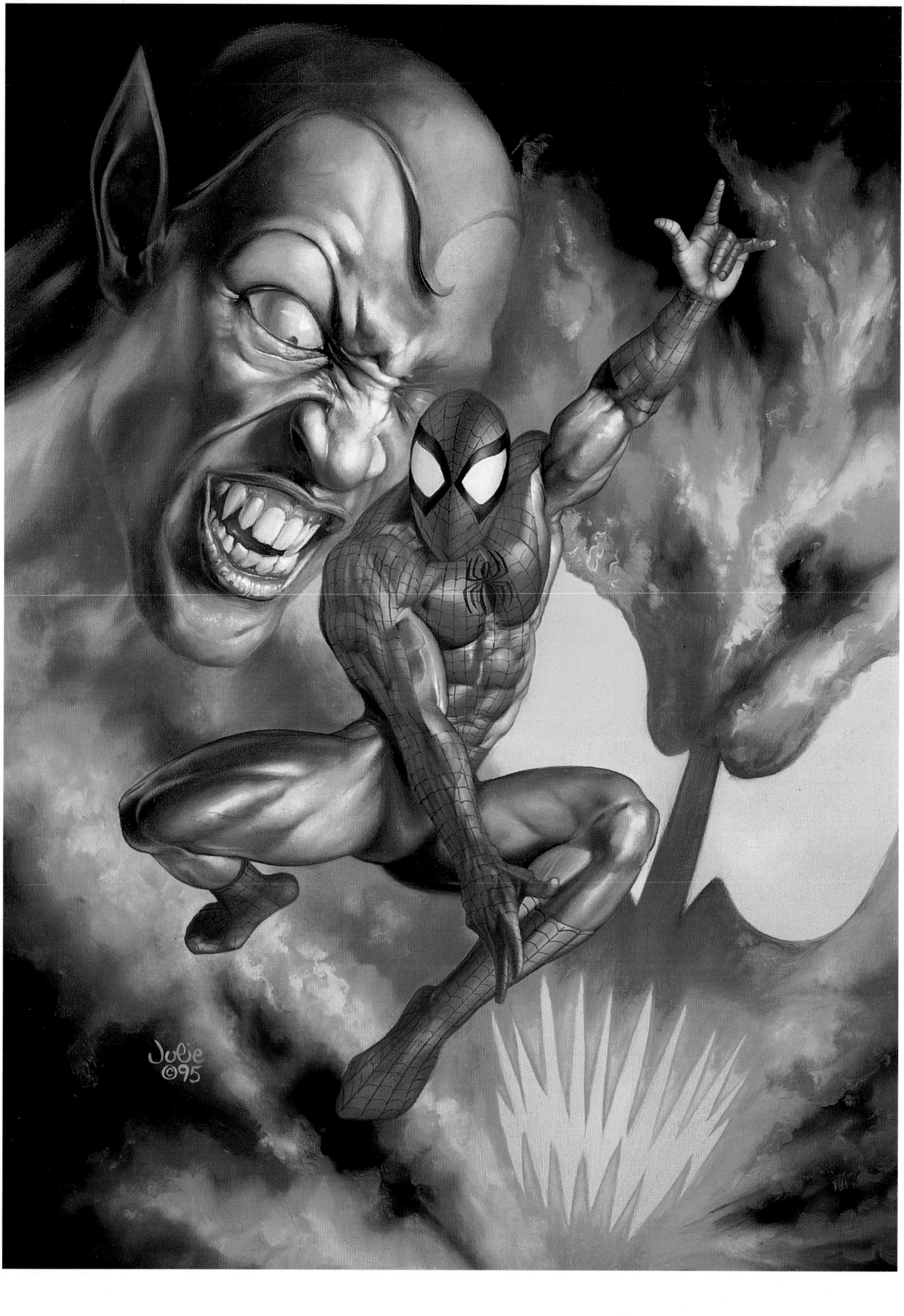
Julie
©95

(far left)

SPIDERMAN VS CARNAGE VS GREEN GOBLIN

1995, Julie

Trading Card. Fleer Publishing Co.

TM & © 1995 Marvel Characters, Inc.

All rights reserved.

One of Julie's first lessons when painting superheroes was that the normal human physique is really not up to the kind of manoeuvres she was expected to portray. Spiderman especially is so flexible that you can't expect any model to reach that degree of contortion. He has no pelvis or spine to speak of, says Julie, or at least they'd have to be made of rubber.

Boris finds that whereas usually one or two good shots of a model are enough for a superhero painting, with Spiderman it usually takes half a dozen. His model is always Julie, because he knows she is supple enough to adopt the right positions.

(above left)

CARNAGE

1996, Julie

Cover. Byron Preiss Multimedia.

TM & © 1996 Marvel Characters, Inc.

All rights reserved.

(left)

GREEN GOBLIN

1995, Julie

Trading Card. Fleer Publishing Co.

TM & © 1995 Marvel Characters, Inc.

All rights reserved.

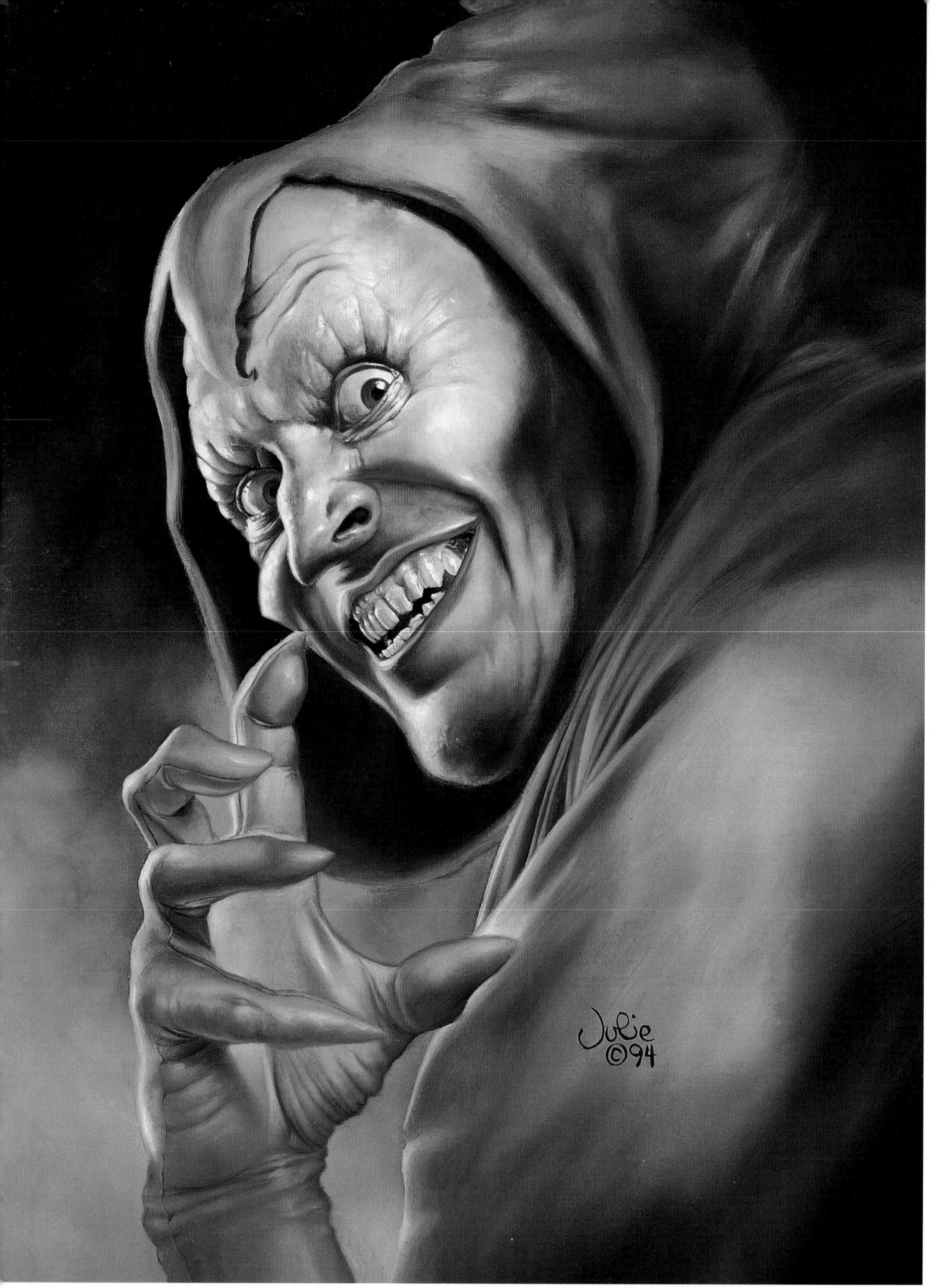
Julie
©94

(left)

HOBGOBLIN

1994, Julie

Trading Card. Fleer Publishing Co.

TM & © 1994 Marvel Characters, Inc.

All rights reserved.

(right)

SCARLET SPIDER

1996, Julie

Trading Card. Fleer Publishing Co.

TM & © 1996 Marvel Characters, Inc.

All rights reserved.

Scarlet Spider, or Ben Reilly, is a genetically engineered clone of Spiderman and was created to destroy him. Reilly had his own ideas though and tried to go his own way. For a confused period he believed he actually was Spiderman, then he came to his senses and moved to Seattle, Washington, where he has been trying to forge his own identity. Complicating this is the discovery that being a clone means he is likely to be hit by a rapid degenerative disease.

(left)
SPIDERMAN VS LIZARD
1997, Julie
Book cover. Byron Preiss Multimedia.

(right)
LIZARD
1996, Boris
Trading Card. Fleer Publishing Co.
At one point Peter Parker tries to rid himself of his spider powers but instead grows four extra arms. In search of a doctor to cure him, he bumps instead into the Lizard, who is a doctor but has no wish to do Spiderman any favours . . .

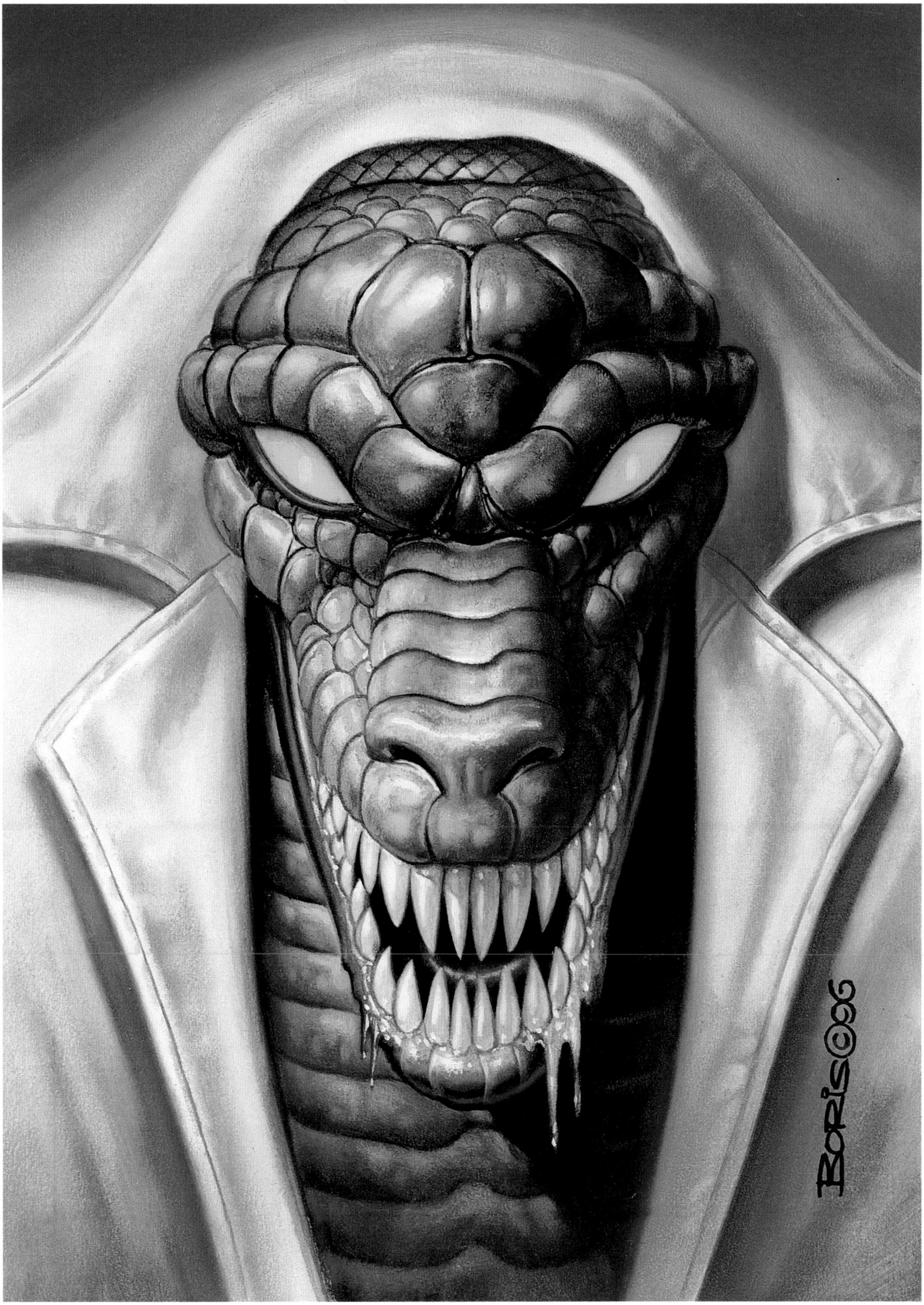
BORIS©96

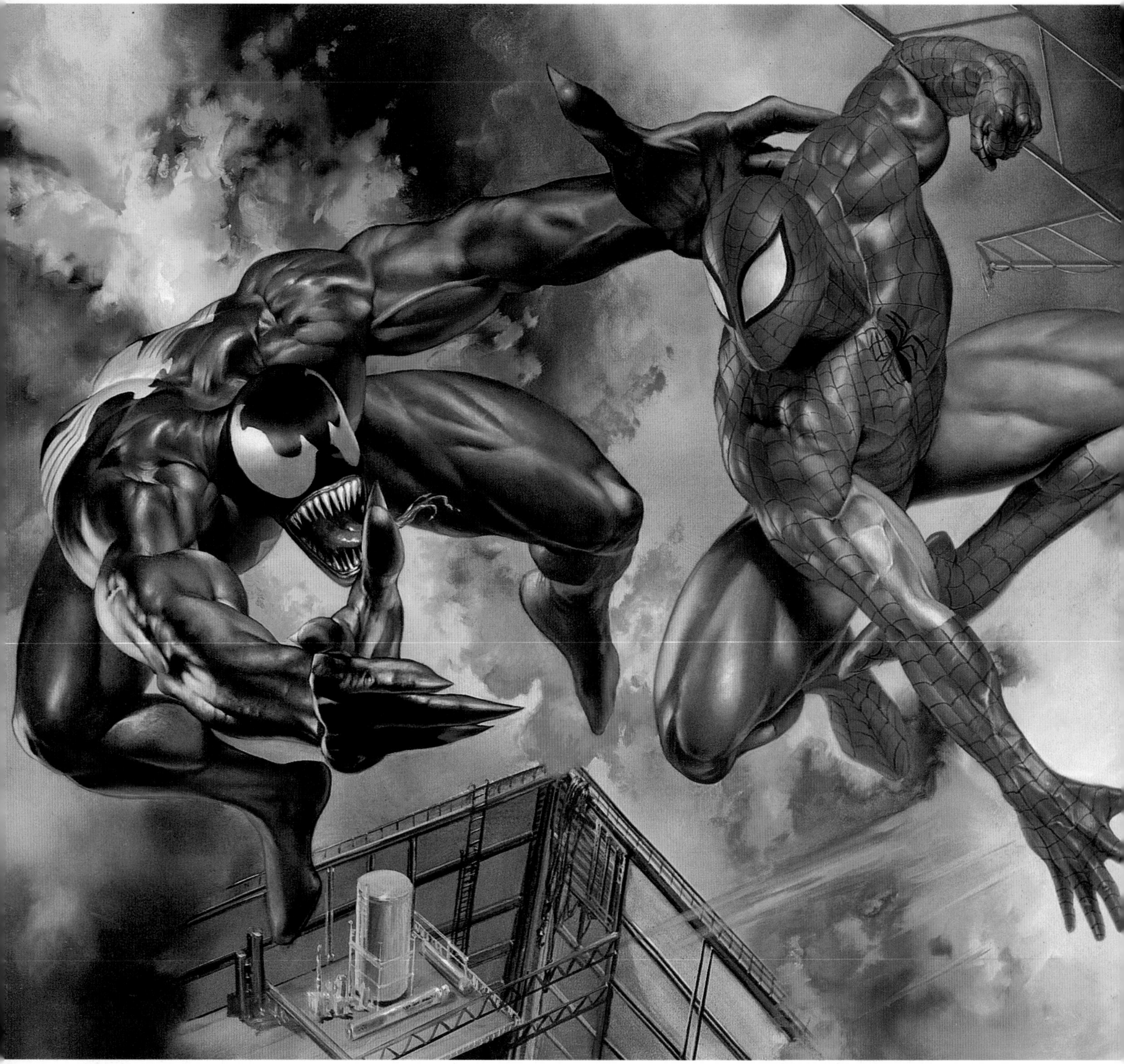

(above)

SPIDERMAN VS VENOM

1996, Julie

Trading Card. Fleer Publishing Co.

(right)

VENOM

1995, Boris

Trading Card. Fleer Publishing Co.

One of the few suggestions Boris and Julie were given for these cards was that there was no need for them all to be full-length figures. This is often very refreshing because it allows them to focus right in on the face.

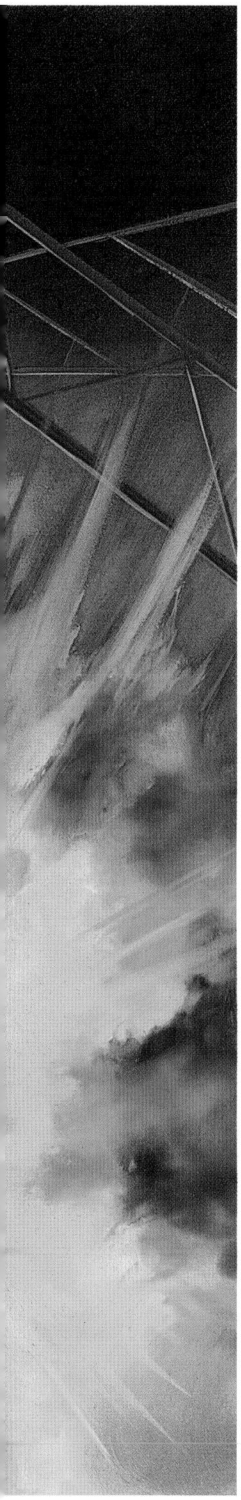

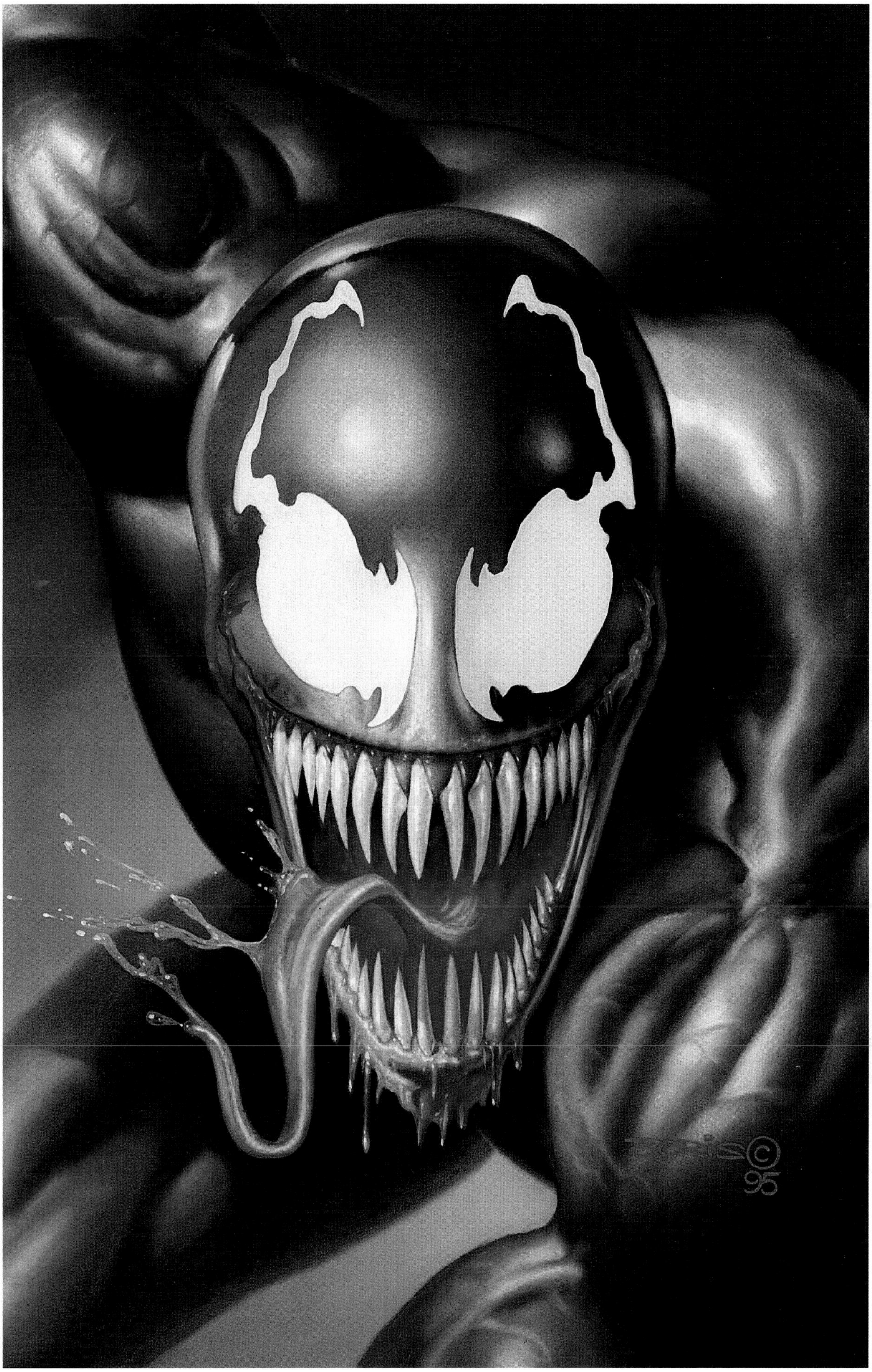
BORIS©
95

(left)

SURFING THE WEB

1995, Boris

Trading Card. Fleer Publishing Co.

TM & © 1995 Marvel Characters, Inc.

All rights reserved.

(right)

READY TO LEAP

1996, Boris

Trading Card. Fleer Publishing Co.

TM & © 1996 Marvel Characters, Inc.

All rights reserved.

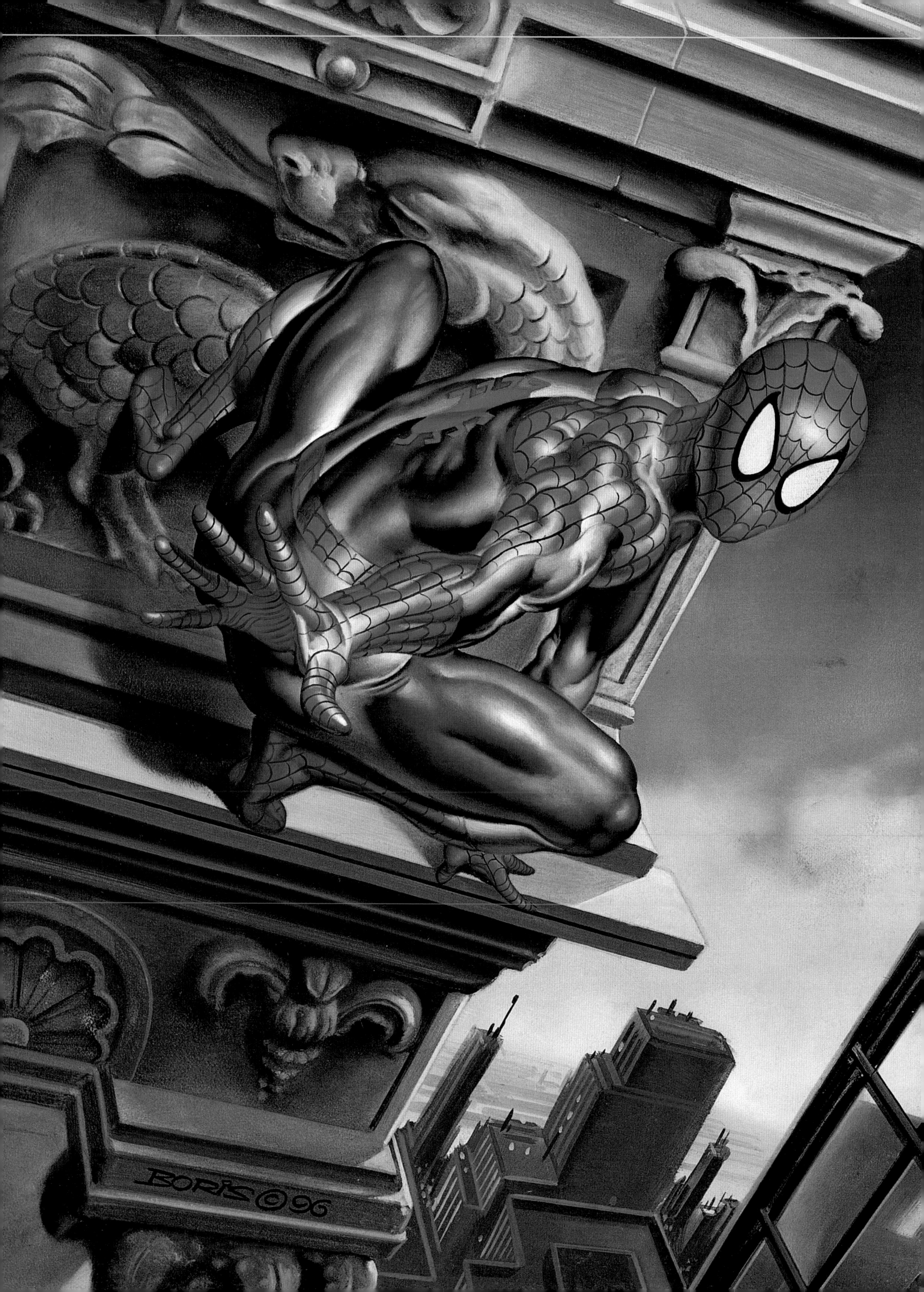
BORIS ©96

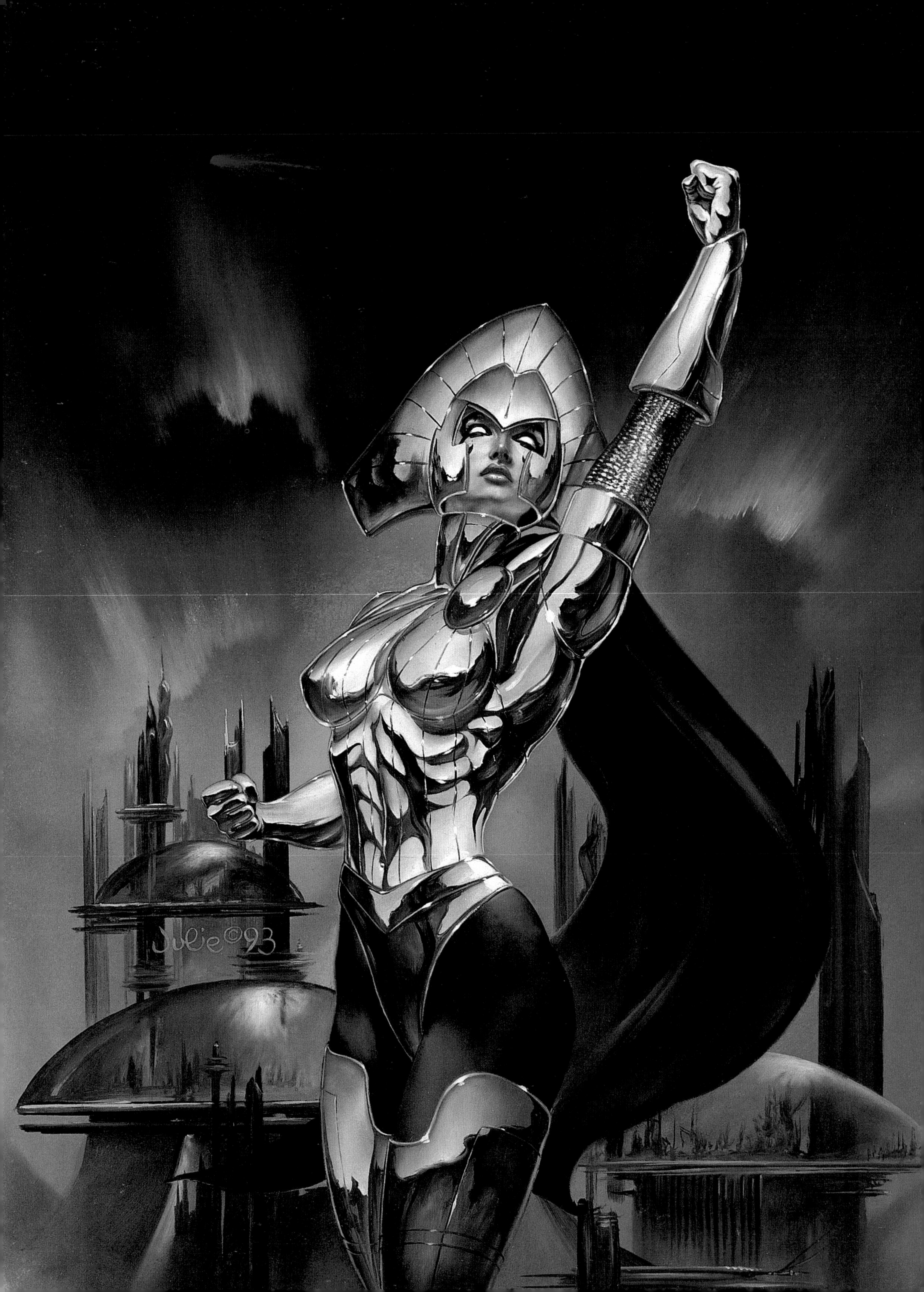
Julie©93

Marvellous Universes

For those few readers who may not already know, Boris Vallejo was born and raised in Peru, but moved to New York as a young man to take advantage of the greater opportunities for artists there. He and Julie now live in nearby Pennsylvania and still make regular visits to the Big Apple for both work and pleasure. Boris still feels he is basically a city person at heart, while Julie is more drawn to the open country. Fortunately they have been able to find a balance that suits them both.

Julie hails from Texas but through various adventures ended up on the East Coast where she met Boris while attending his studio as a model. He encouraged her previously neglected artistic talent and to everyone's astonishment she was soon turning out paintings every bit as good as his; as you can see in this collection where for almost the first time they appear side by side.

Often it is impossible to tell their work apart, but there are differences in emphasis if you look closely. Many people assume they often work on paintings together, but they rarely have, until a few recent experiments. Previously the only contribution they generally made to each other's work was perhaps to offer an opinion on how they felt a painting was taking shape.

Many people have a problem with Boris and Julie's paintings, especially over the virtual (or actual) nudity in many of them, and I must confess that I did too at the outset. I was first confronted with it in Julie's book, *Hard Curves,* when the only question that came to mind regarding one picture was: 'So this is you and your sisters with your tops off?'.

Julie seemed to sense my difficulty, probably having encountered it before, because she quickly came to my rescue. Somehow in the way she explained things I grasped the angle that she and Boris were coming from. It is very much like naturism, a body-building attitude to nudity which they explore in their art. There is nothing salacious about it at all. The nudity they portray is often meant to be sexy, but not in a particularly personal way. As Julie once said: 'You're invited to look but not touch.' It is a celebration of sensuality with nothing sordid about it at all. In fact it's probably a much healthier attitude than normal prudishness. To Julie and Boris any awkwardness is purely in the eye (or inhibitions) of the beholder.

(left)

LILANDRA

1993, Julie
Trading Card. Fleer Publishing Co.
TM & © 1993 Marvel Characters, Inc.
All rights reserved.
Lilandra was the first Julie Bell painting I came across and it remains one of my favourites. I just love the character's defiant, take-on-the-world attitude. This is, of course, a characteristic of both Julie's paintings and her attitude to life. She celebrates these bold, sexy women and aims to be as much like them as she can. The great thing about this is that it frees the viewer to enjoy them without the danger of feeling part of any exclusively male club.

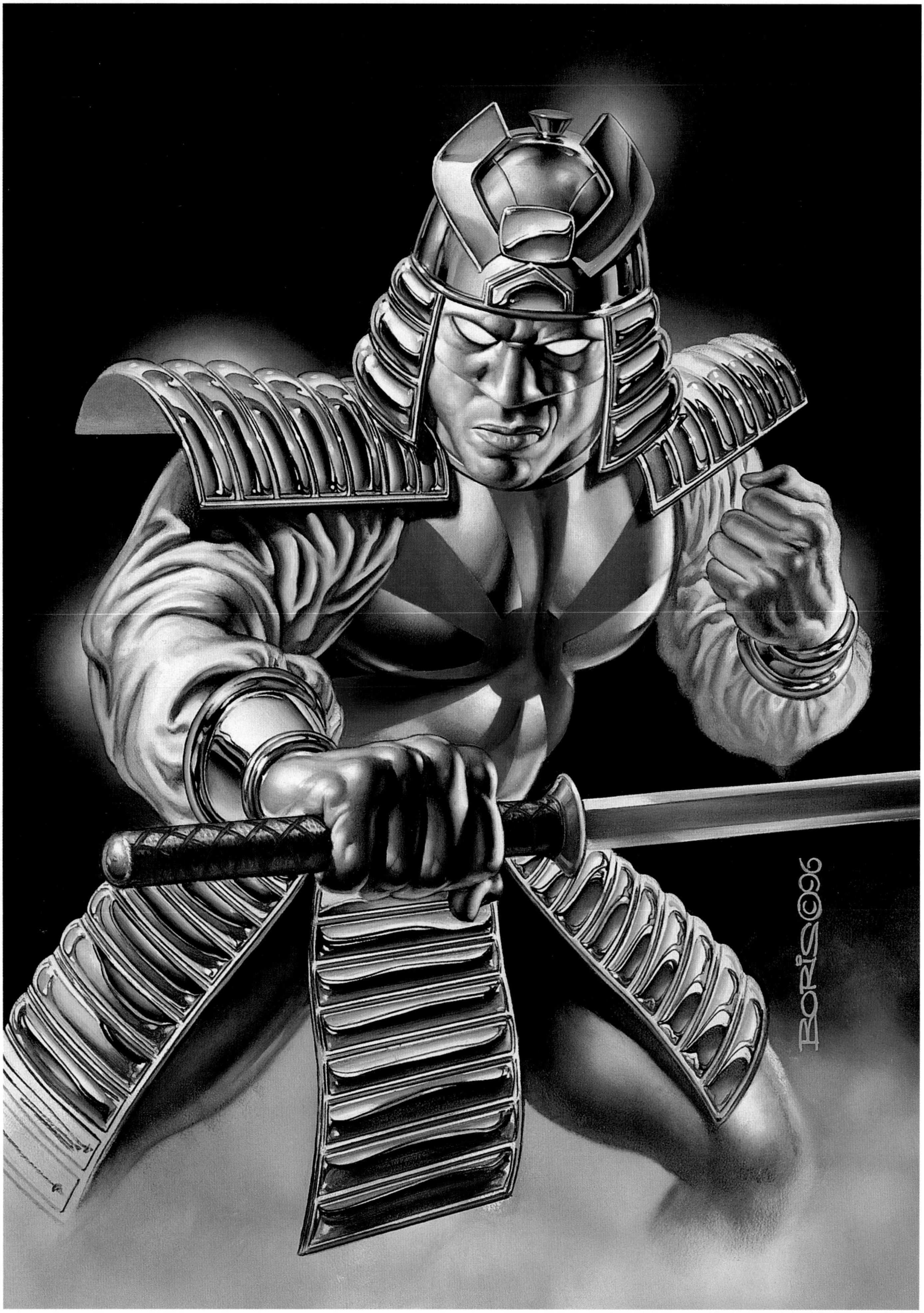
BORIS©96

(left)

SILVER SAMURAI

1996, Boris

Trading Card. Fleer Publishing Co.

(right)

SHI

1995, Julie

Cover. Crusade Comics

Most characters in this chapter are from various Marvel teams, but a few have strayed from other comic universes. Here we see Shi, the creation of William Tucci, who founded Crusade Comics purely as her vehicle when other publishers rejected the idea. She repaid his confidence by becoming an immediate and continuing hit.

Shi is Ana Ishikawa, an intelligent, sensitive, spiritual half-Japanese living in New York. She's torn between her mother's Catholic upbringing and her grandfather's martial arts training, under which she is pledged to avenge her father and brother's deaths. Resolving this conflict and realizing who she was became the theme of the first Way of the Warrior series, the character has since moved on to putting into practice what she learnt.

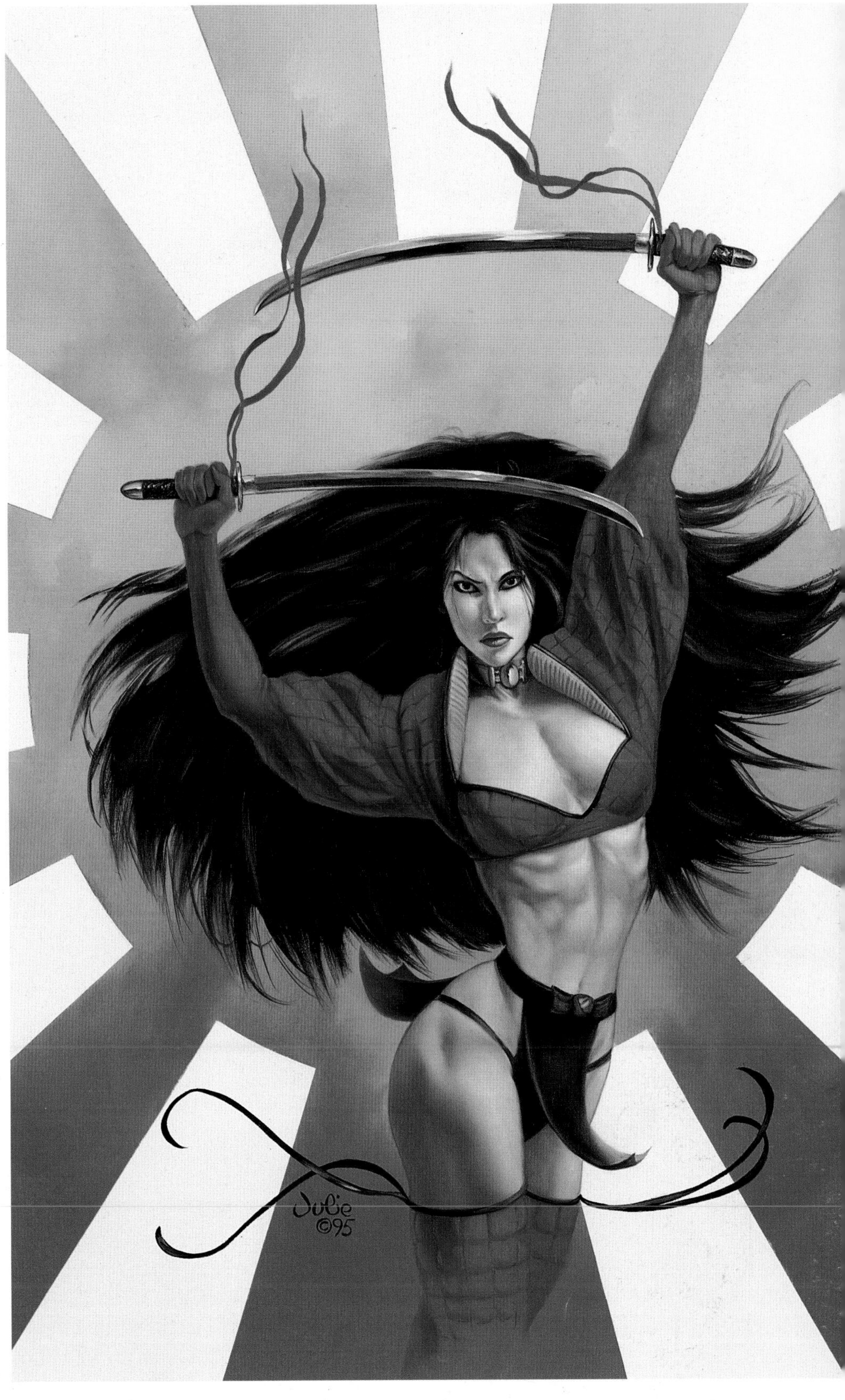
Julie
©95

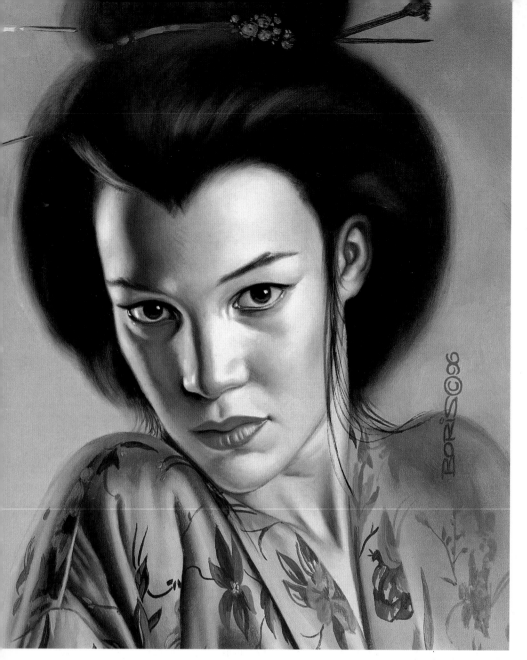

(left)

YUKIO

1996, Boris

Trading Card. Fleer Publishing Co.

TM & © 1996 Marvel Characters, Inc.

All rights reserved.

Here's a spread of pictures with a nice Oriental feel. Some real-life cultures can look as exotic as any fantasy with just a little exaggeration. Most fantasy art is rooted in what was the mainstream at some time or another. Celtic art also lends itself very easily to fantasy, much more so than, say, the Roman variety.

(right)

MARIKO

1995, Boris

Trading Card. Fleer Publishing Co.

TM & © 1995 Marvel Characters, Inc.

All rights reserved.

(left)

OGUM

1996, Boris

Trading Card. Fleer Publishing Co.

TM & © 1996 Marvel Characters, Inc.

All rights reserved.

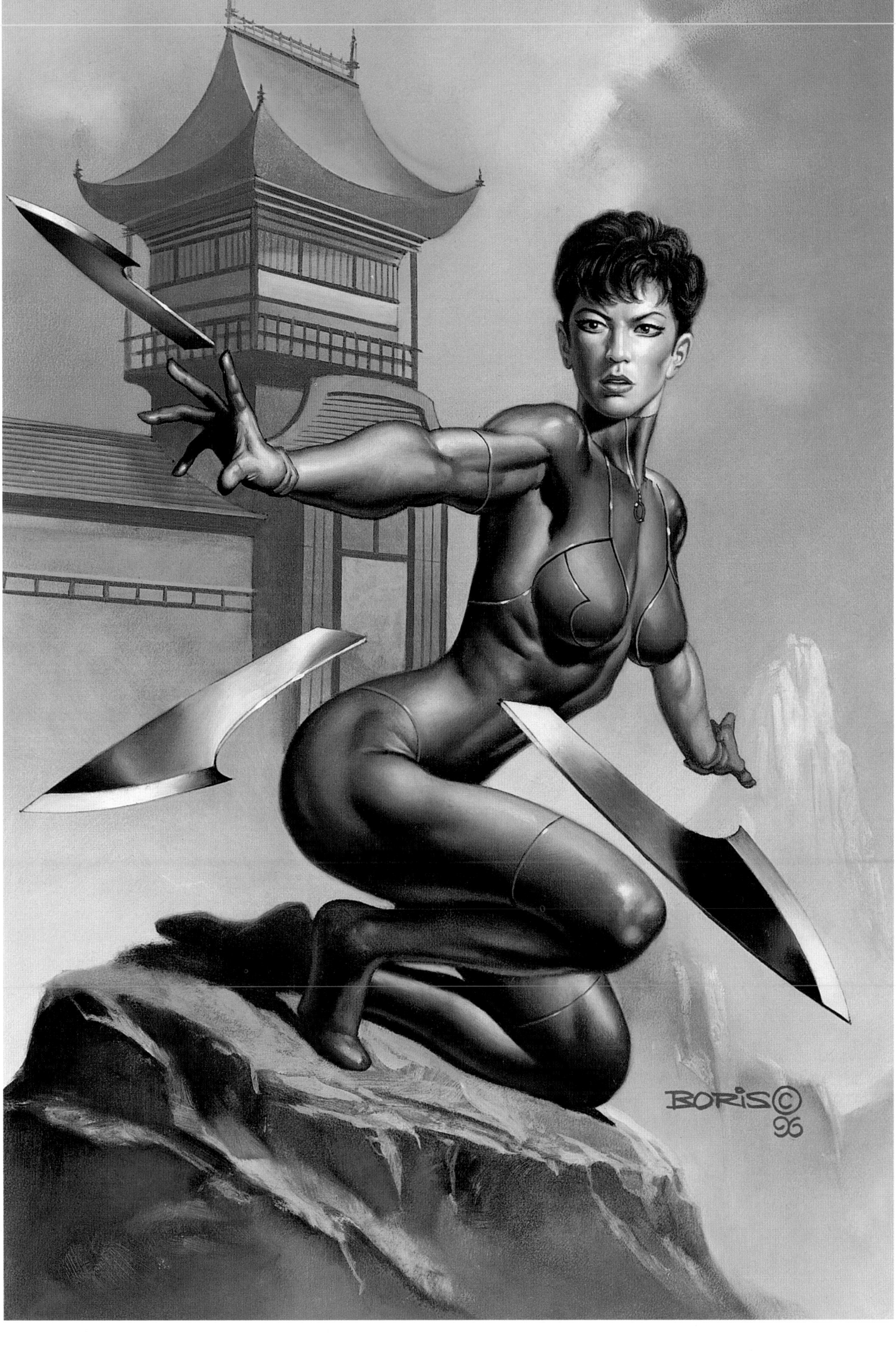
BORIS©
96

(left)

ADAM WARLOCK

1995, Julie

Trading Card. Fleer Publishing Co.
TM & © 1995 Marvel Characters, Inc.
All rights reserved.

Adam Warlock is a fascinating Marvel character, whose life and origins have uncanny parallels with, well, you tell me: he was once omnipotent and became known as God; he died and was resurrected, and he was heavily involved with the Fallen Angels.

However, Adam's origins are rather more prosaic. He was genetically engineered on earth, by a group of scientists known as the Enclave, to be the perfect human being. This didn't quite work of course and they were destroyed when their prodigy went out into the world. Known only as Him, this being got into various scrapes, notably with the god Thor, before retreating into his birth-cocoon. He was woken by a being known as the High Evolutionary and taken to a counter-Earth on the opposite side of the sun where he was greeted as a Messiah and acquired the name Adam Warlock.

(right)

THANOS

1996, Boris

Trading Card. Fleer Publishing Co.
TM & © 1996 Marvel Characters, Inc.
All rights reserved.

Although evil by definition, Thanos often ends up helping the good guys and is Adam Warlock's ally almost as much as his enemy. Such contradictions are part of his appeal. He suffers from an instability that occasionally tips him onto the wrong side.

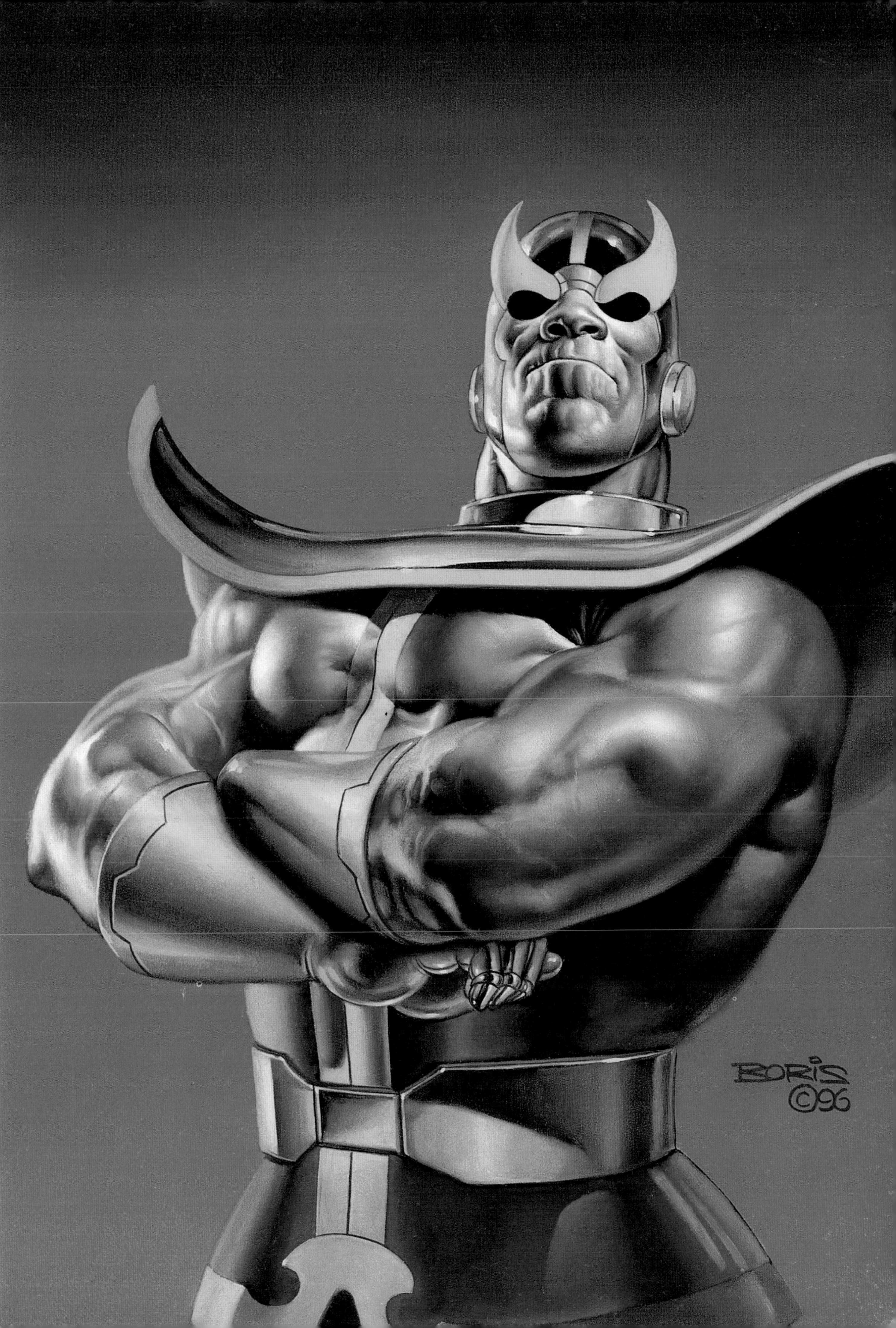
BORIS
©96

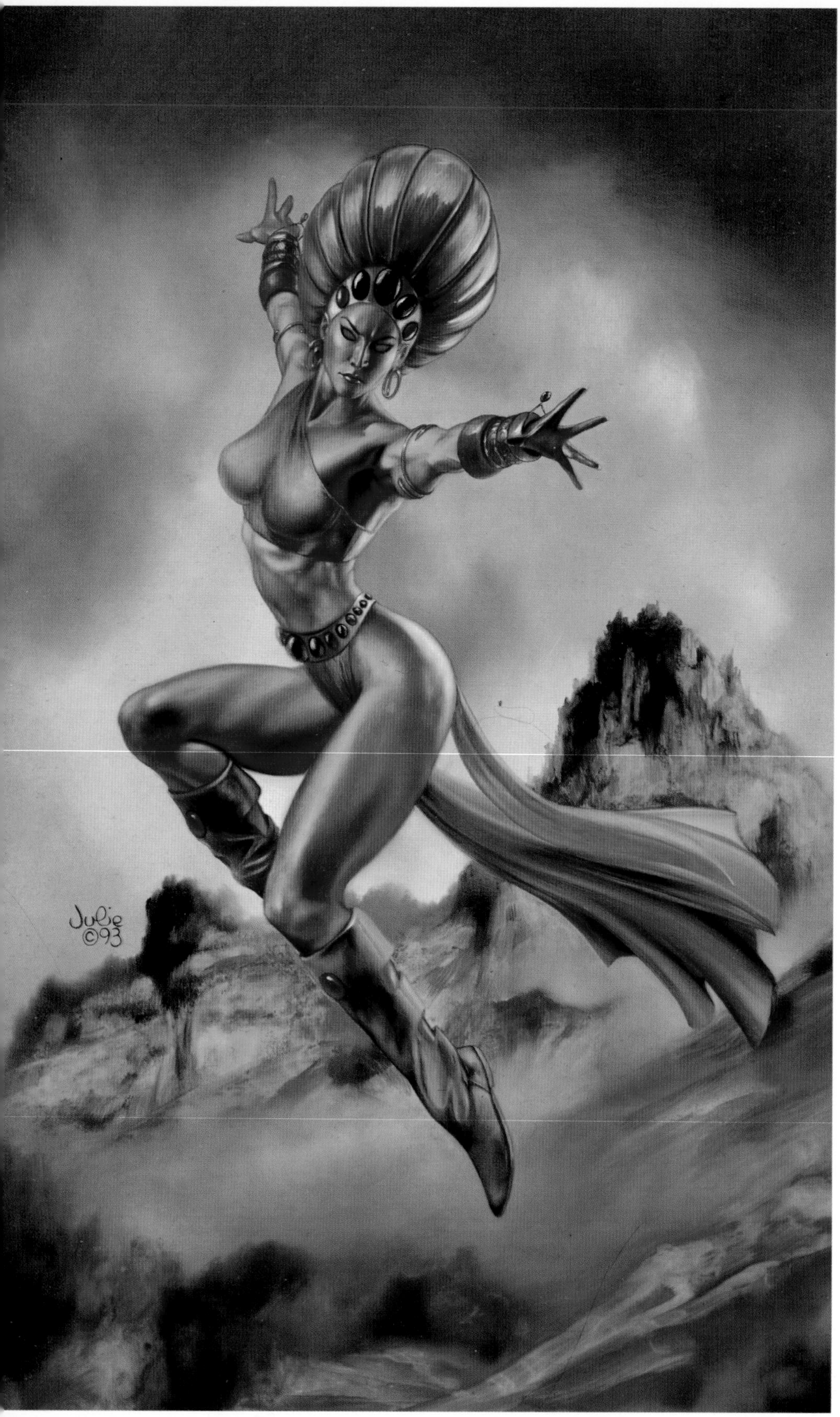
Julie
©93

(left)

YRIAL

1993, Julie

Trading Card.

TM & © 1993 Malibu Comics

(right)

NAMORITA

1995, Julie

Trading Card. Fleer Publishing Co.

TM & © 1995 Marvel Characters, Inc.

One of the New Warriors, a youthful new superhero team that includes Aegis, Bolt, Nova, Speedball and Turbo. Namorita is from Atlantis but passes as a student named Prentiss at the Empire State University. Having gills, she is equally at home on land or in the sea.

(far right)

LOCUS

1993, Julie

Trading Card. Fleer Publishing Co.

TM & © 1993 Marvel Characters, Inc.

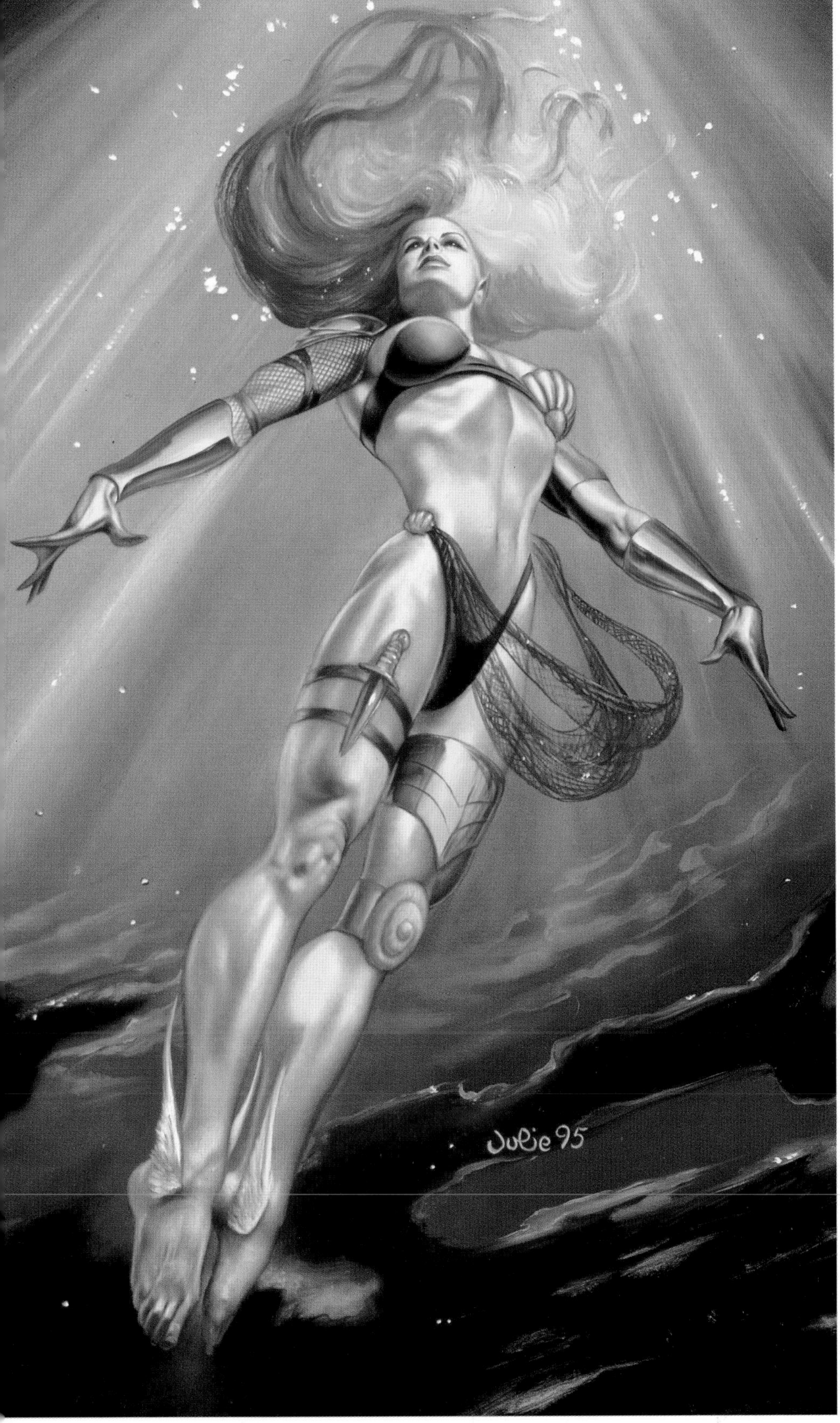
Julie 95

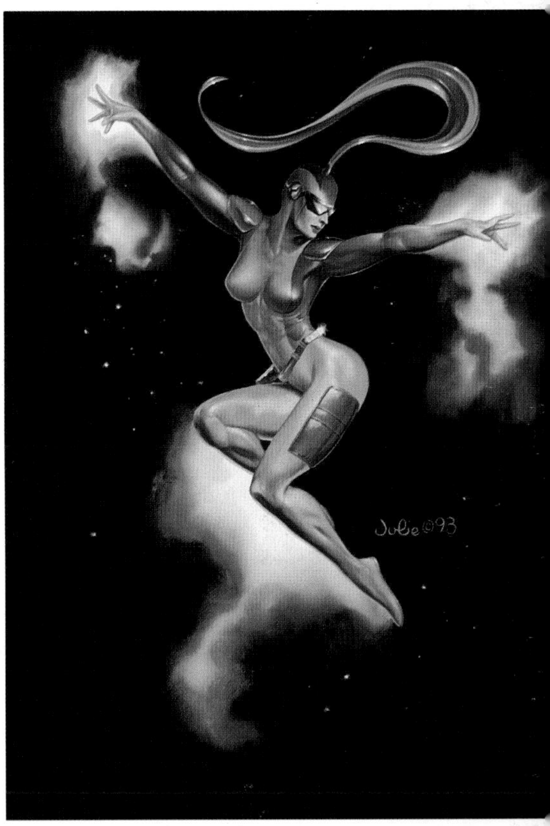
Julie©93

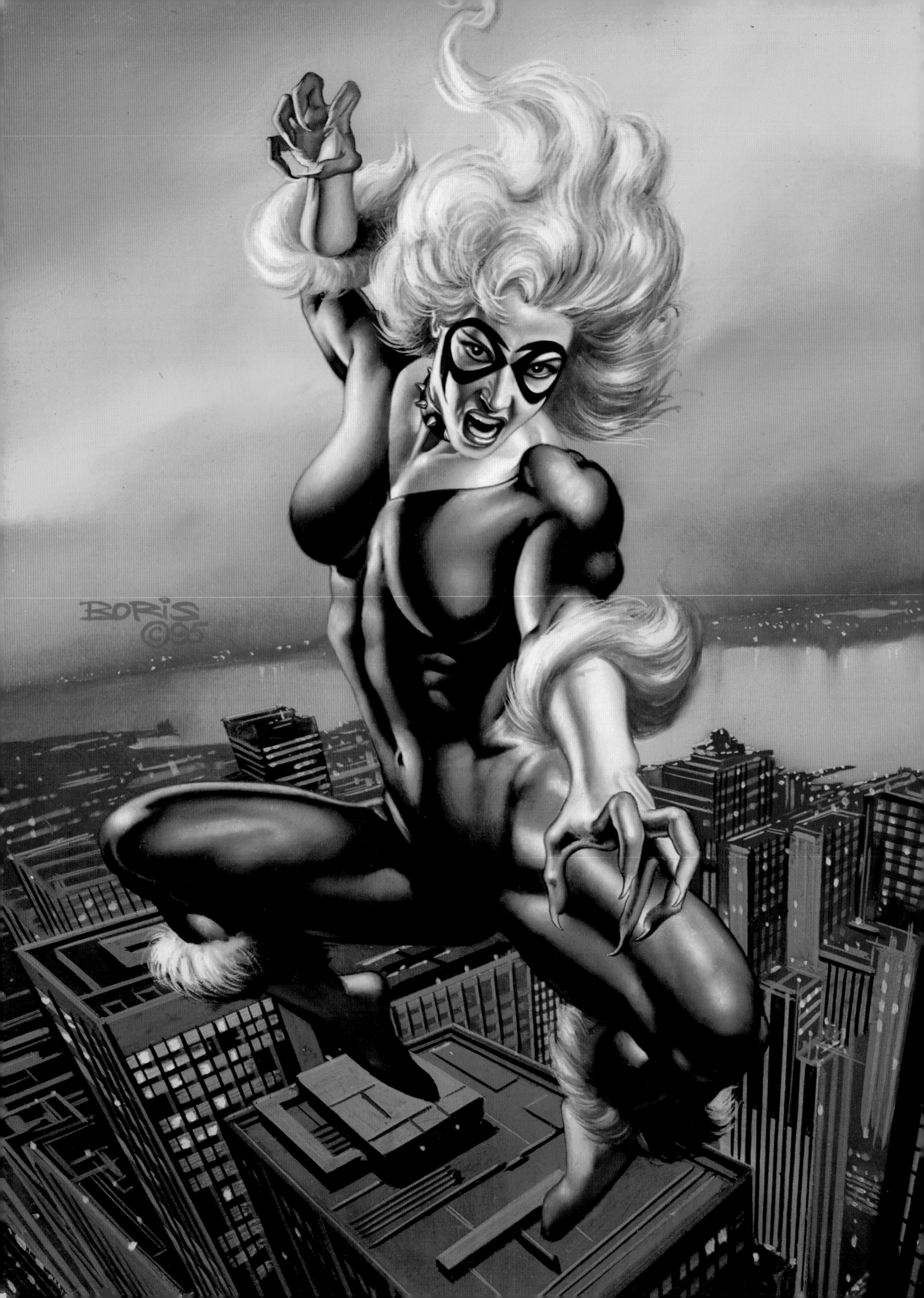
BORIS
©95

(left)

BLACK CAT 1

1995, Boris

Trading Card. Fleer Publishing Co.

(right)

BLACK CAT 2

1994, Boris

Trading Card. Fleer Publishing Co.

Often voted the sexiest Marvel heroine, Black Cat was involved with Spiderman for a while but is generally a loner. As Felicia Hardy she started life as a jewel thief but decided to join the good guys.

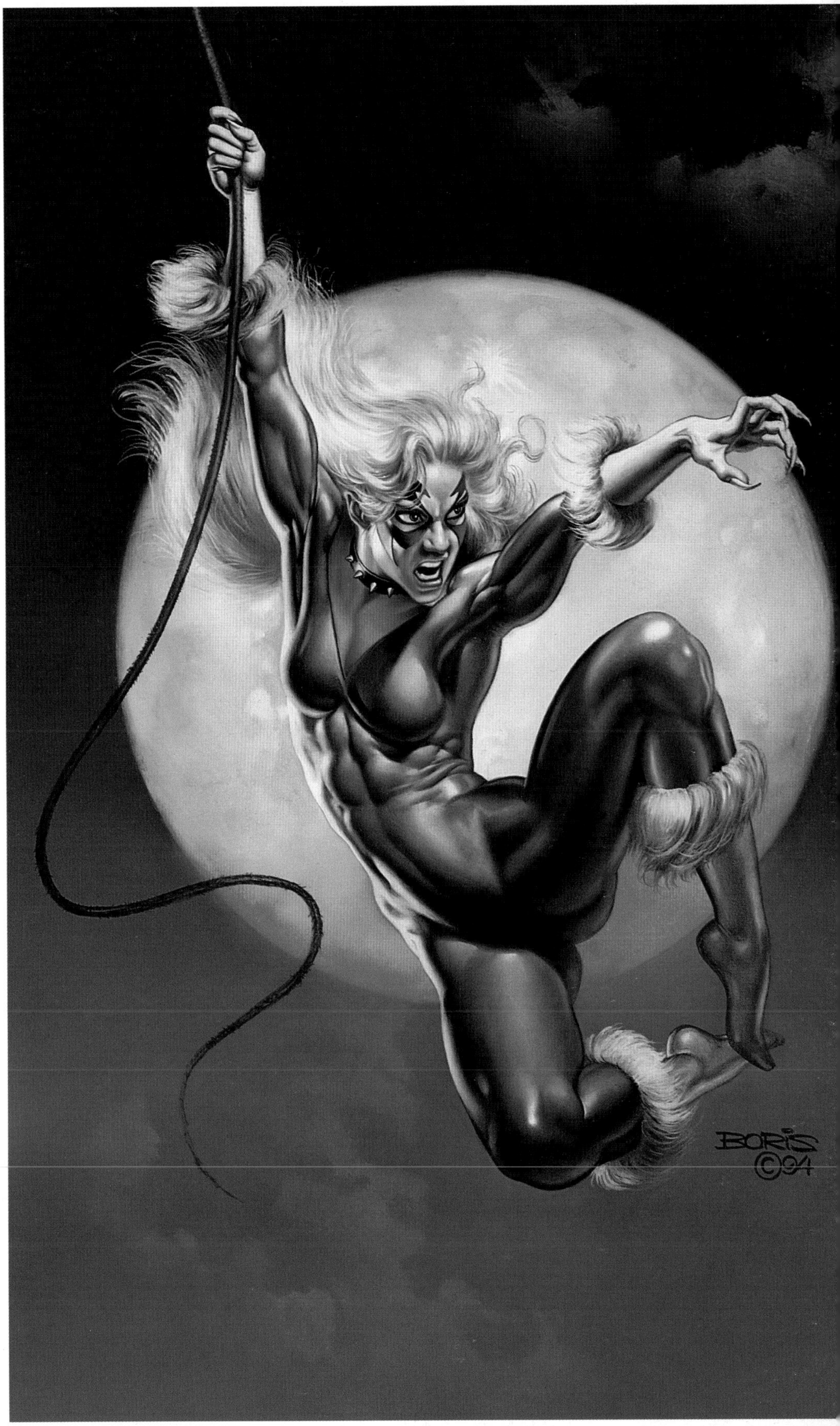
BORIS
©94

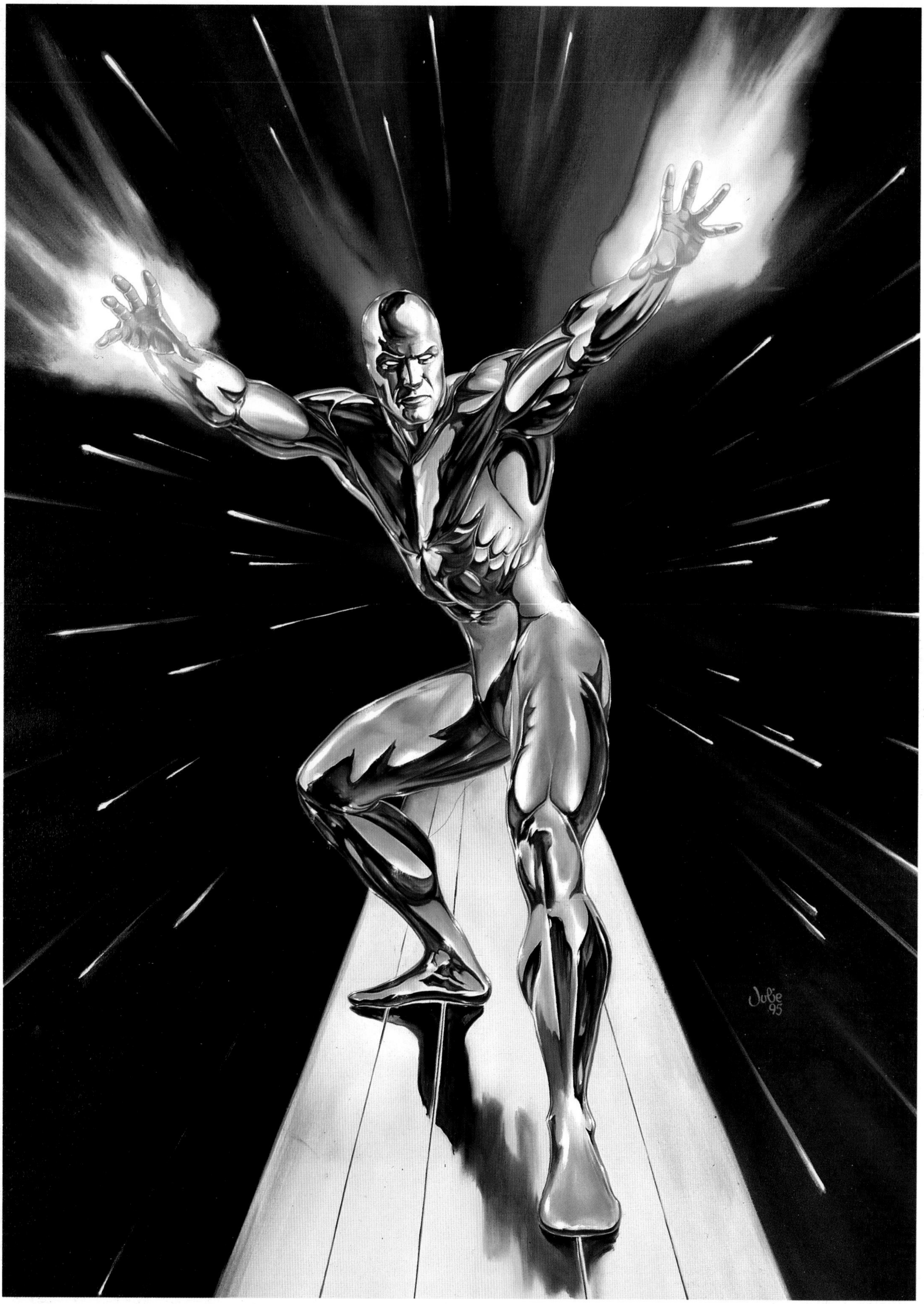
Julie
95

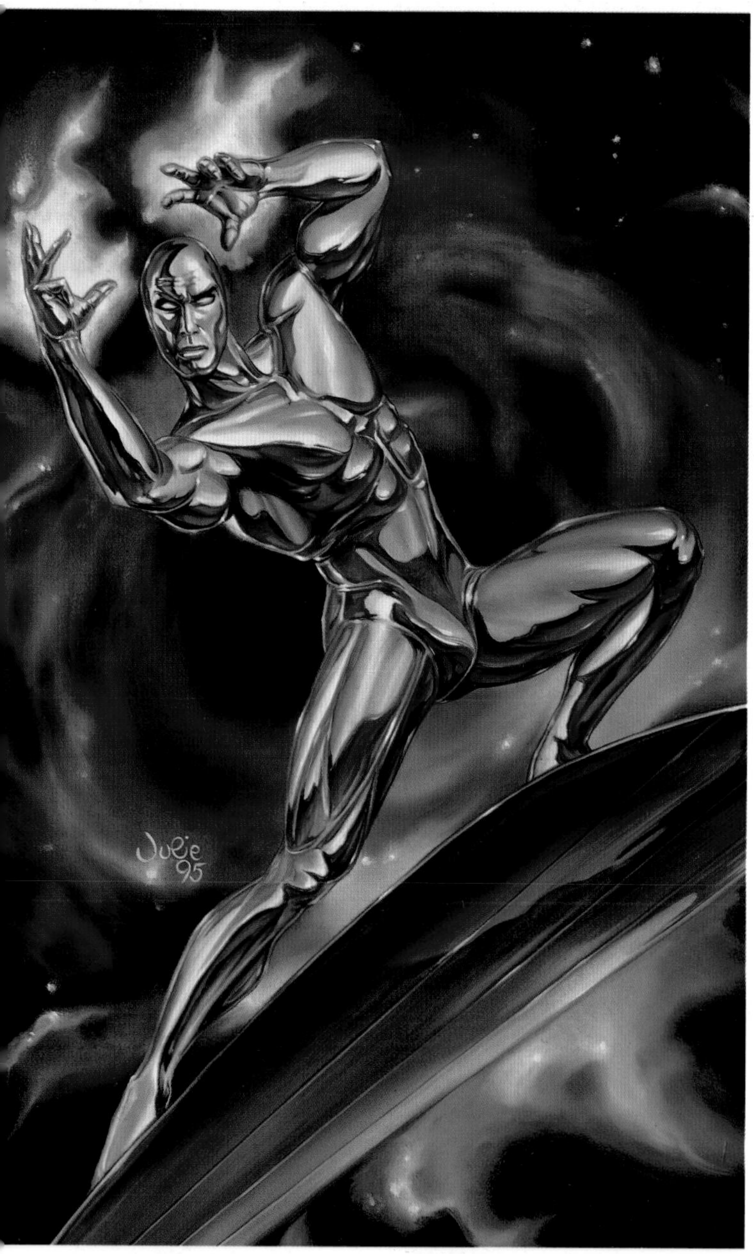
Julie
95

(left)

SILVER SURFER 2

1995, Julie

Trading Card. Fleer Publishing Co.

(below)

SILVER SURFER 1

1993, Julie

Trading Card. Fleer Publishing Co.

This was one of Julie's first three trading card images for Marvel and as she was then a completely unknown quantity they were completely stunned by the quality of her work.

(left)

SILVER SURFER 3

1995, Julie

Trading Card. Fleer Publishing Co.

The Silver Surfer is one of Stan Lee's most enduring superheroes from the 60s. As the herald of Galactus he ploughs his lonely furrow through the universe, feeding off pure cosmic energy that he can channel at will. The surfboard was created by the planet-devourer Galactus, along with his metallic flesh. The Surfer was originally a human called Norrin Radd born on the utopian planet Zenn-La.

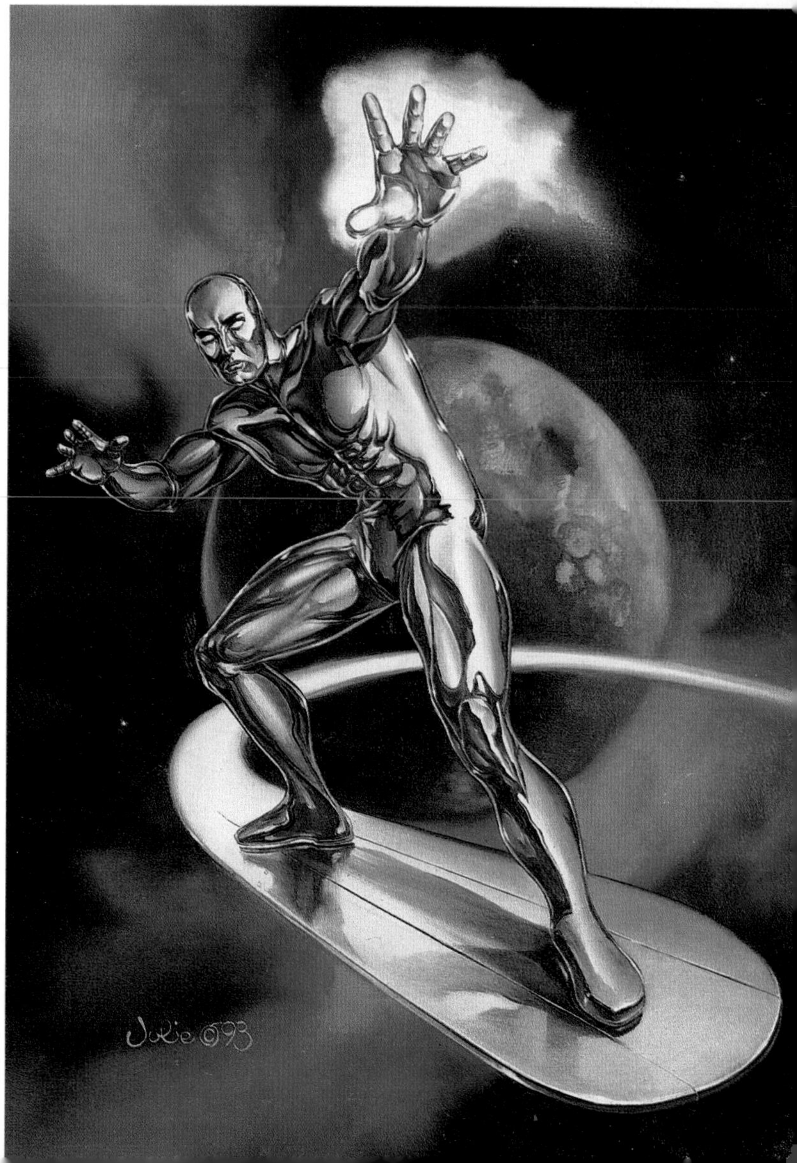
Julie ©93

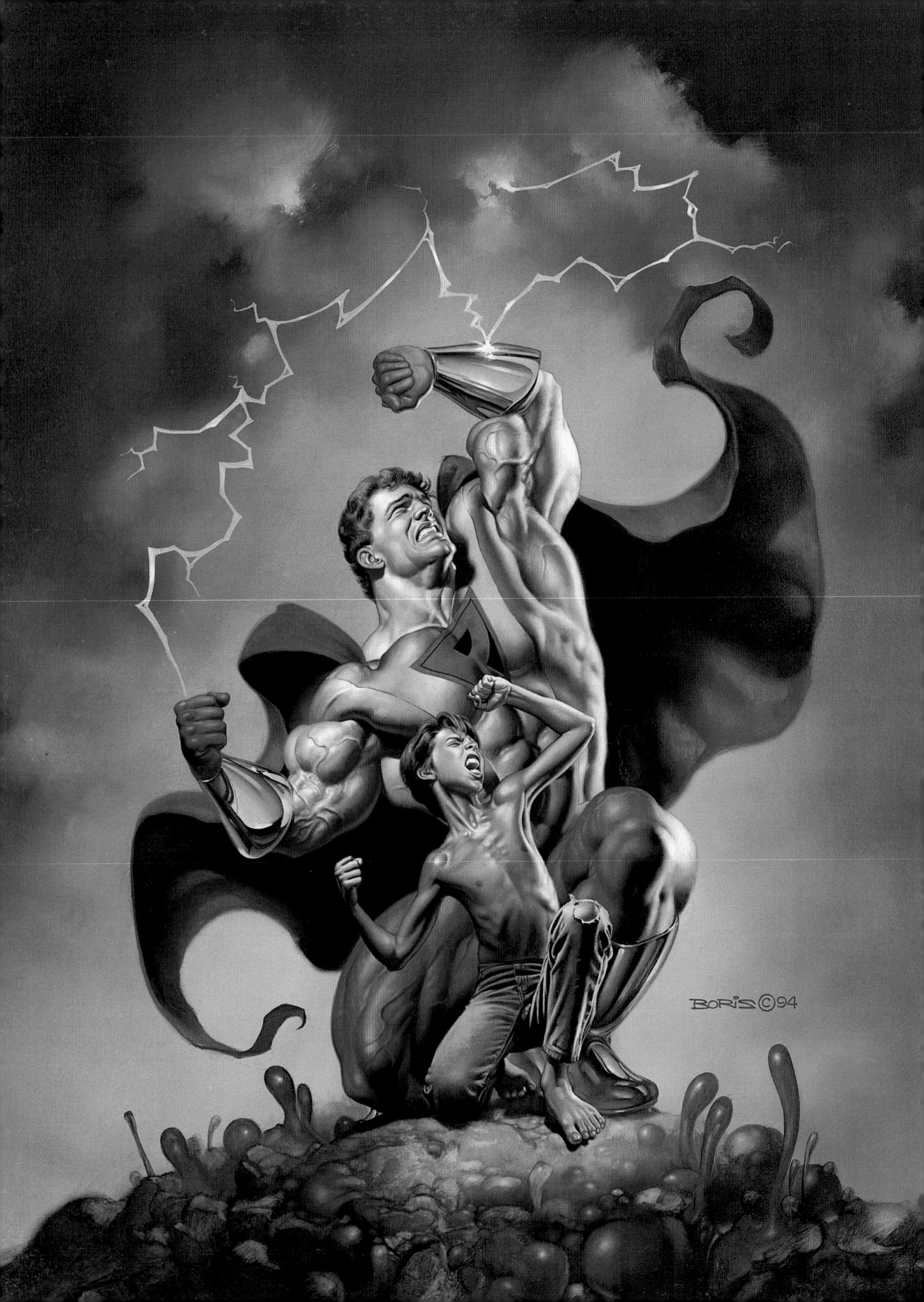
BORIS ©94

(left)

PRIME

1994, Boris

Cover. Malibu Comics

(right)

PSI LORD

1996, Boris

Trading Card. Fleer Publishing Co.

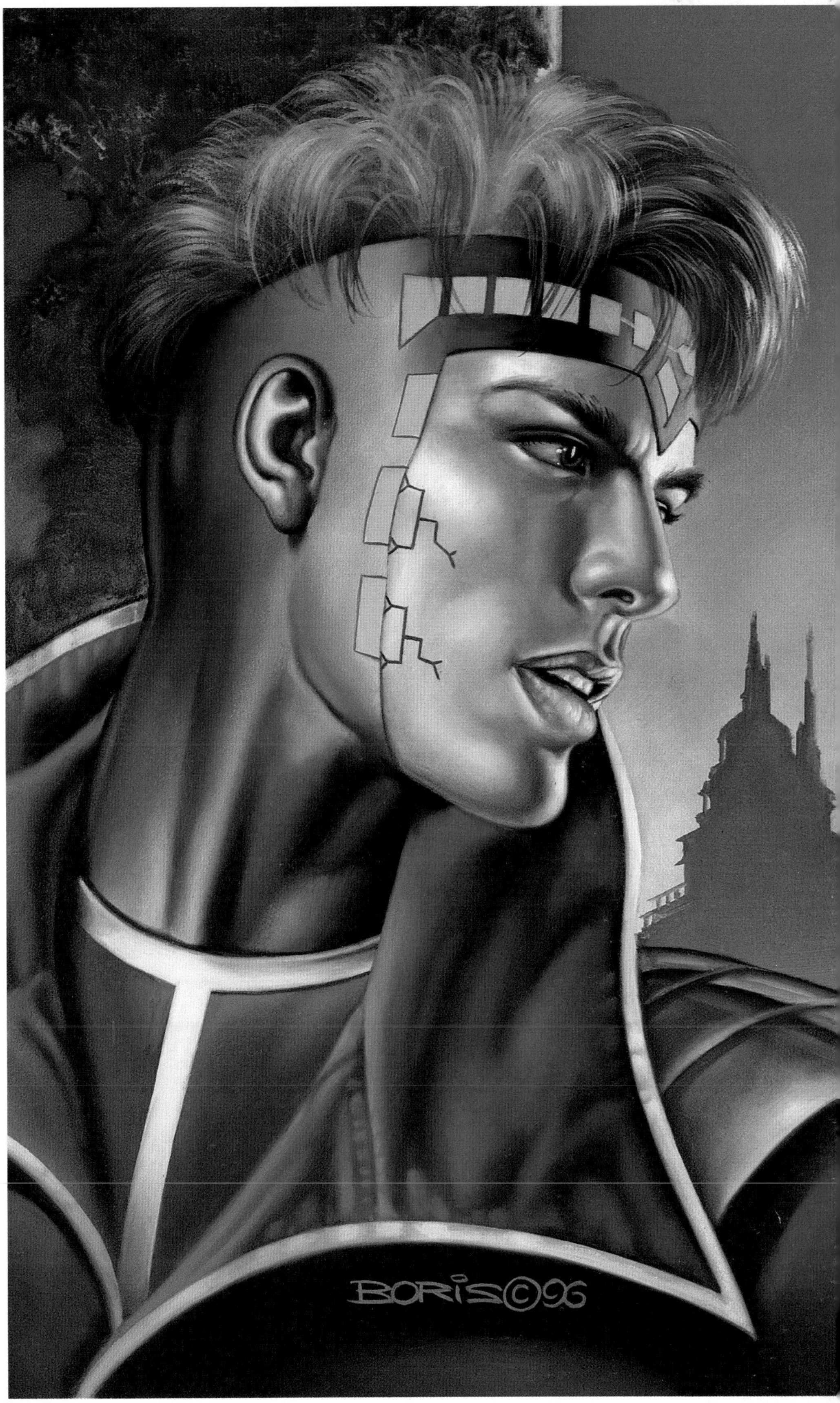
BORIS©96

(left)

VOID

1994, Julie

Trading card. Image Comics

© Aegis Entertainment

For a while silver flesh became almost
a trademark of Julie's, and shiny metal
in some form or another featured in
about half the pictures in her first book
Soft As Steel.

(right)

SILVER SABLE

1995, Julie

Trading Card. Fleer Publishing Co.

TM & © 1995 Marvel Characters, Inc.

All rights reserved.

Silver Sable is one of the more hard-
headed superheroes who believes
in getting paid for her good deeds and
is not too scrupulous about methods.
She considers real selfless do-gooders,
like Spiderman, to be 'amateurs'.

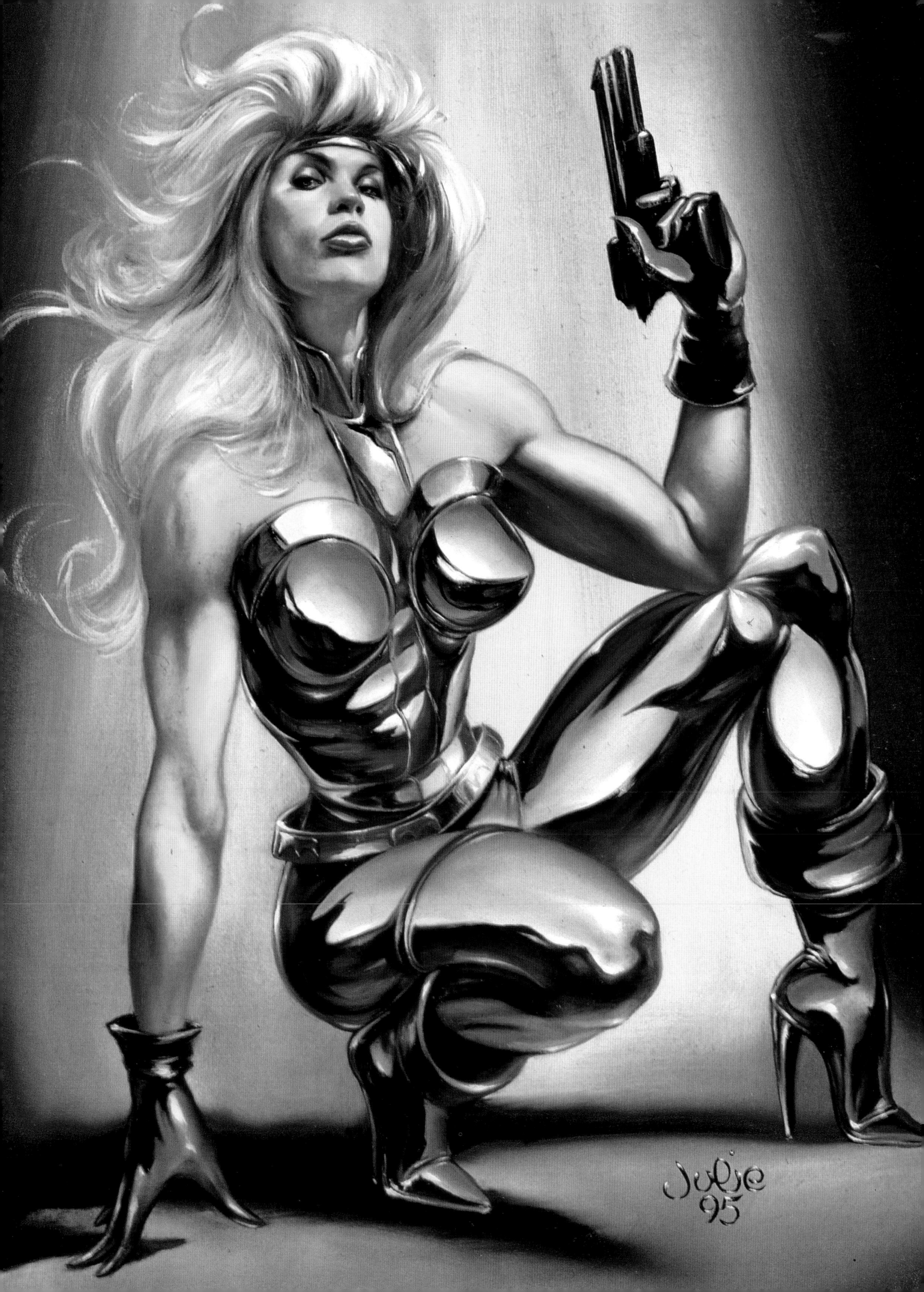
Julie
95

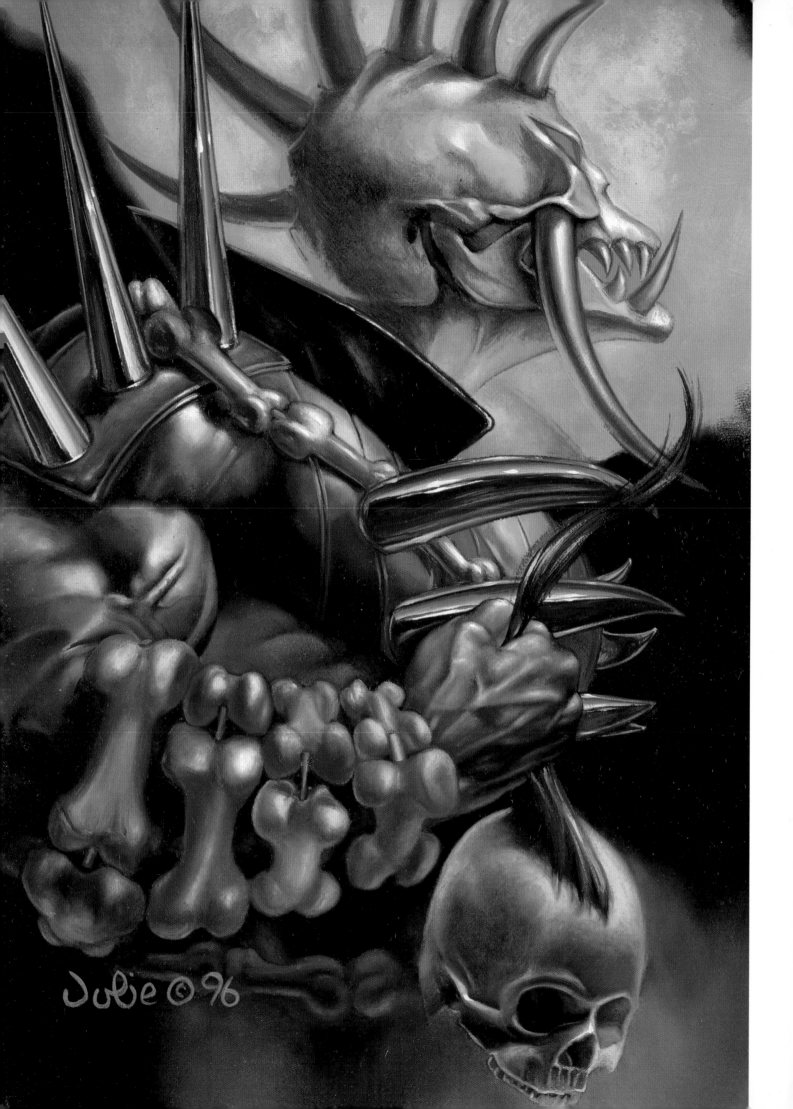

Julie © 96

(far left)
VENGEANCE
1996, Julie
Trading Card. Fleer Publishing Co.
TM & © 1996 Marvel Characters, Inc.
All rights reserved.
One of the few pictures on which Boris and Julie have worked together. Boris came up with the overall layout and 'message', and the idea of showing the character in silhouette; Julie took it from there and really enjoyed playing with the textures. The character is one of Ghost Rider's fellow biking avengers.

(left)
LADY DEMON
1995, Boris
Cover. Chaos! Comics
TM & © 1995 Lady Death.
All rights reserved.

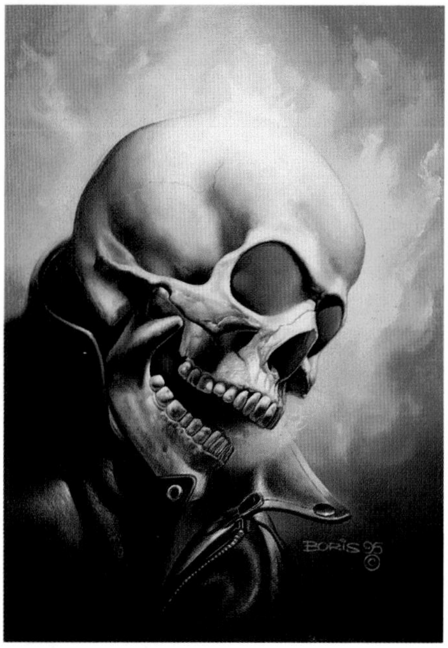
BORIS 95 ©

(above)

GHOST RIDER

1995, Boris

Trading Card. Fleer Publishing Co.

TM & © 1995 Marvel Characters, Inc.

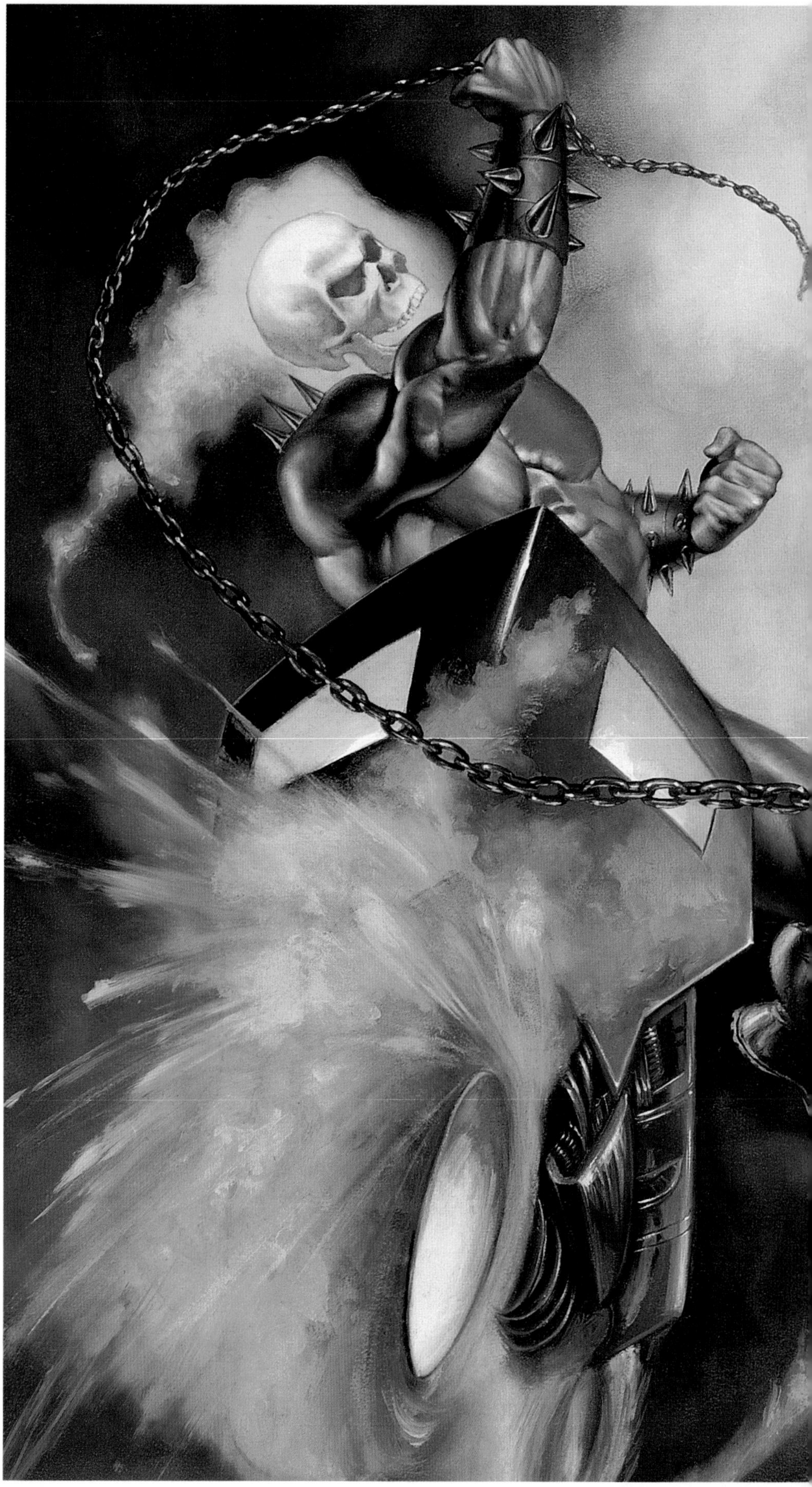

(right)

GHOST RIDER VS BLACKOUT

1996, Julie

Trading Card. Fleer Publishing Co.

TM & © 1996 Marvel Characters, Inc.

Ghost Rider was originally created in the 70s but was relaunched by Marvel in the early 90s. Besides his flaming-wheeled motorbike his main weapon is an extending chain with which he lays low drug barons and other assorted baddies that cross his path. His alter ego is mild-mannered Dan Ketch who was first possessed by the flame-headed Spirit of Vengeance after the murder of his sister. He and Ghost Rider are in fact two quite separate beings alternately sharing the same body, which makes for an interestingly complex relationship.

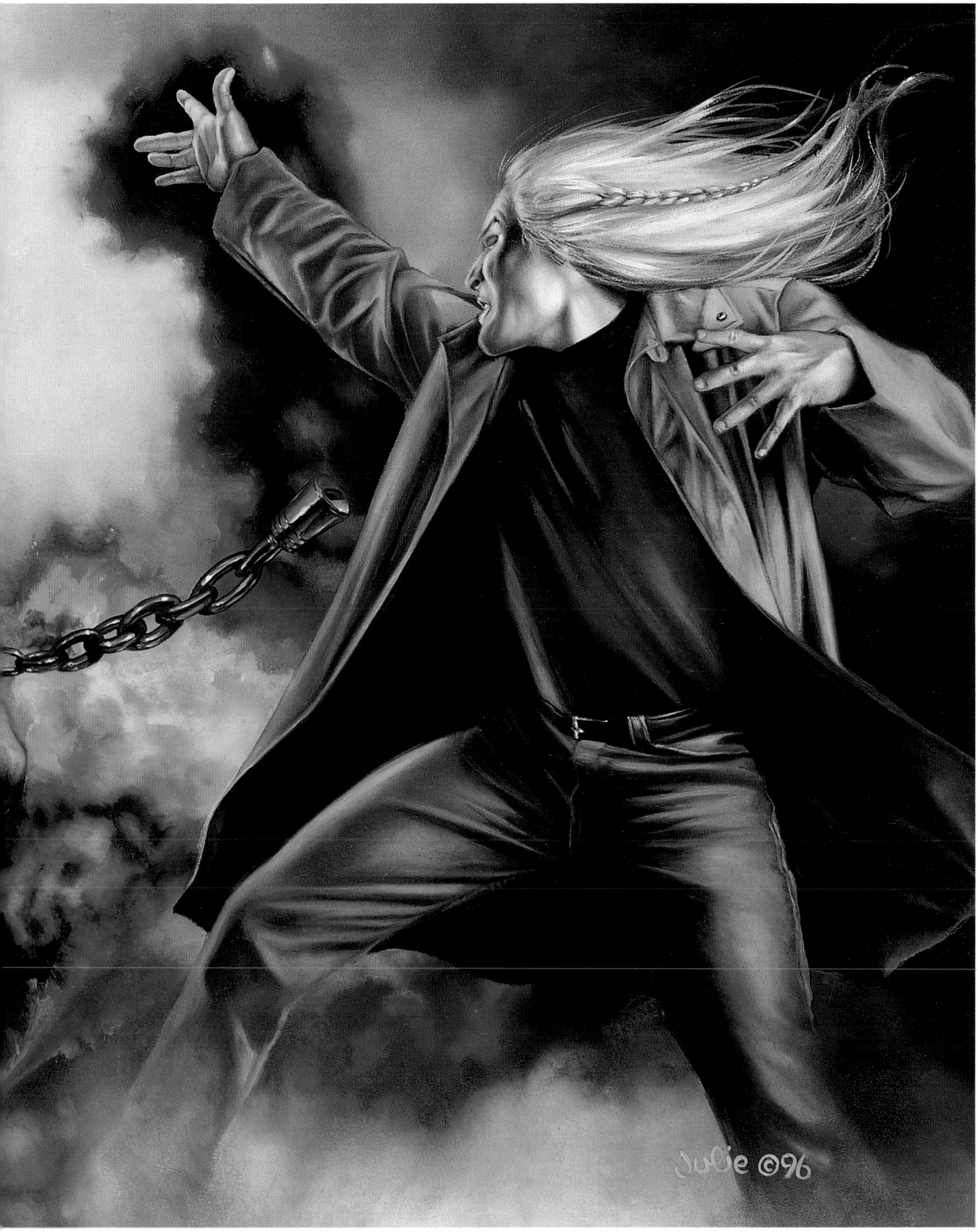
Julie ©96

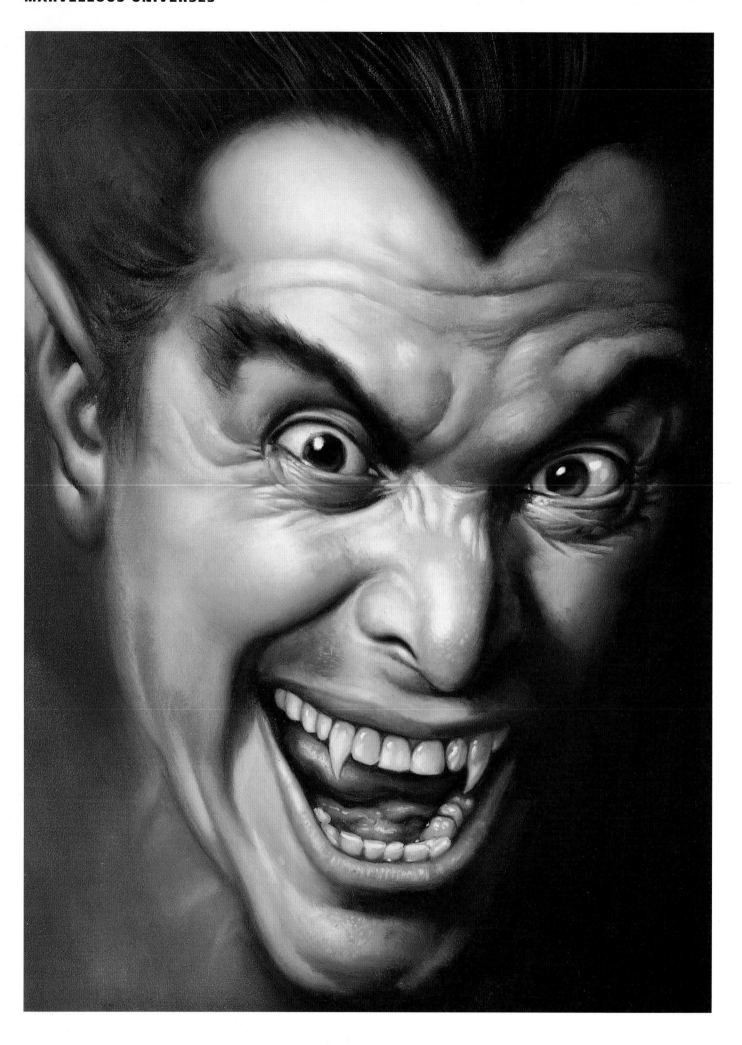

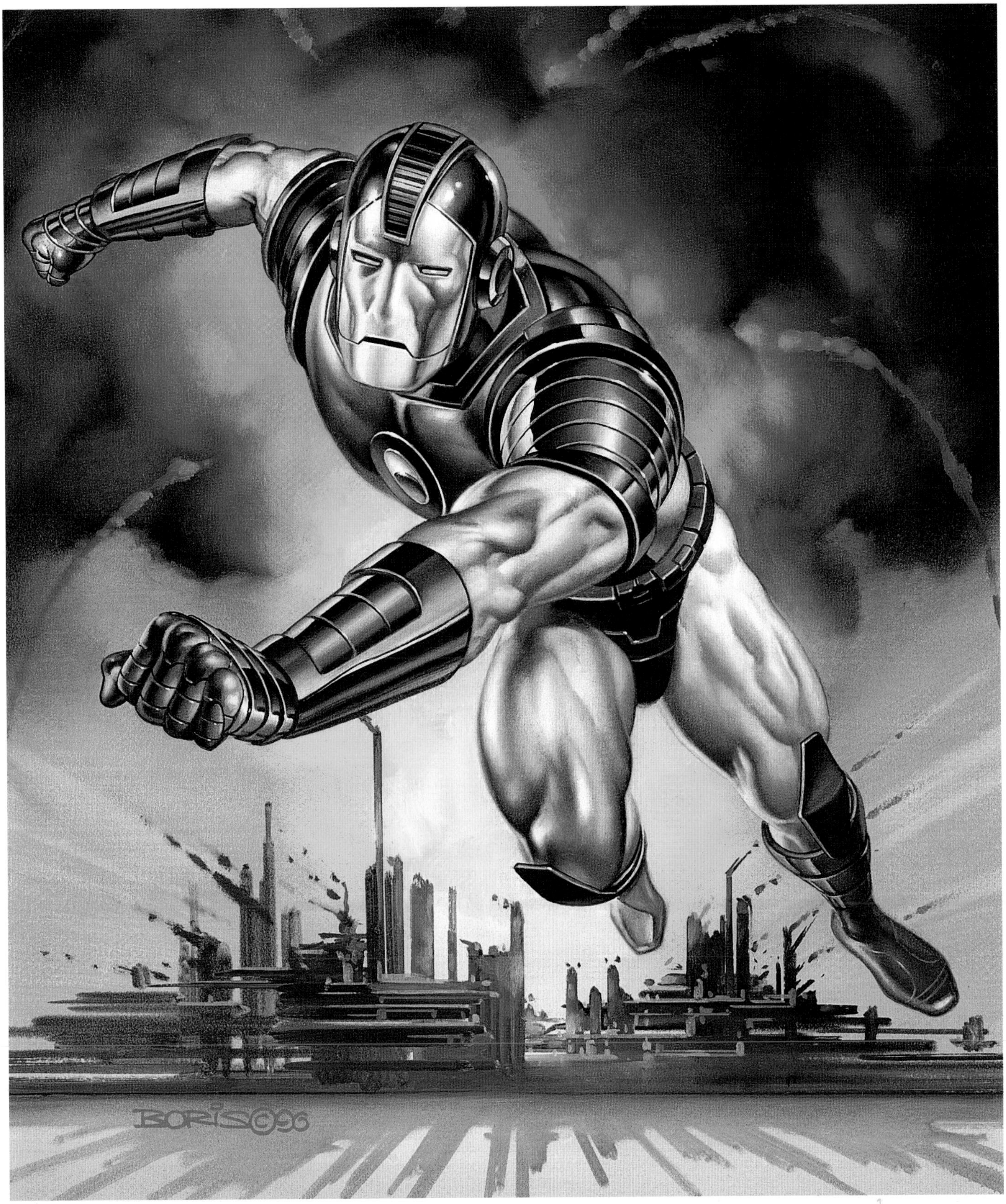
BORIS©96

(left)

JACKAL

1996, Boris

Trading Card. Fleer Publishing Co.

(above)

WAR MACHINE

1995, Boris

Trading Card. Fleer Publishing Co.

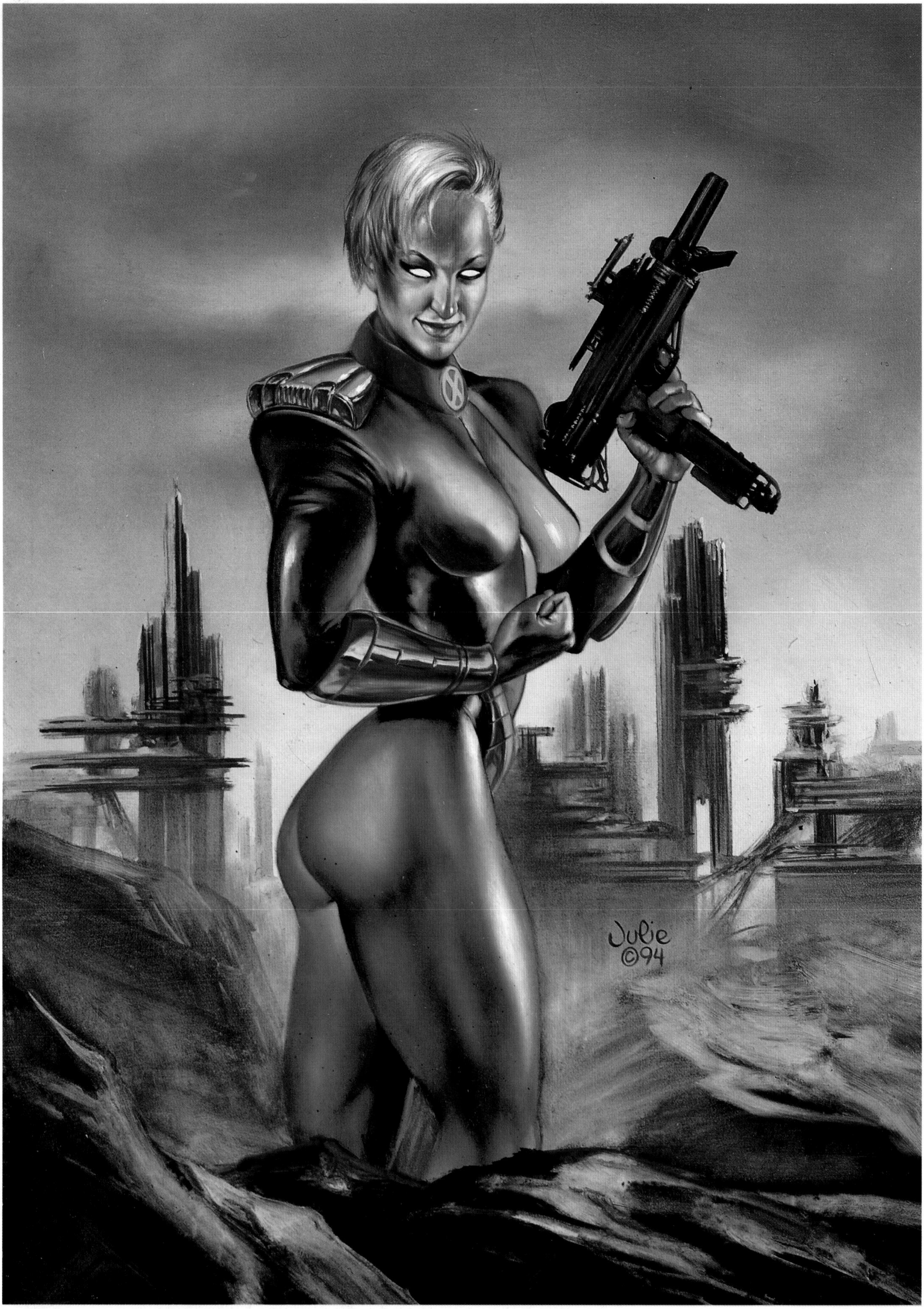
Julie
©94

(left)

ASKANTE

1994, Julie

Trading Card. Fleer Publishing Co.

(right)

GENESIS

1996, Boris

Trading Card. Fleer Publishing Co.

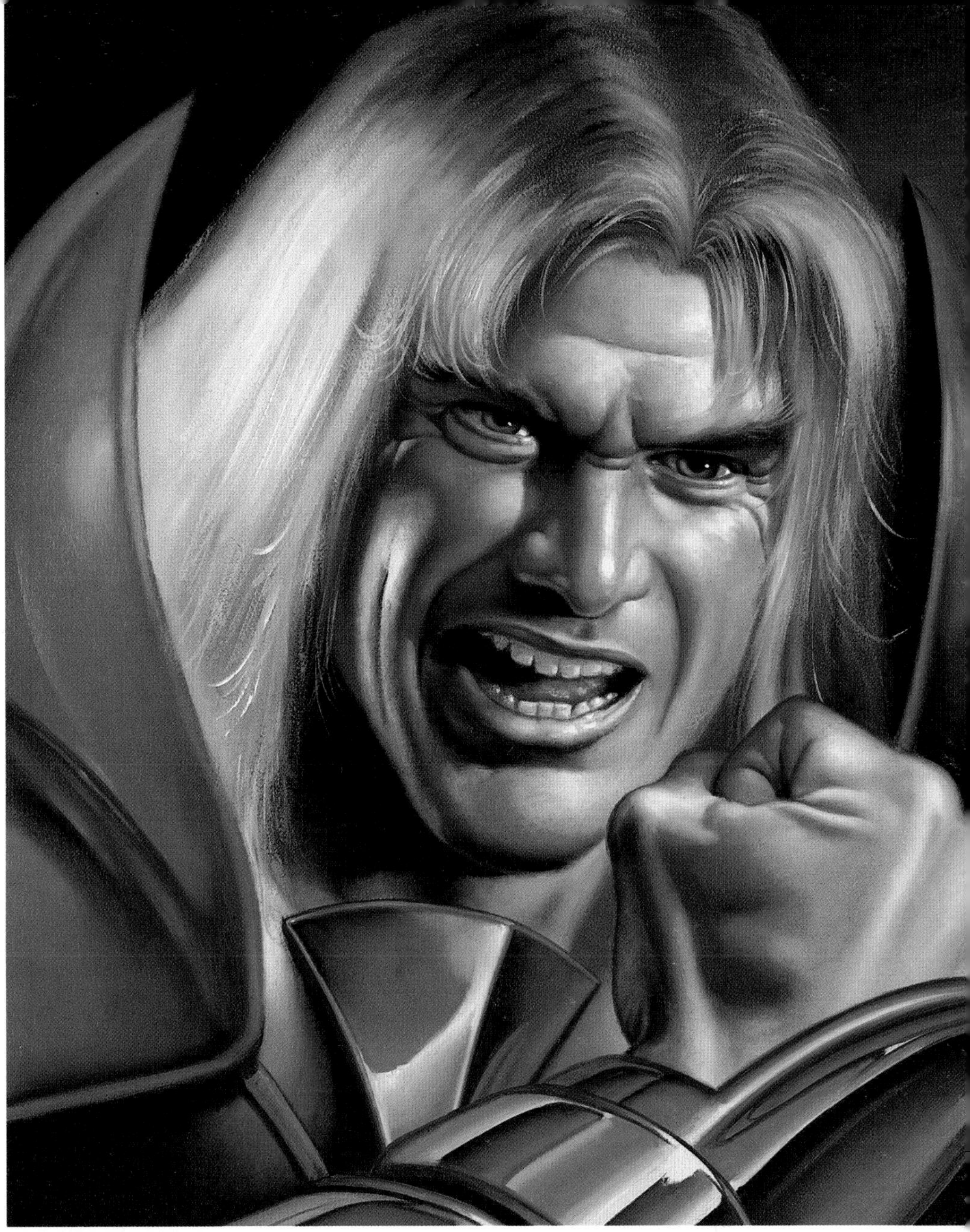

(right)

ASTARTE

1994, Boris

Trading Card. Fleer Publishing Co.

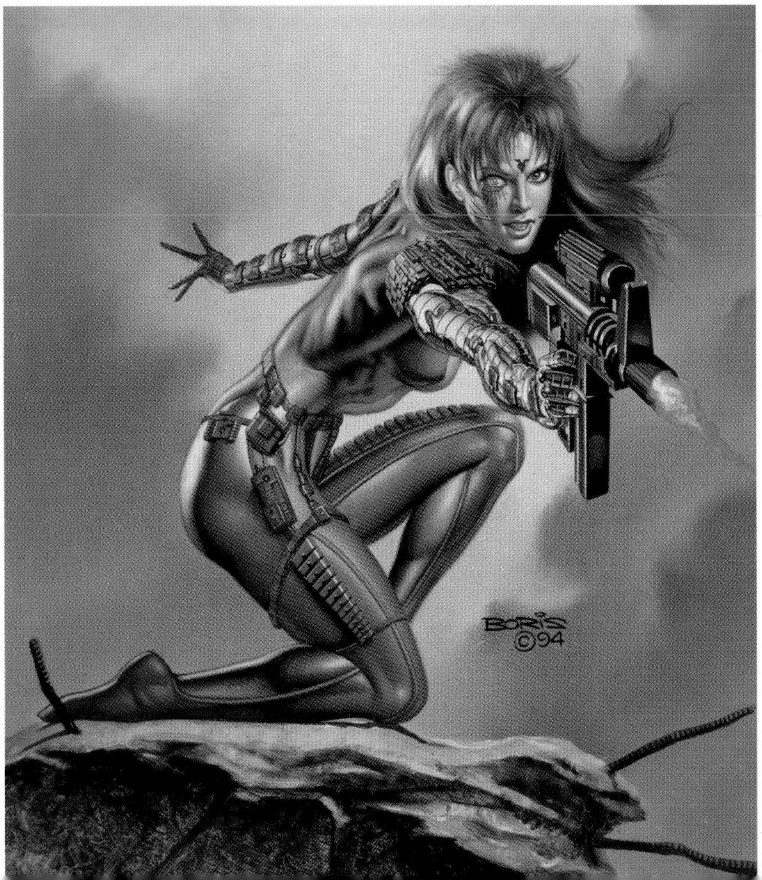
BORIS
©94

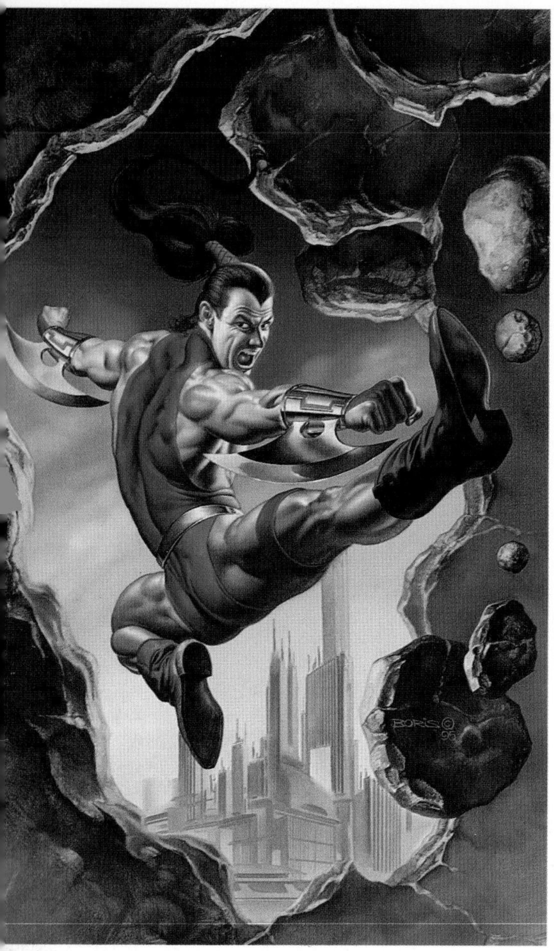

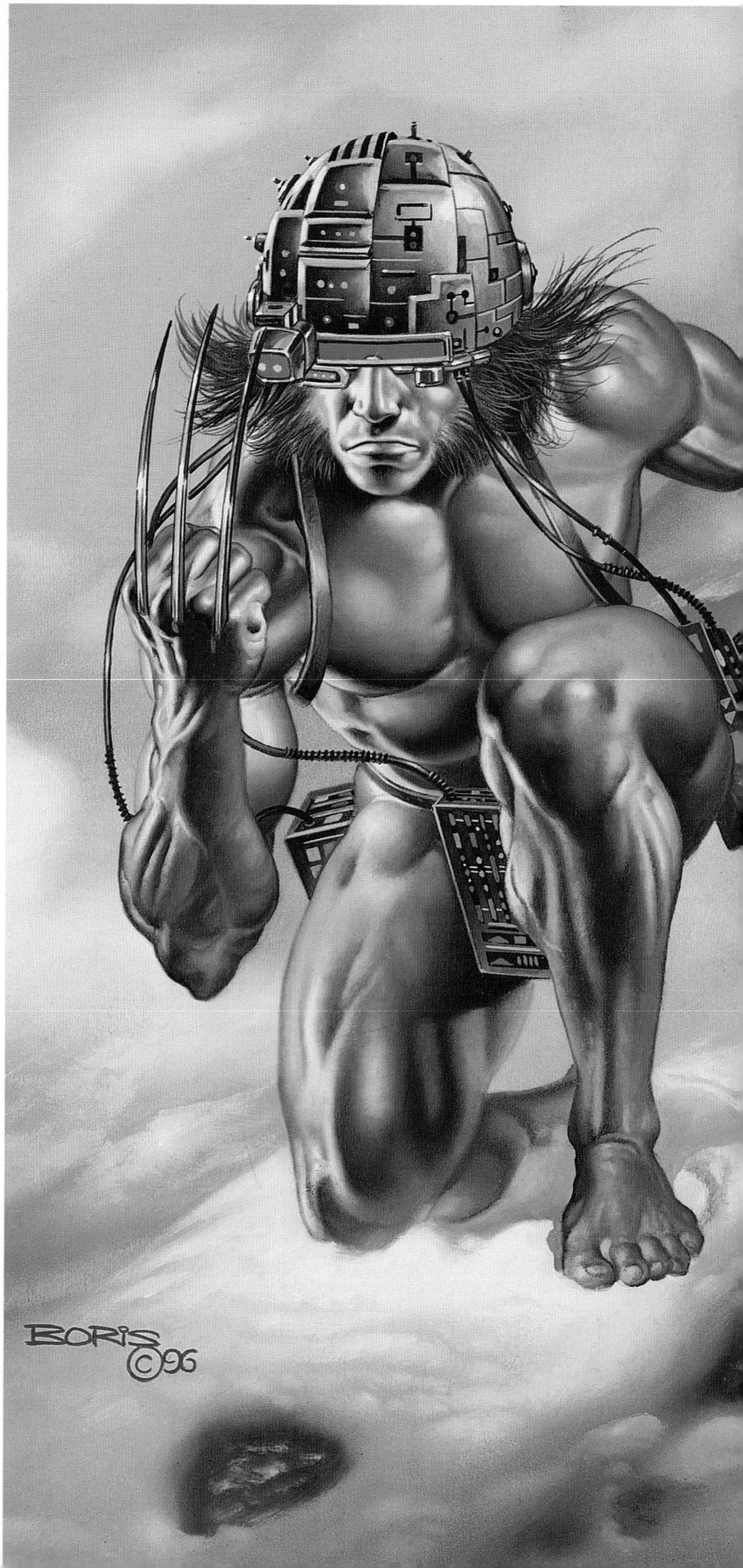
BORIS
©96

(above)

ALLISTER THE SLAYER

1995, Boris

Cover. Midnight Press

(right)

WEAPON X

1996, Boris

Trading Card. Fleer Publishing Co.

(far right)

PROPHET

1995, Boris

Cover. Image Comics

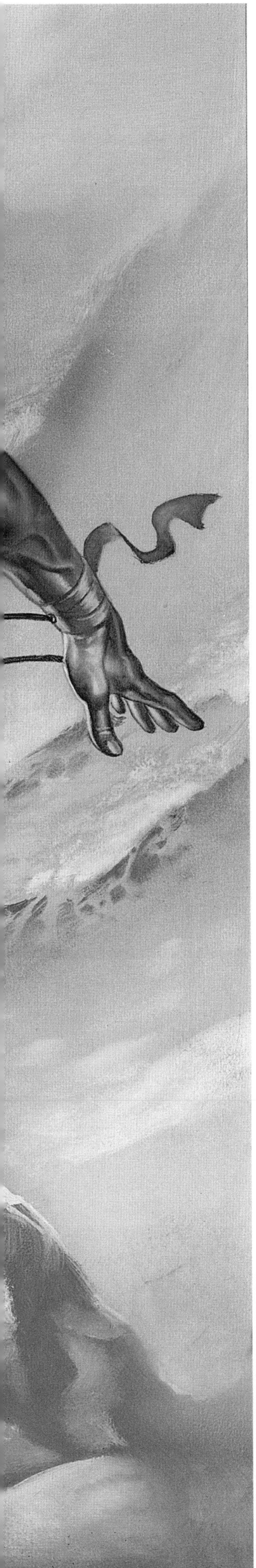

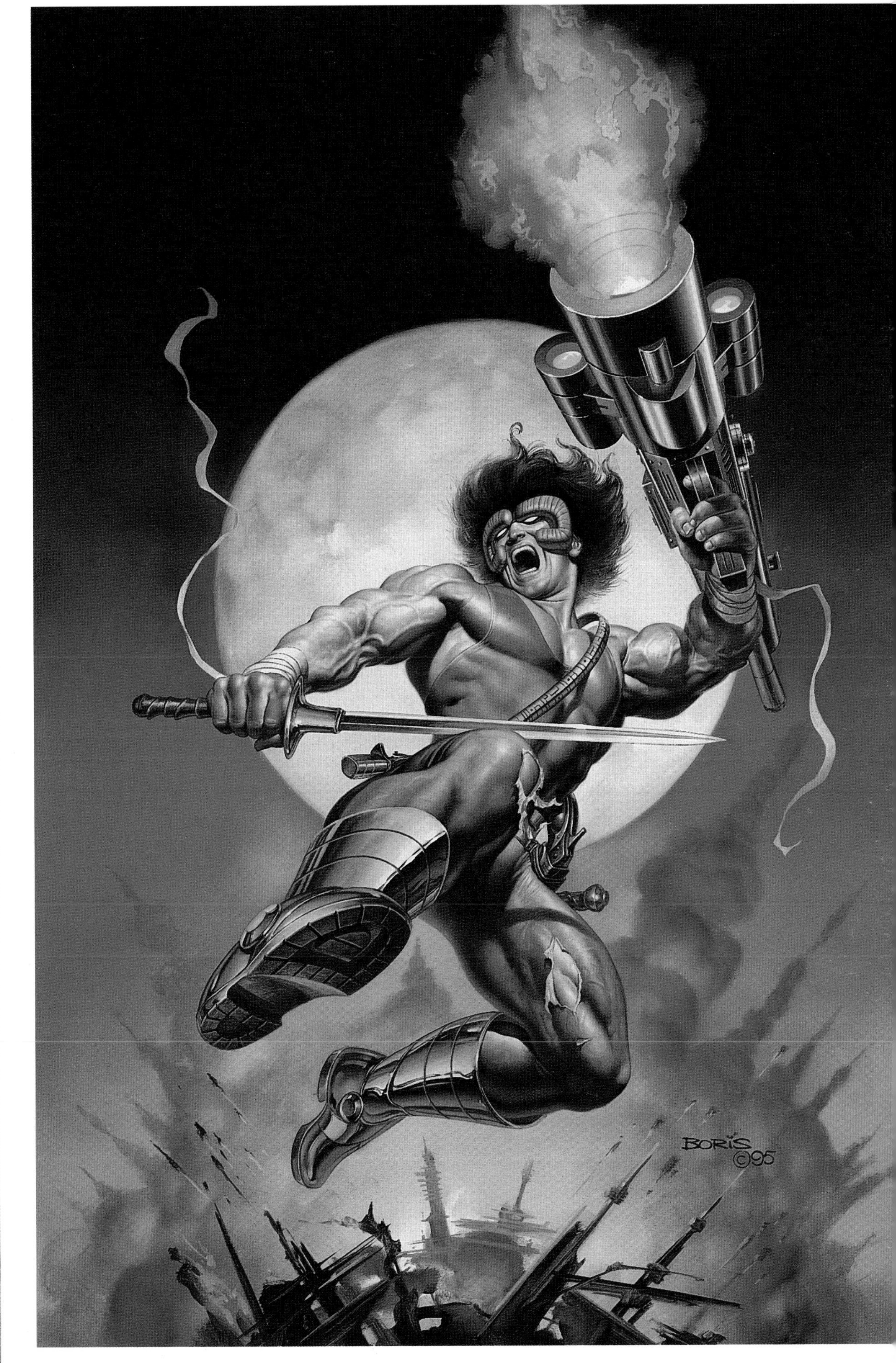
BORIS
©95

(right)

HOLOCAUST

1996, Boris

Trading Card. Fleer Publishing Co.

TM & © 1995 Marvel Characters, Inc.

All rights reserved.

Holocaust is a refugee from the Age of
Apocalypse timeline, where his temper
was not improved when he was
physically destroyed and forced to adopt
a suit of armour to contain his energies.
His aim is to make the universe
uninhabitable to any but himself, but
luckily he gets repeatedly thwarted by
various bands of superheroes.

(far right)

SIENA BLAZE

1994, Boris

Trading Card. Fleer Publishing Co.

TM & © 1994 Marvel Characters, Inc.

All rights reserved.

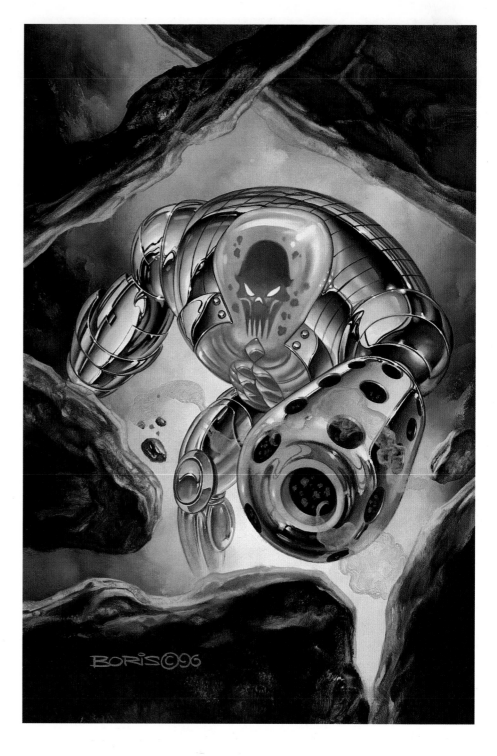

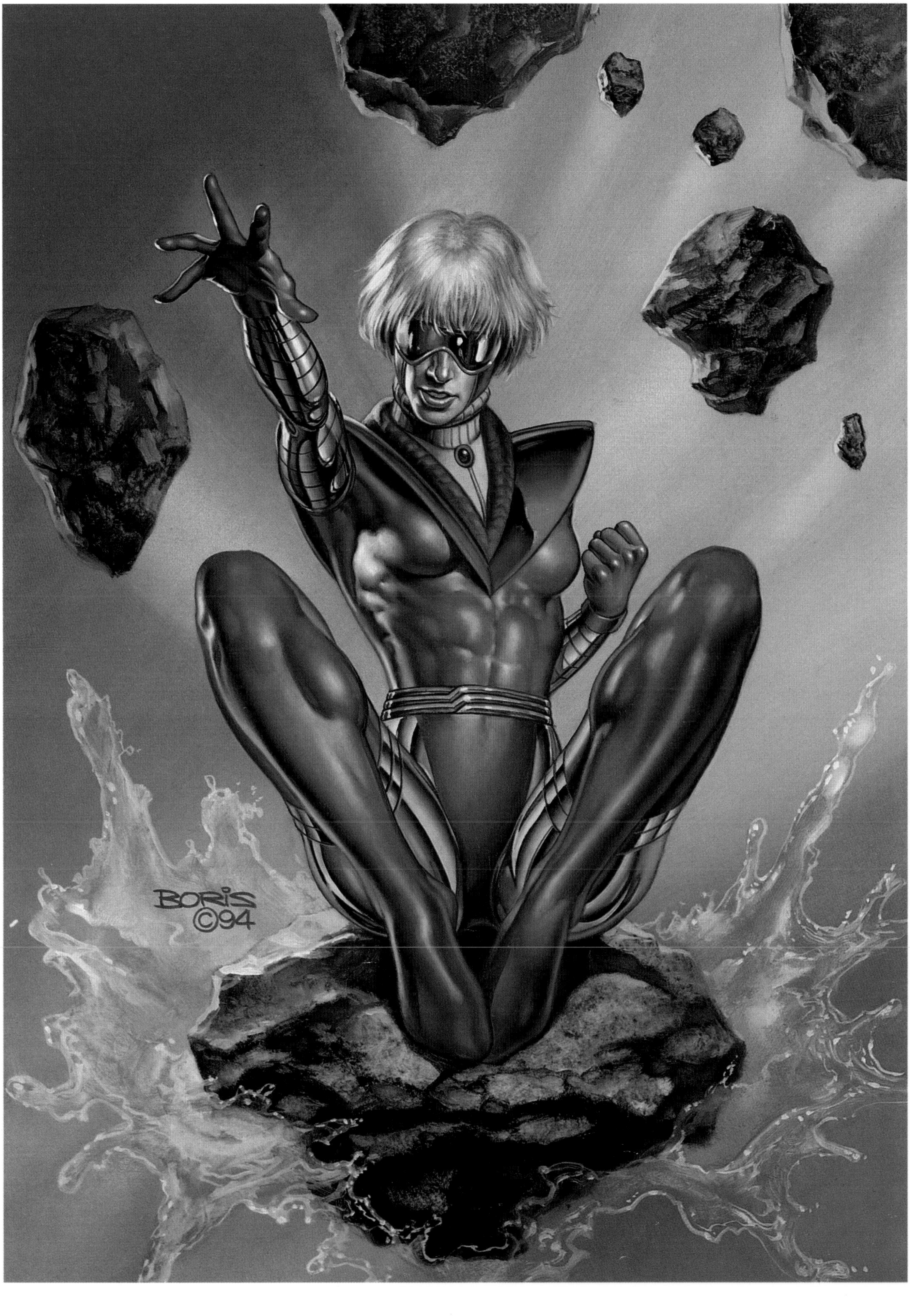
BORIS
©94

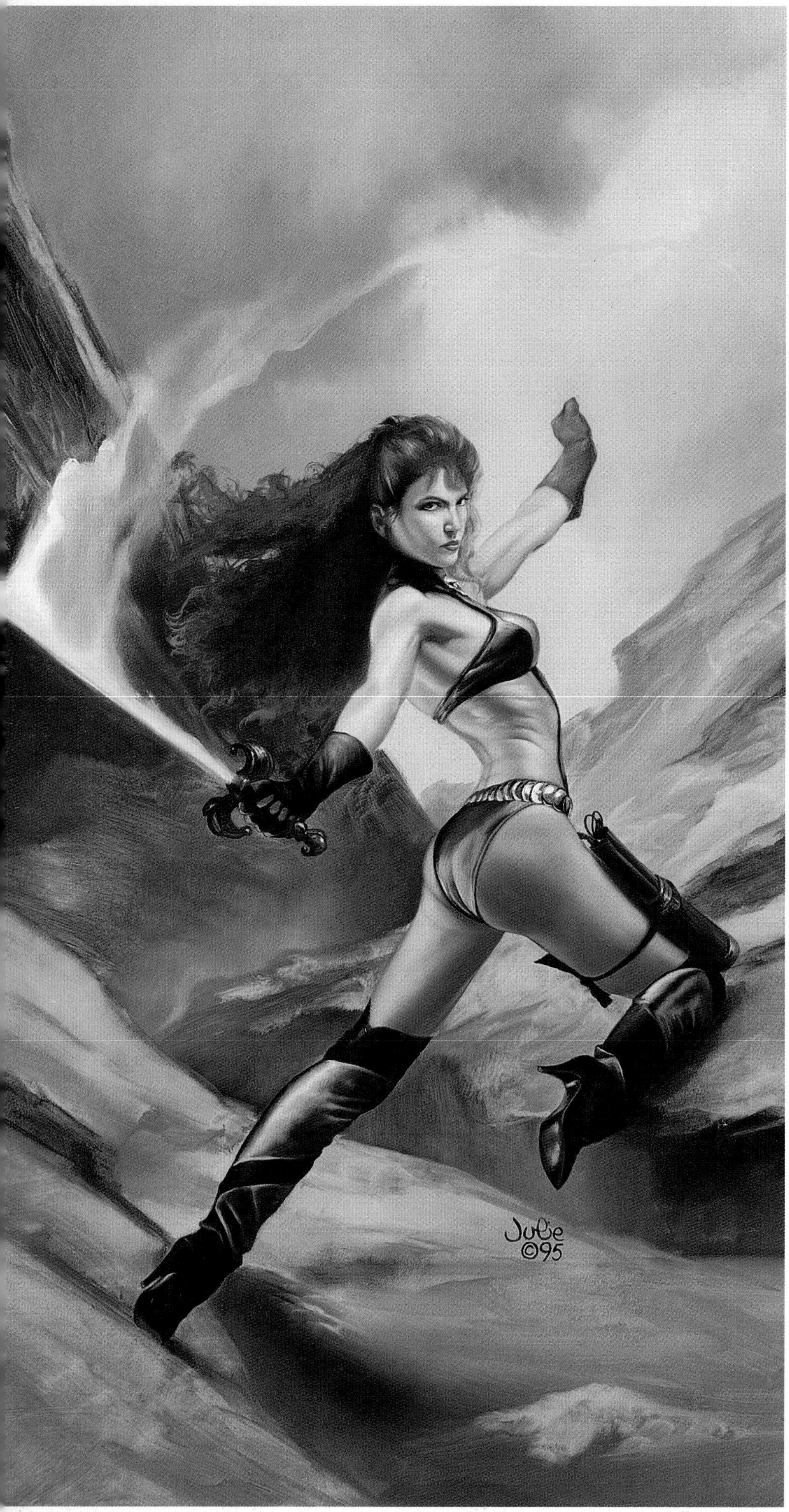
Julie
©95

(left)

BRINKE OF DESTRUCTION

1995, Julie

Cover. Chaos! Comics

(right)

BRINKE

1995, Boris

Cover. Chaos! Comics

Besides writing and starring in her own comics, Brinke Stevens is a cult 'Scream Queen' of B-movies. She almost broke into the A-list by being short-listed for the role of one of Dracula's brides in Coppola's 1994 film *Bram Stoker's Dracula* but didn't quite make it into the final three. She has few regrets though, saying she prefers B-movies anyway, because they are so quickly made. She first broke into movies by finding that being prepared to undress for a shower scene opens many doors in Hollywood. From there she progressed to her first Roger Corman horror movie, *Slumber Party Massacre* in which, well, you can guess really. She also has a Master's degree in Marine Biology and worked in that field for a while until the bright lights beckoned.

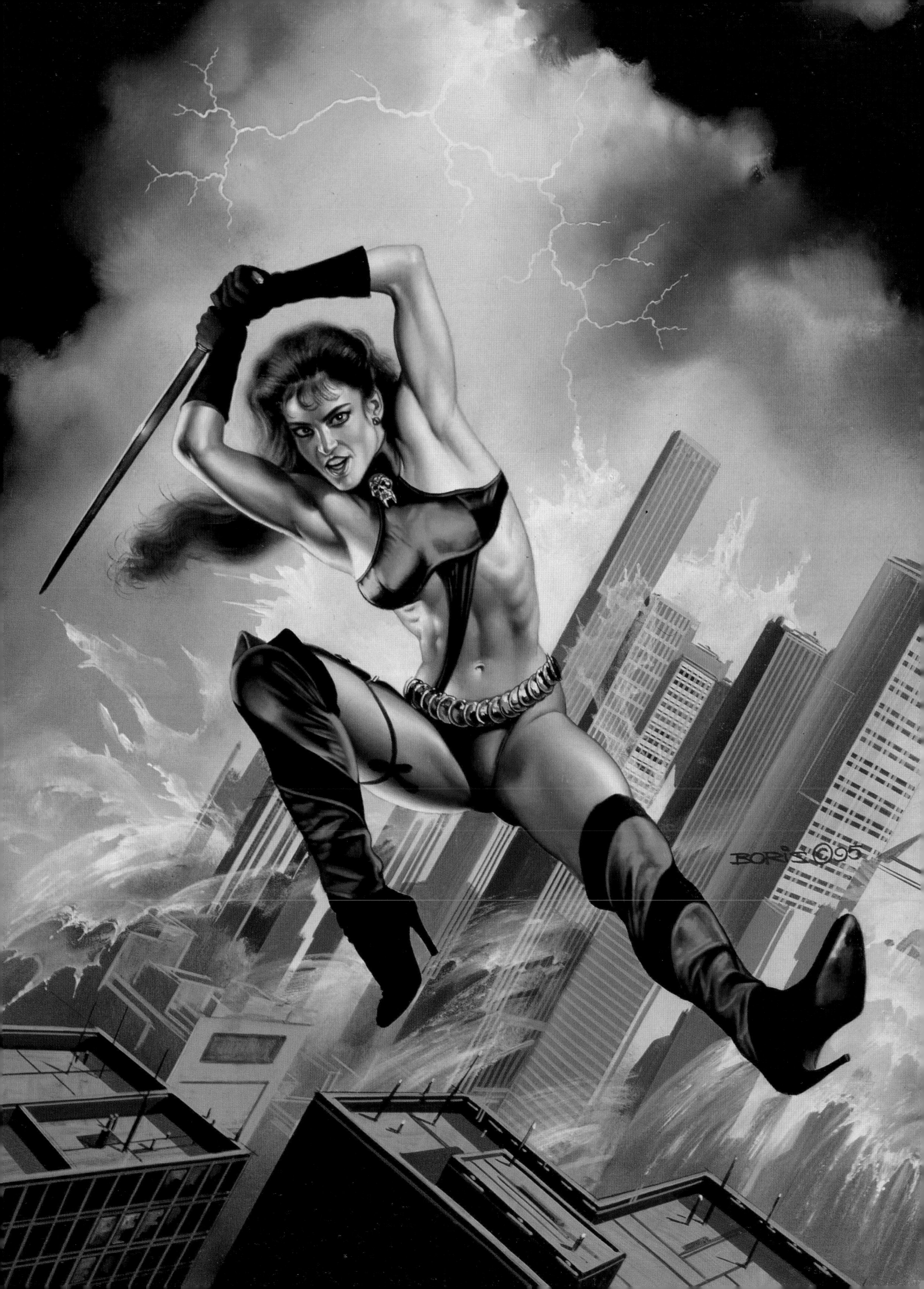
BORIS ©95

(right)

ZEALOT

1994, Boris

Trading Card. Image Comics

(far right)

US AGENT

1996, Boris

Trading Card. Fleer Publishing Co.

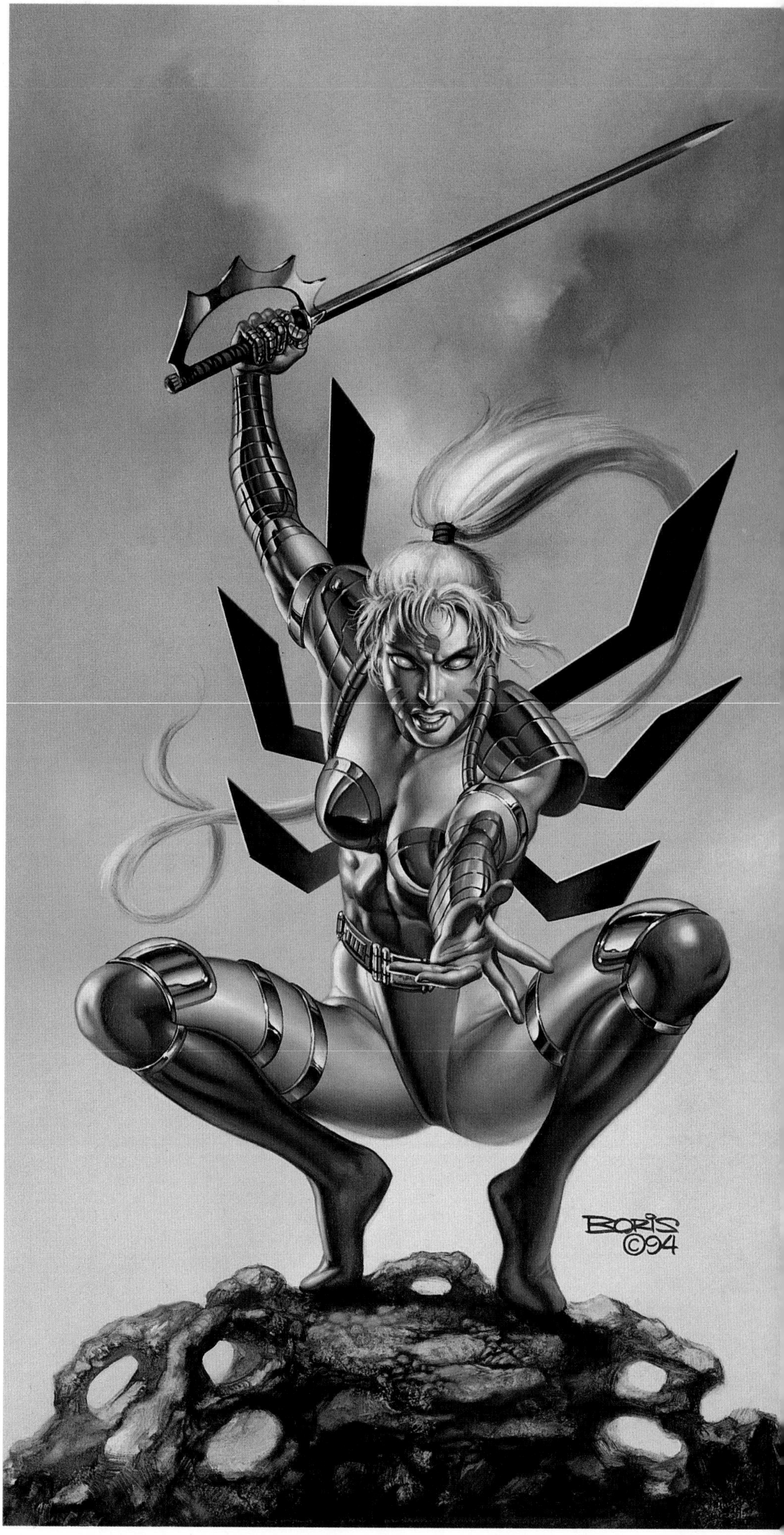
BORIS
©94

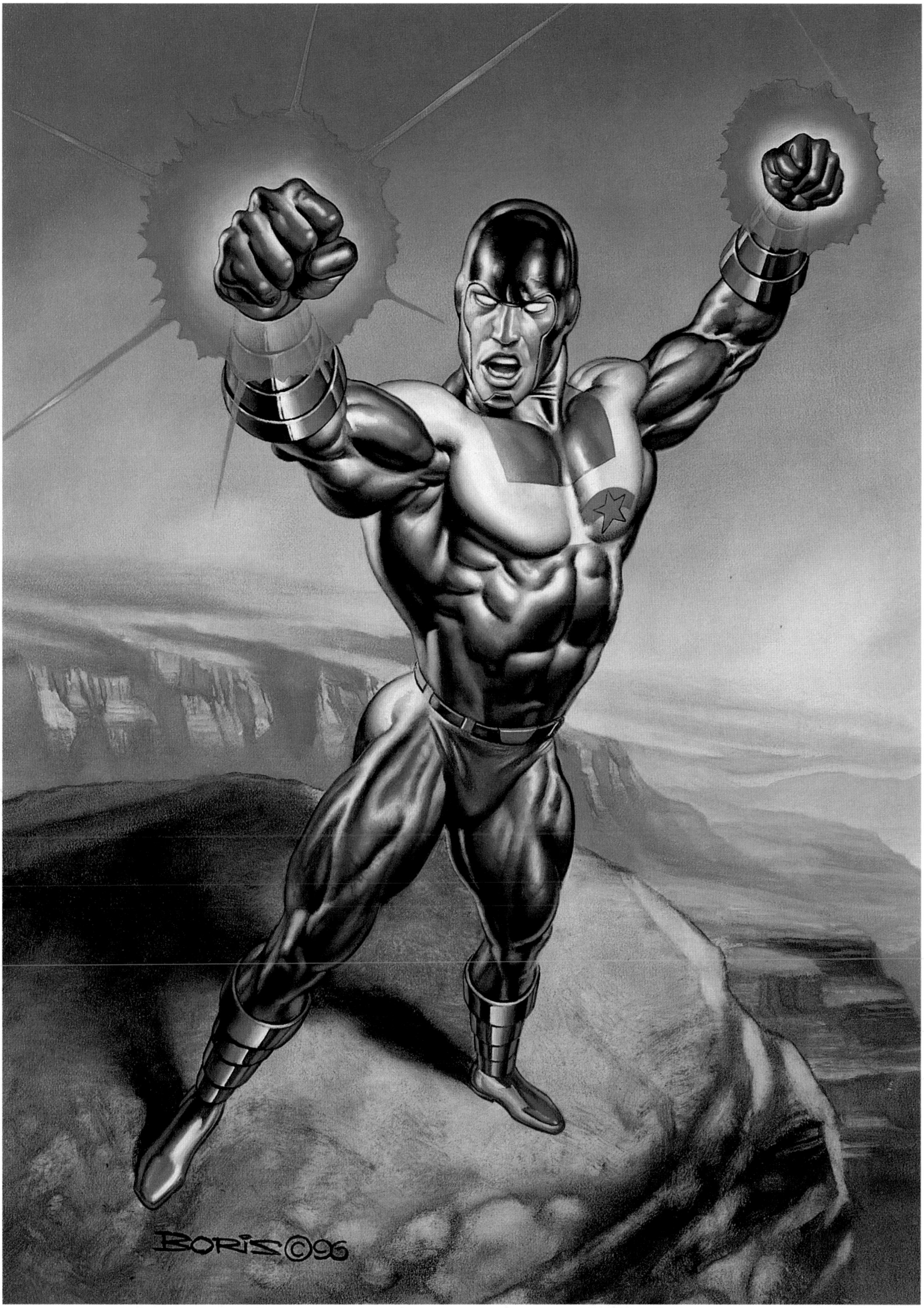
BORIS©96

THUNDERSTRIKE
1996, Julie
Trading Card. Fleer Publishing Co.
TM & © 1996 Marvel Characters, Inc.
All rights reserved.

LADY DEATHSTRYKE
1996, Julie
Trading Card. Fleer Publishing Co.
TM & © 1996 Marvel Characters, Inc.
All rights reserved.

Lady Deathstryke is one of the more colourful villains of the Marvel universe. As Yuriko Oyama, she first appeared in the Daredevil comics, allied with him against her own father, Dark Wind (Kenji Oyama), a Japanese crime lord and inventor. But after killing Dark Wind she has a change of heart and takes on his mantle of crime herself. Believing Wolverine to have stolen the secret of his unbreakable bones from her father, she hunts him down with the aid of the psychotic Reavers. She also willingly suffers transformation into a cybernetic hybrid in order to be on a more equal footing with him.

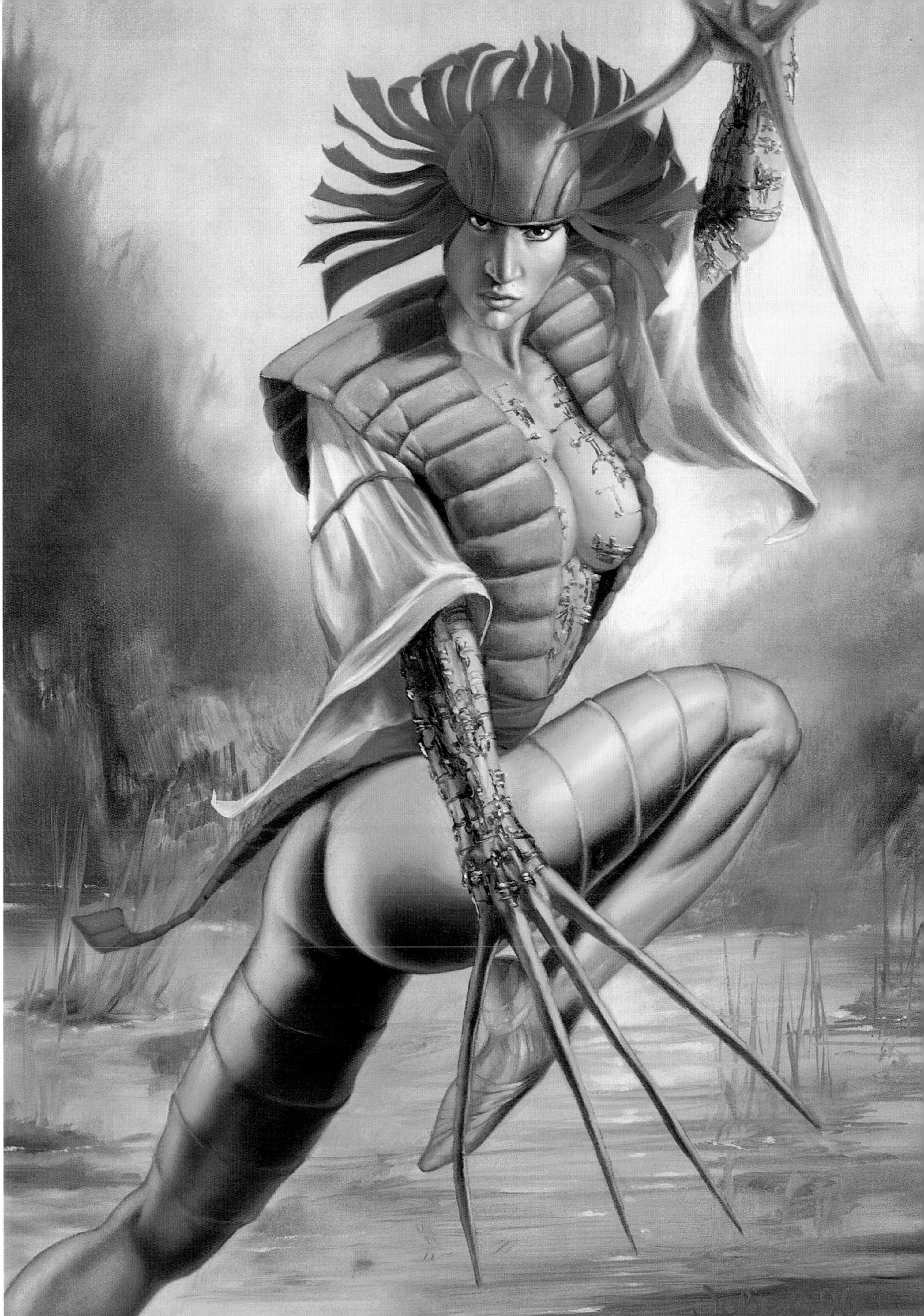

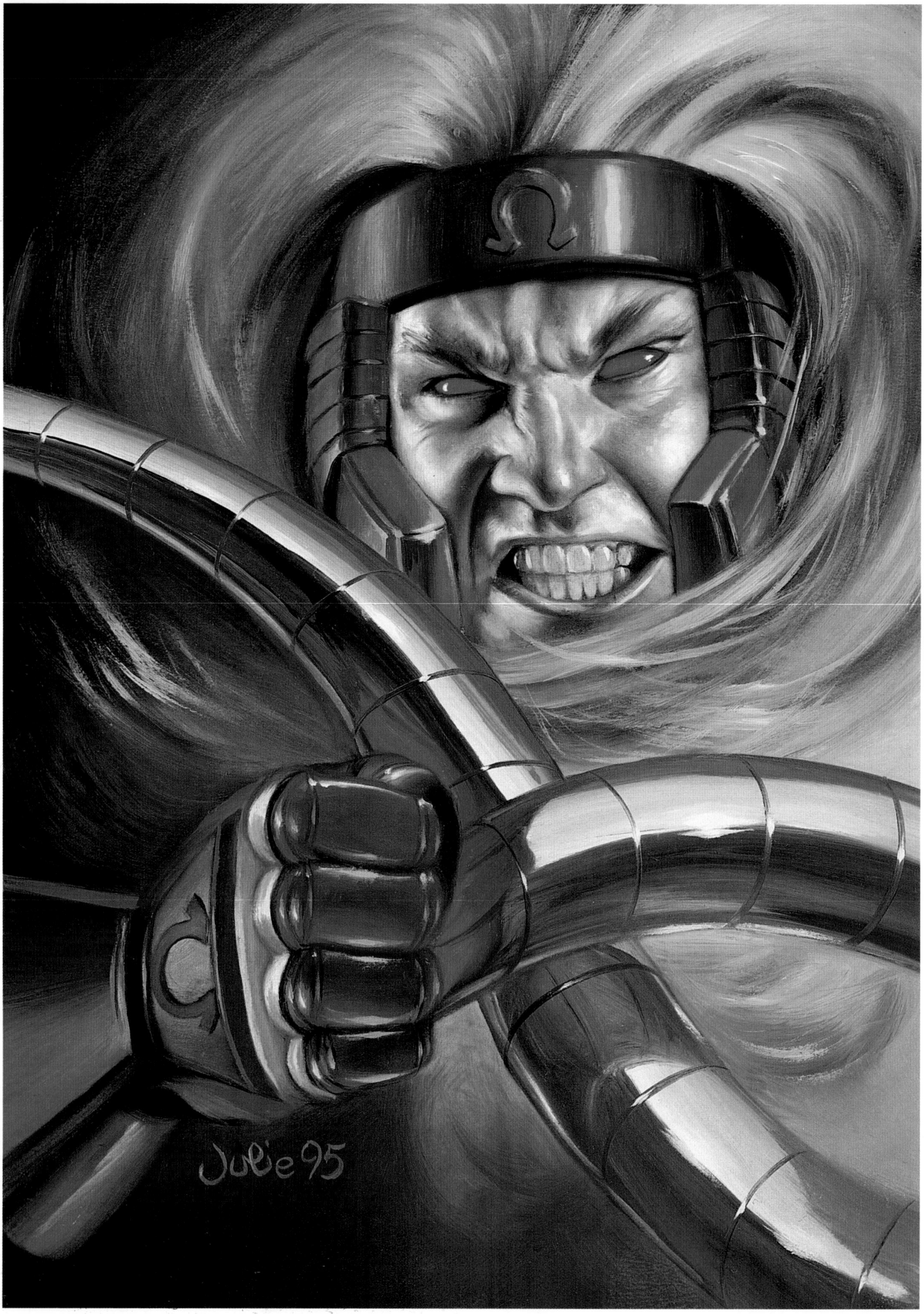
Julie 95

(left)
OMEGA RED

1995, Julie

Trading Card. Fleer Publishing Co.

TM & © 1995 Marvel Characters, Inc.

All rights reserved.

(right)
GEN 13

1998, Julie

Book cover. Byron Preiss Multimedia

© Aegis Entertainment Inc.

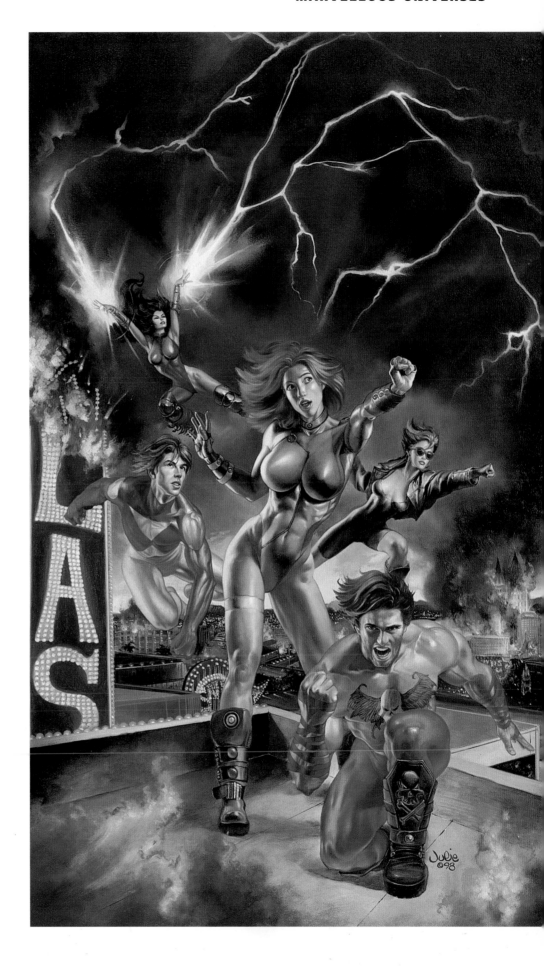

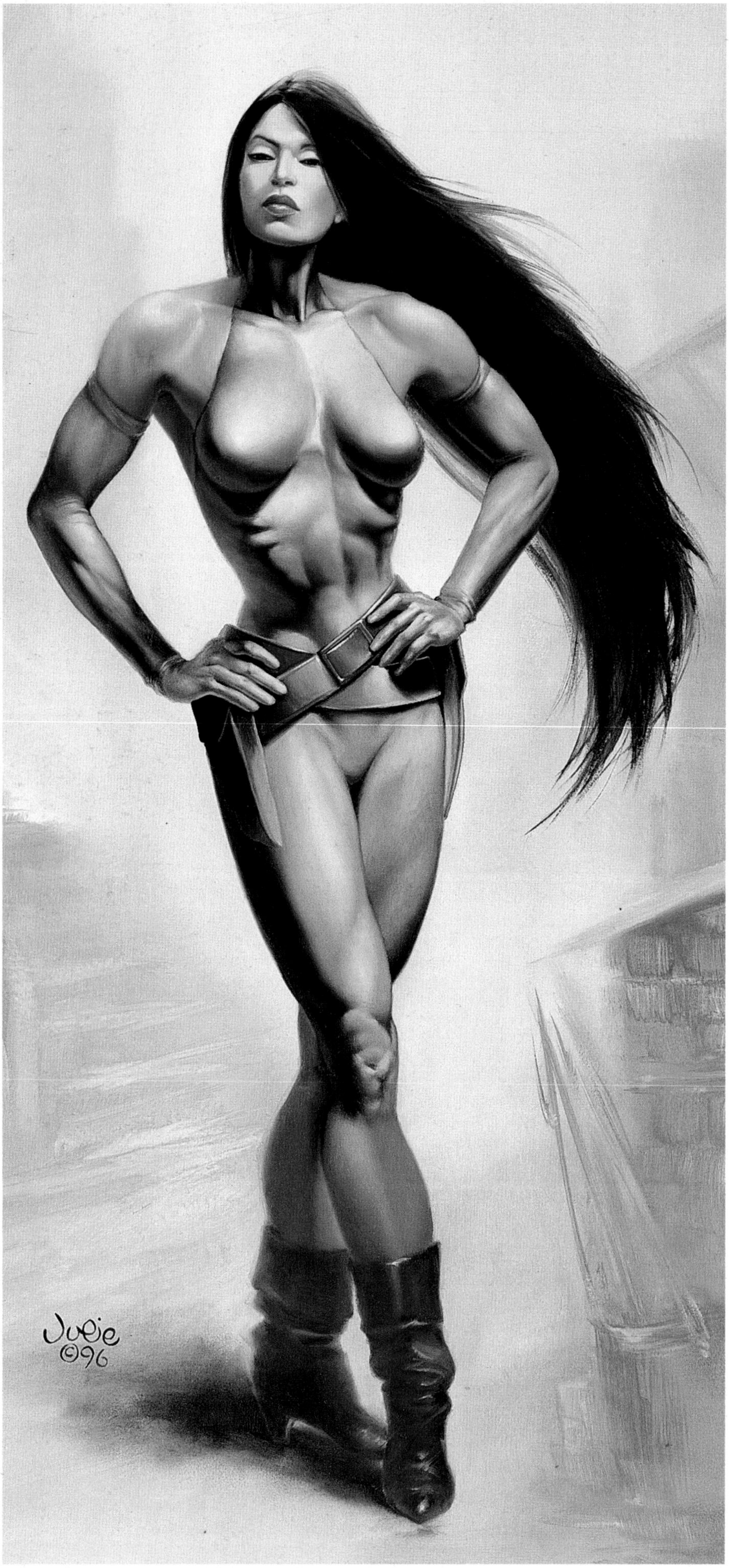
Julie
©96

(left)

HYDRA

1996, Julie

Trading Card. Fleer Publishing Co.

(right)

ACTION FIGURES

1995, Boris

Cover. Penthouse Comix

Not exactly standard superheroes, these vampire hunters were painted for the cover of a Penthouse publishing venture that Boris and Julie both had fun with for a while. The tone of these 'adult' comics was very tongue-in-cheek and light-hearted. In this case, it's plainly more important that the girls look sexy than that they are even faintly equipped to take on a vampire, but that was kind of the joke.

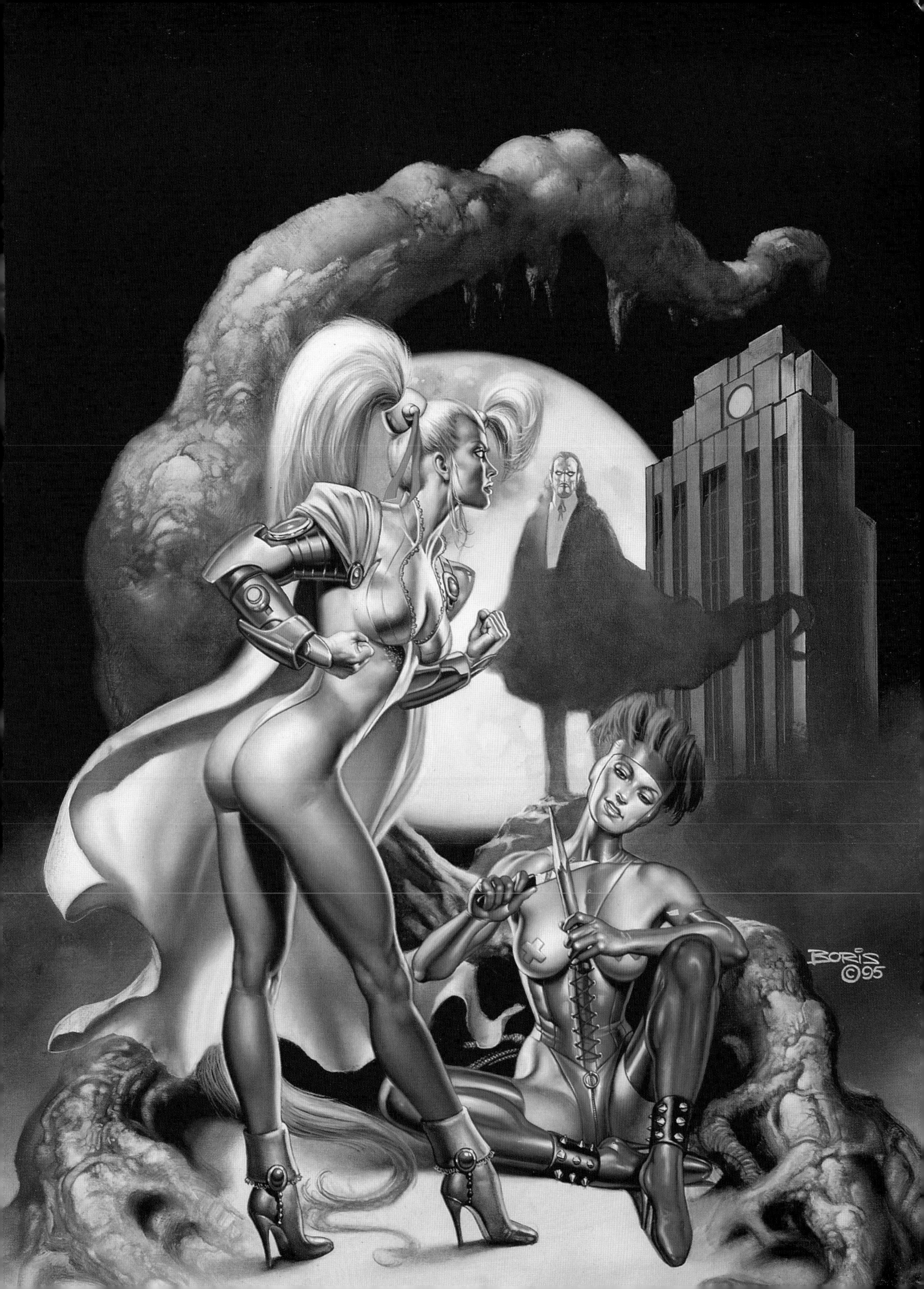
BORIS
©95

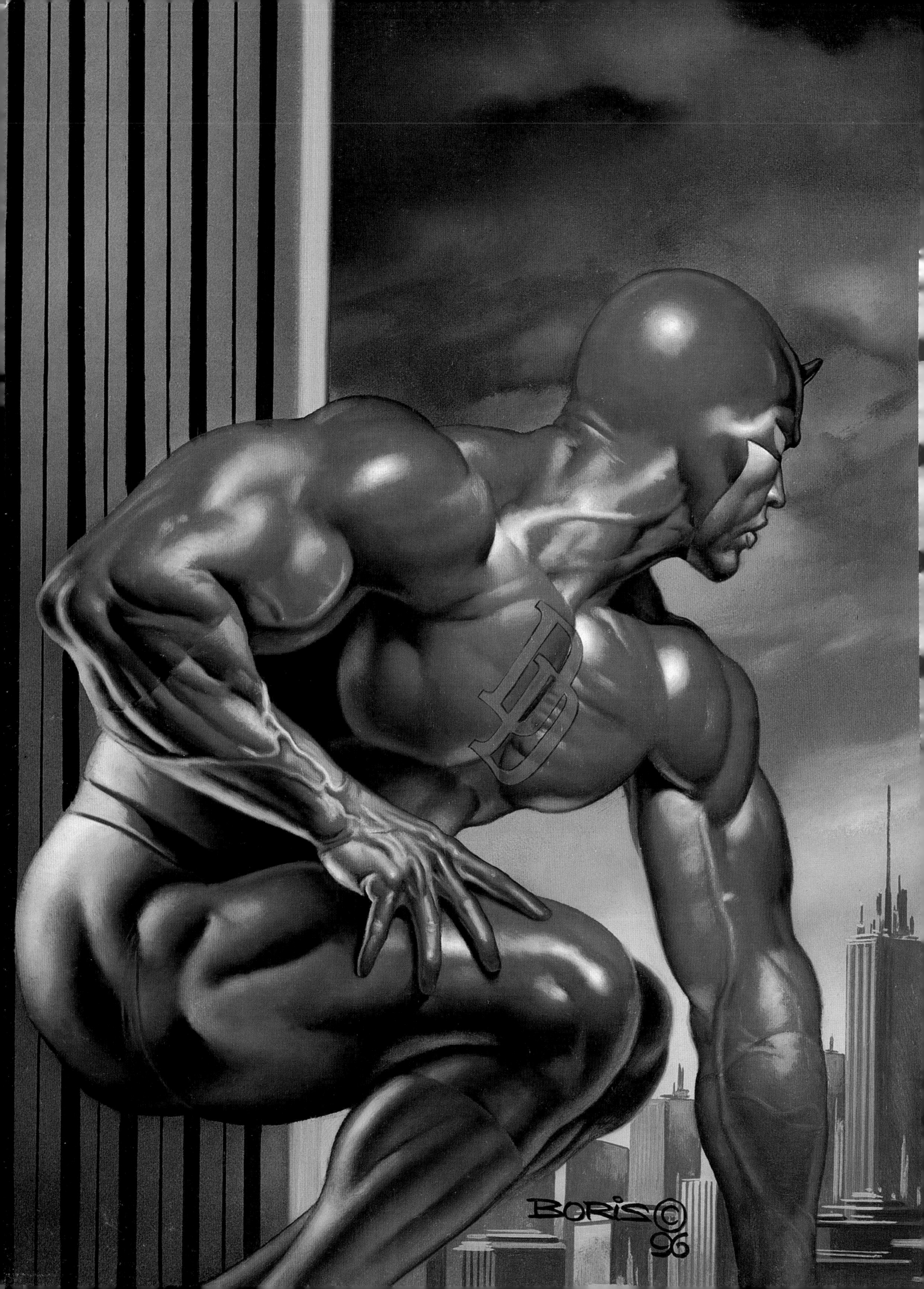
BORIS ©
96

Marvel Knights and DC Days

So here's a million-dollar question: if this book happened to sell a million copies, what would be Boris and Julie's reaction? Boris laughs: 'It may sound funny but it wouldn't surprise me. I'd be delighted of course but I always believe everyone has the potential to do as well as anyone else. A million copies? Well yes that would be wonderful, but our main reaction would be that the next book has to be even better.' Julie adds: 'You can't ever just let it slide. Having success is no reason to stop trying as hard.'

So they wouldn't be tempted to take a year off to lie in the sun? This provokes incredulous laughter from both. 'If anything it is the exact opposite. We both thrive on work. We paint because we love it. We're always competing with ourselves to do better. We just love the challenge.'

Boris goes on: 'Sometimes we decide to take the evening off after dinner to do nothing. Then after a while it's like, so OK, what now? We don't feel comfortable not working. Art is a great stimulant, it's not just a job.' Julie: 'It's what we enjoy, we're just lucky also to be paid for it.'

So would they be happy painting nothing but superheroes for the rest of their days? Julie: 'Superheroes are just perfect for us with their emphasis on the figure and so on. Also we can always find an angle that makes the pictures personal to us as well as pleasing our clients. But if they were the only thing we were allowed to do, it would be frustrating.'

(left)

DAREDEVIL 2

1996, Boris

Trading Card. Fleer Publishing Co.

TM & © 1996 Marvel Characters, Inc.

All rights reserved.

(right)

PATROLLING NEW YORK

1996, Julie

Trading Card. Fleer Publishing Co.

TM & © 1996 Marvel Characters, Inc.

All rights reserved.

The Marvel Knights are a fairly new superhero team that has quickly gained a devoted following. They began as an offshoot of the Fantastic Four and Dr Strange sagas but now have their own titles and fan base.

Daredevil is one of the main characters. His attributes, as the name suggests, include fearlessness but according to Marvel mythology, the nickname was first given in mockery because he was such a wimp. Matthew Murdock is the son of a prize fighter who made him promise not to follow in his footsteps. So all violent activity was banned and young Matthew buckled down to his studies and became a geek in the eyes of his fellow students. Finally their taunts grew too much and he began training to fight in secret. Then one day he threw himself in front of a truck to save a blind man and was drenched in radioactive waste that spilled out of the wreck, which was how he acquired his superpowers.

(far right)

DAREDEVIL 1

1995, Boris

Trading Card. Fleer Publishing Co.

TM & © 1995 Marvel Characters, Inc.

All rights reserved.

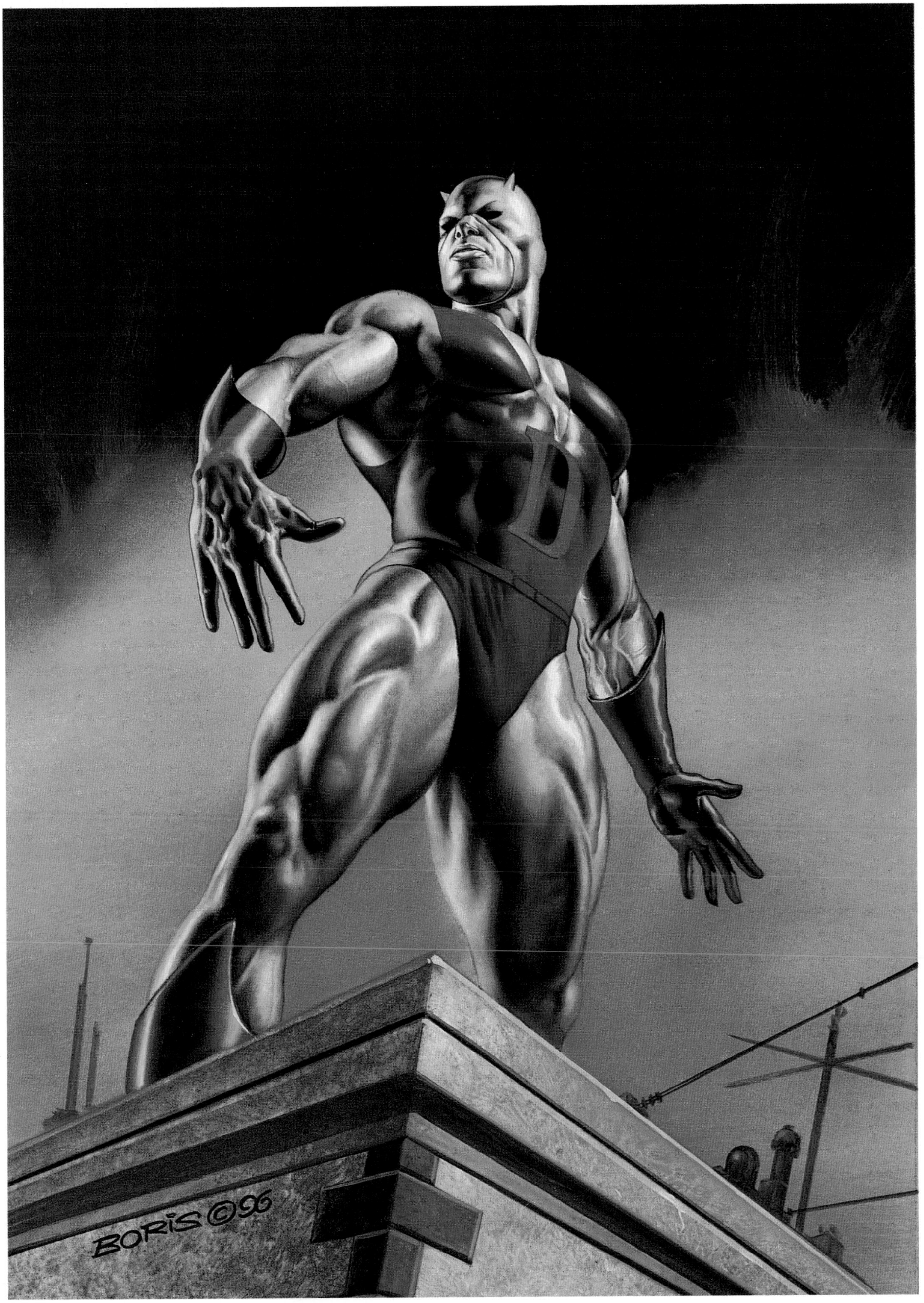
BORIS ©96

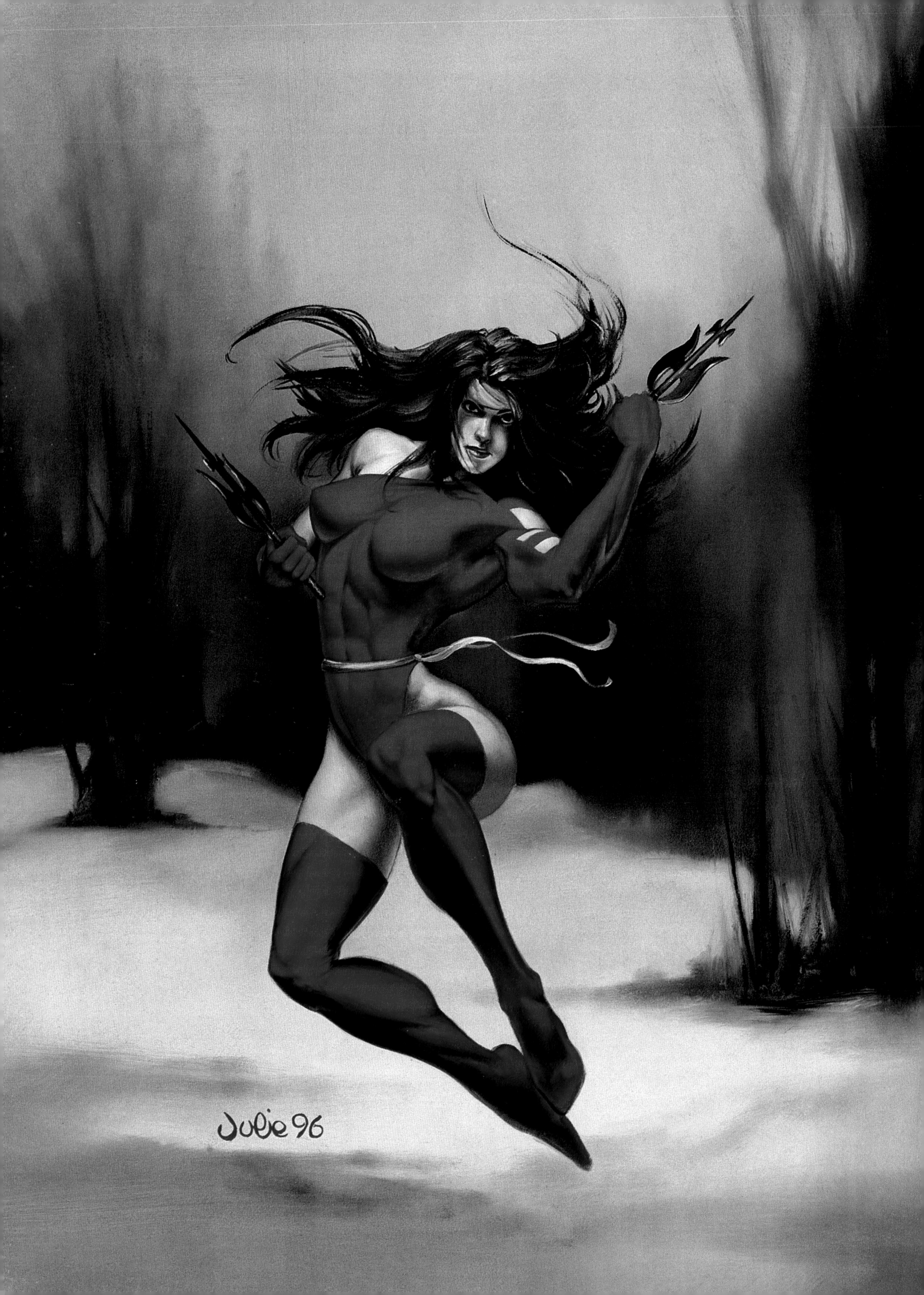
Julie 96

(far left)

ELEKTRA

1996, Julie

Trading Card. Fleer Publishing Co.

TM & © 1996 Marvel Characters, Inc.

All rights reserved.

Like her ancient Greek namesake, Elektra has an intense relationship with her father and when he's killed by terrorists she turns to the ninja arts to avenge him. Poisoned by bitterness, she also turns nasty and becomes a mercenary herself; but Daredevil, who loved Elektra in her innocent youth, still holds a soft spot for her. Assassinated by Bullseye, she dies in Daredevil's arms but he later manages to revive her as a reformed character.

(left)

BLACK WIDOW

1996, Julie

Trading Card. Fleer Publishing Co.

TM & © 1996 Marvel Characters, Inc.

All rights reserved.

The Black Widow started out as a spy for her native Russia but was drawn into the superhero game through a clash with Iron Man. She has no natural superpowers but her suit is packed with gadgets that let her act as one. The most famous is her Widow's Bite, an electronic discharge weapon that stuns her enemies. Black Widow has belonged to many teams, including the Champions and Avengers, and has partnered several other heroes including Daredevil, whose lover she became for a while.

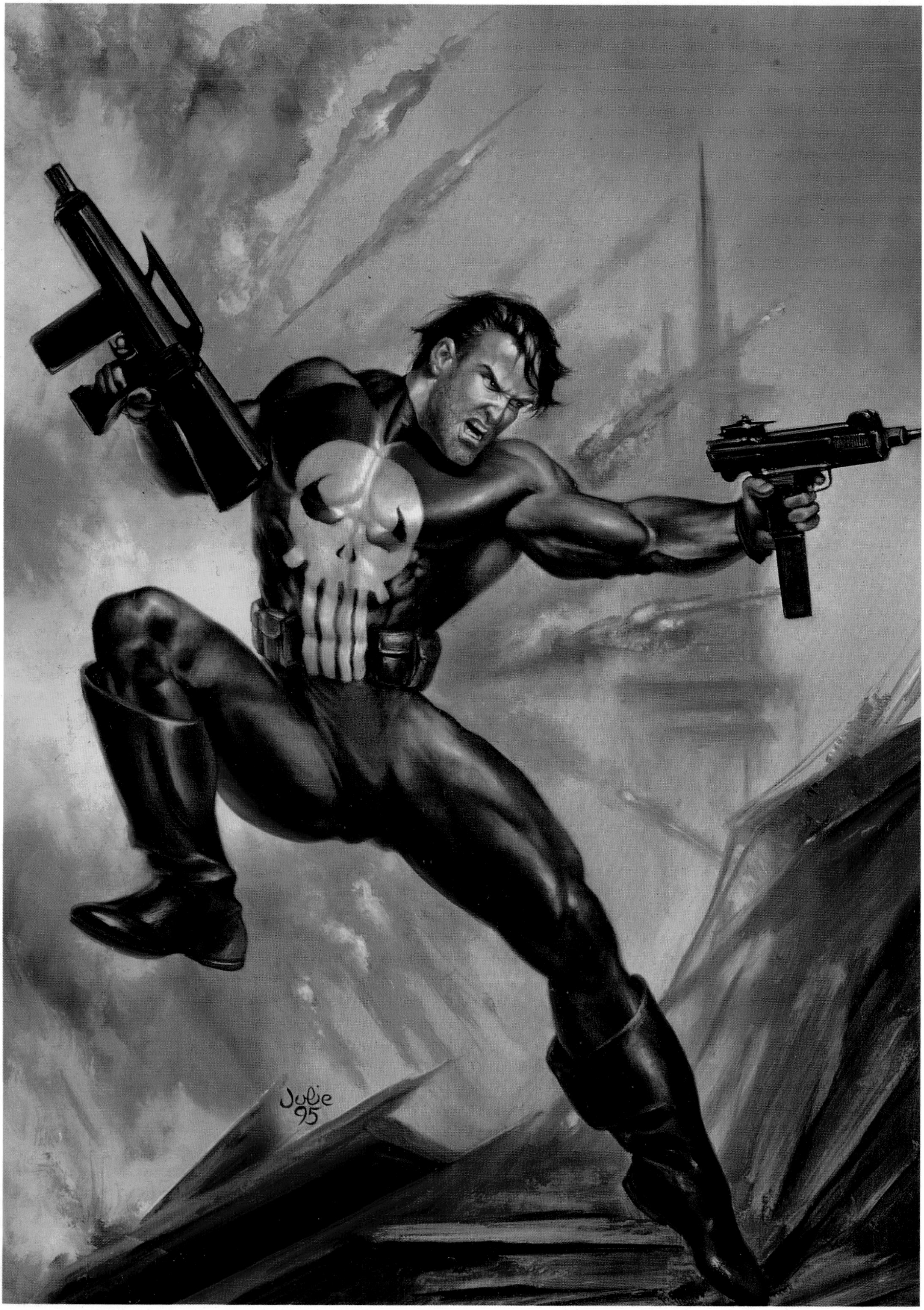
Julie
95

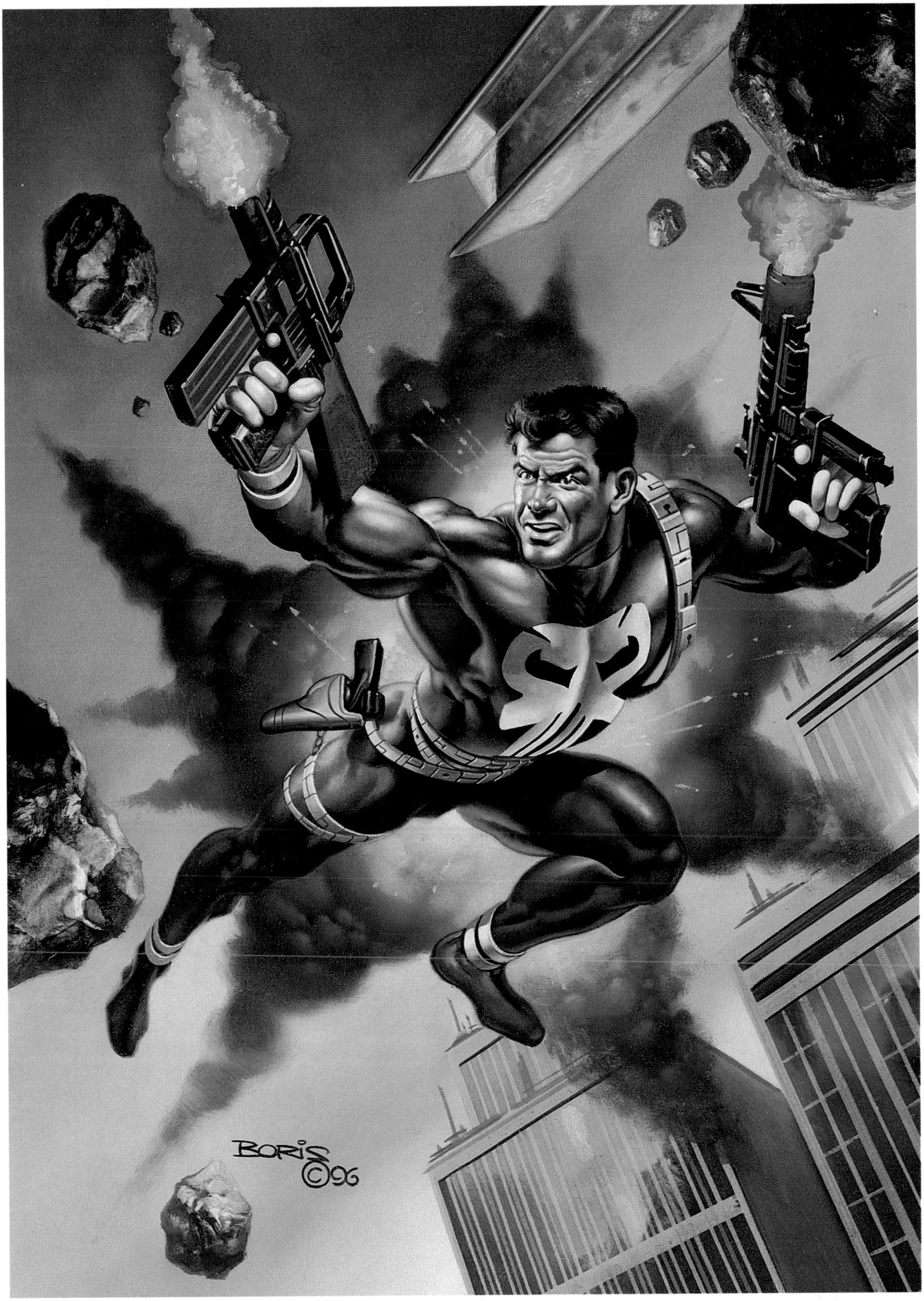
BORIS ©96

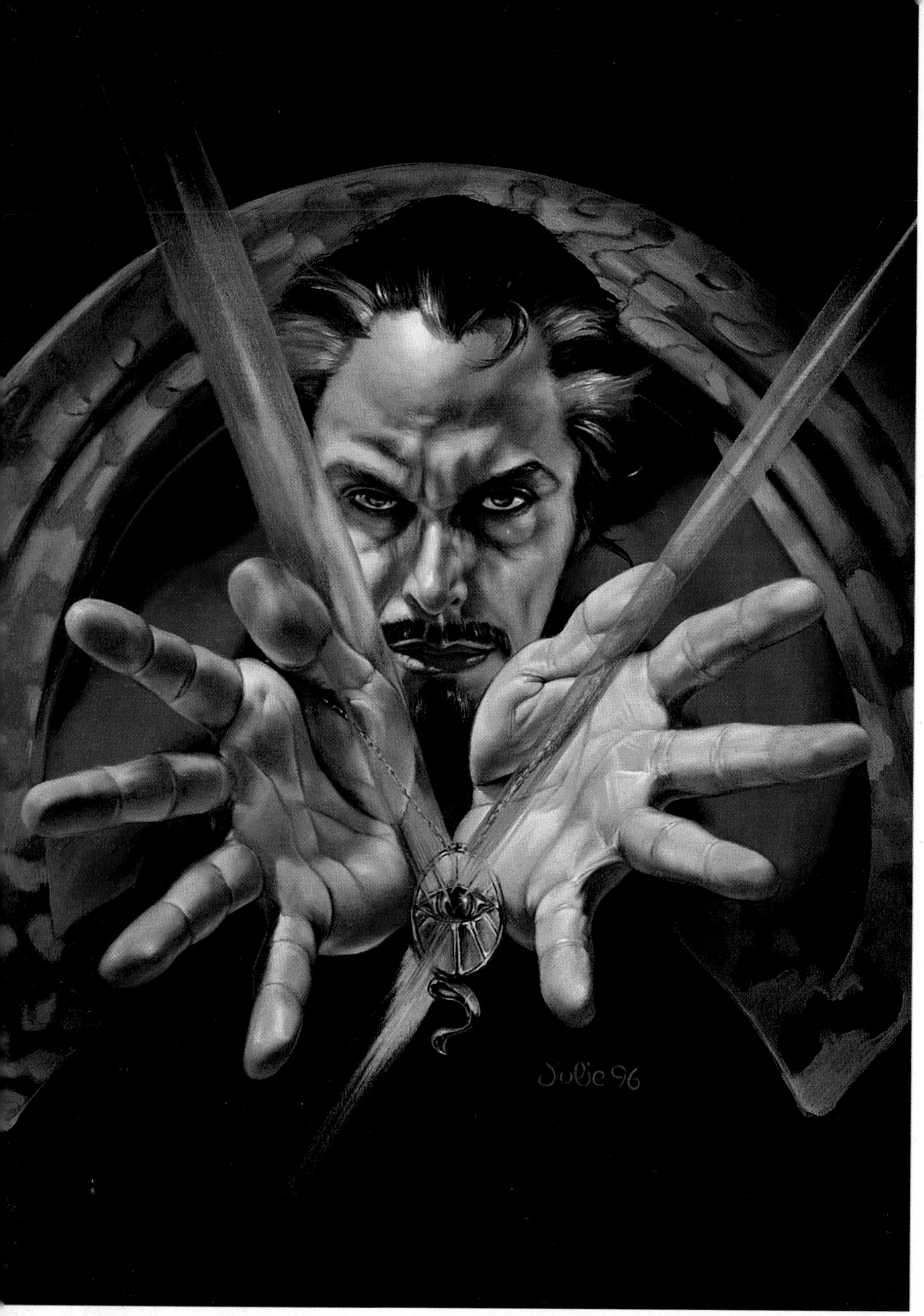
Julie 96

(page 72)

PUNISHER 1

1995, Julie

Trading Card. Fleer Publishing Co.

(page 73)

PUNISHER 2

1996, Boris

Trading Card. Fleer Publishing Co.

The Punisher is a former war hero and marine who deserted and turned vigilante when warring gangsters wiped out his family in Central Park. His extreme methods often bring him into conflict with Daredevil and other heroes, but he is basically on their side. Lacking any special powers beyond his natural fighting ability, he compensates with a vast arsenal of weapons. His base is a converted truck disguised as a TV repair van.

(right)

CRYSTAL

1996, Boris

Trading Card. Fleer Publishing Co.

Crystal is one of the Inhumans along with Black Bolt, Gorgon, Karnak, Medusa, Triton and Lockjaw. The Inhumans are the result of genetic experimentation on humans some 25,000 years ago. They made their home on the mysterious island of Attilan in the North Atlantic where they somehow managed to keep their existence hidden from humans. The Inhumans themselves have indulged in genetic manipulation, often with disastrous results that have led to wars. They first made an appearance in the Fantastic Four comics.

(above)

DR STRANGE

1996, Julie

Trading Card. Fleer Publishing Co.

Strange was originally a brilliant but vain surgeon who suddenly became a much nicer person when he lost his talent. Deprived of the skill of his fingers, he turned to magic and developed an even greater skill at that, which he uses to defend the world against the dark forces of the occult.

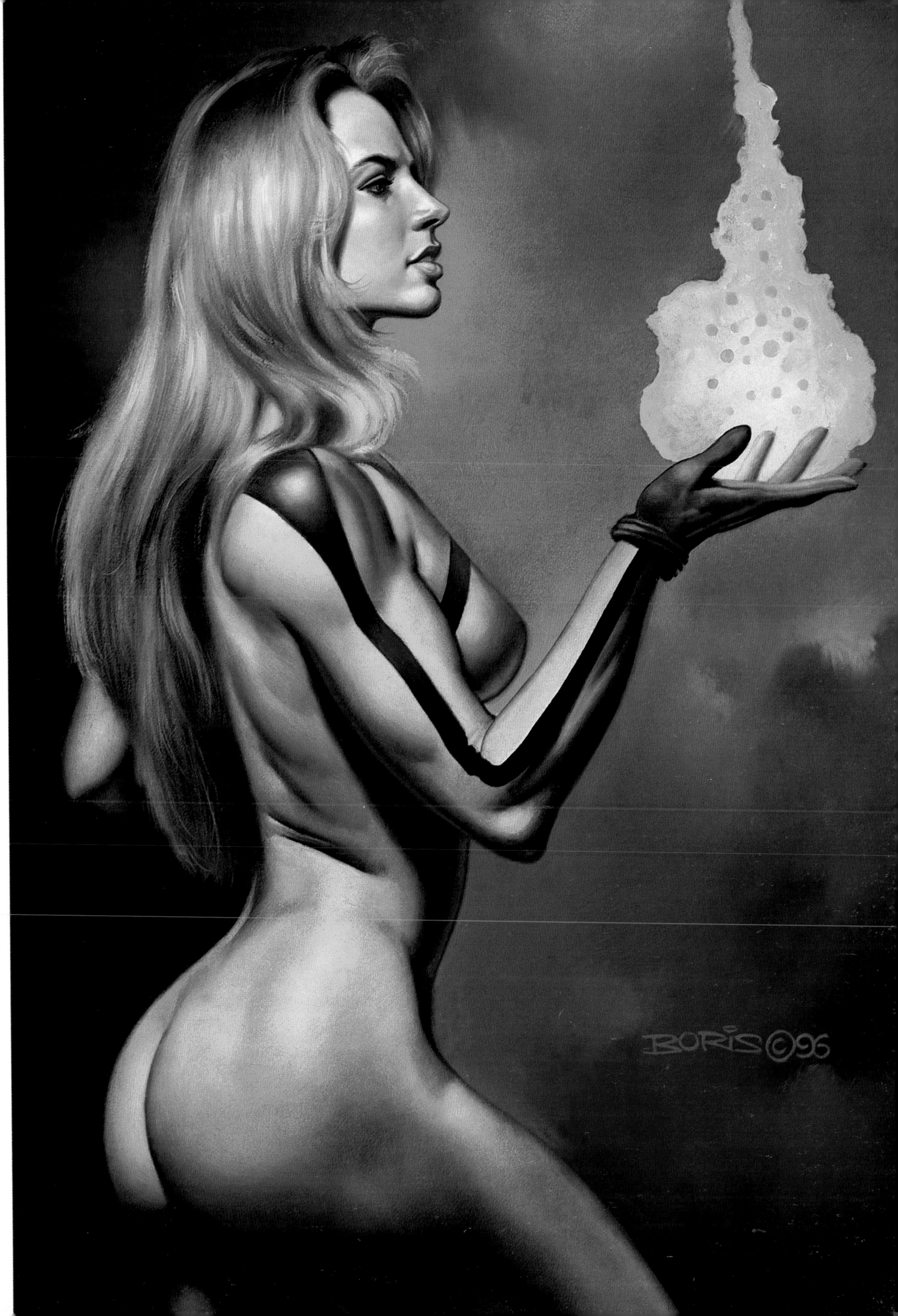
BORIS ©96

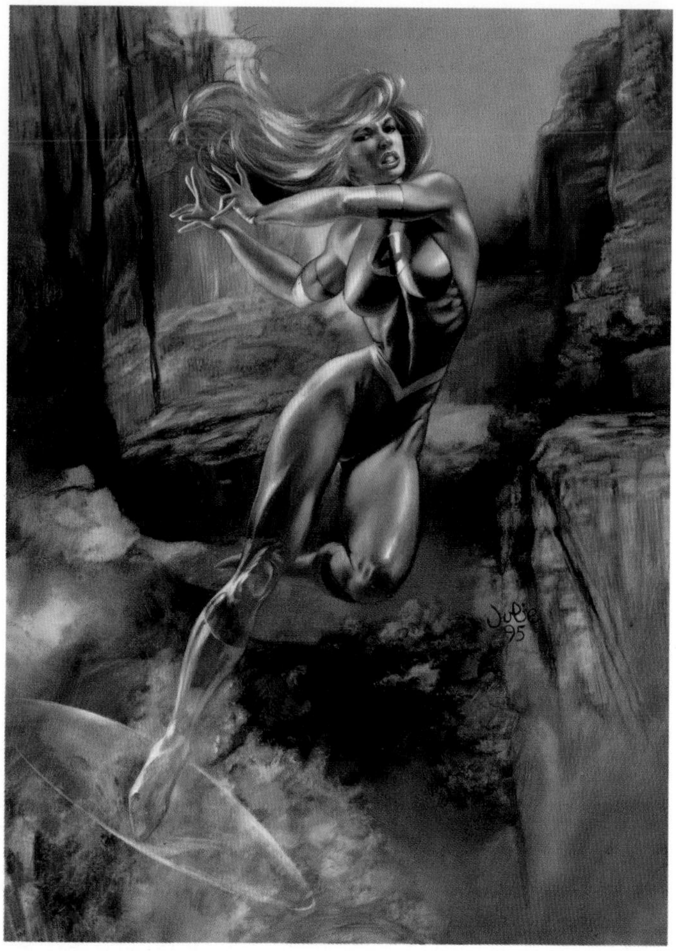
Julie 95

(left)

INVISIBLE WOMAN

1995, Julie

Trading Card. Fleer Publishing Co.

(below)

HUMAN TORCH

1995, Boris

Trading Card. Fleer Publishing Co.

Here we see three of the Fantastic Four team. The members are Mr Fantastic (Reed Richards), Invisible Woman (Sue Richards), Human Torch (Johnny Storm) and Thing (Ben Grimm). Reed Richards was originally a rocket scientist working on an interstellar rocket design that was axed by the government. Rather than see their work wasted, he and his three colleagues took the ship out for a premature trial run. It crashed back to earth and when they emerged from the wreckage they found that radiation had given them superpowers that they have since used for the benefit of mankind.

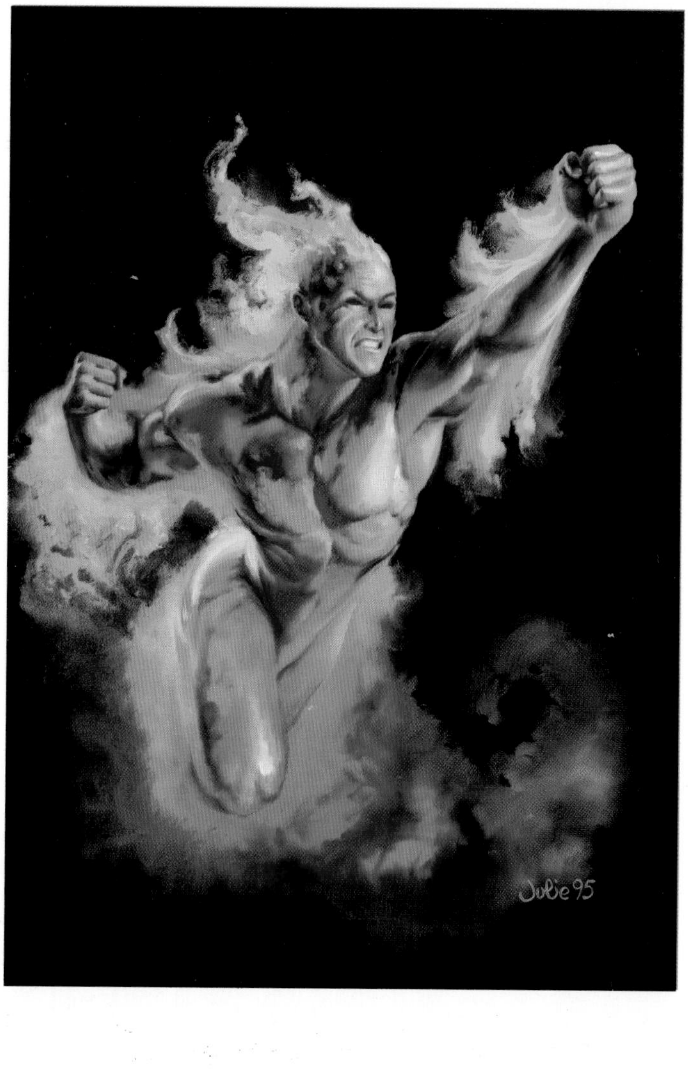
Julie 95

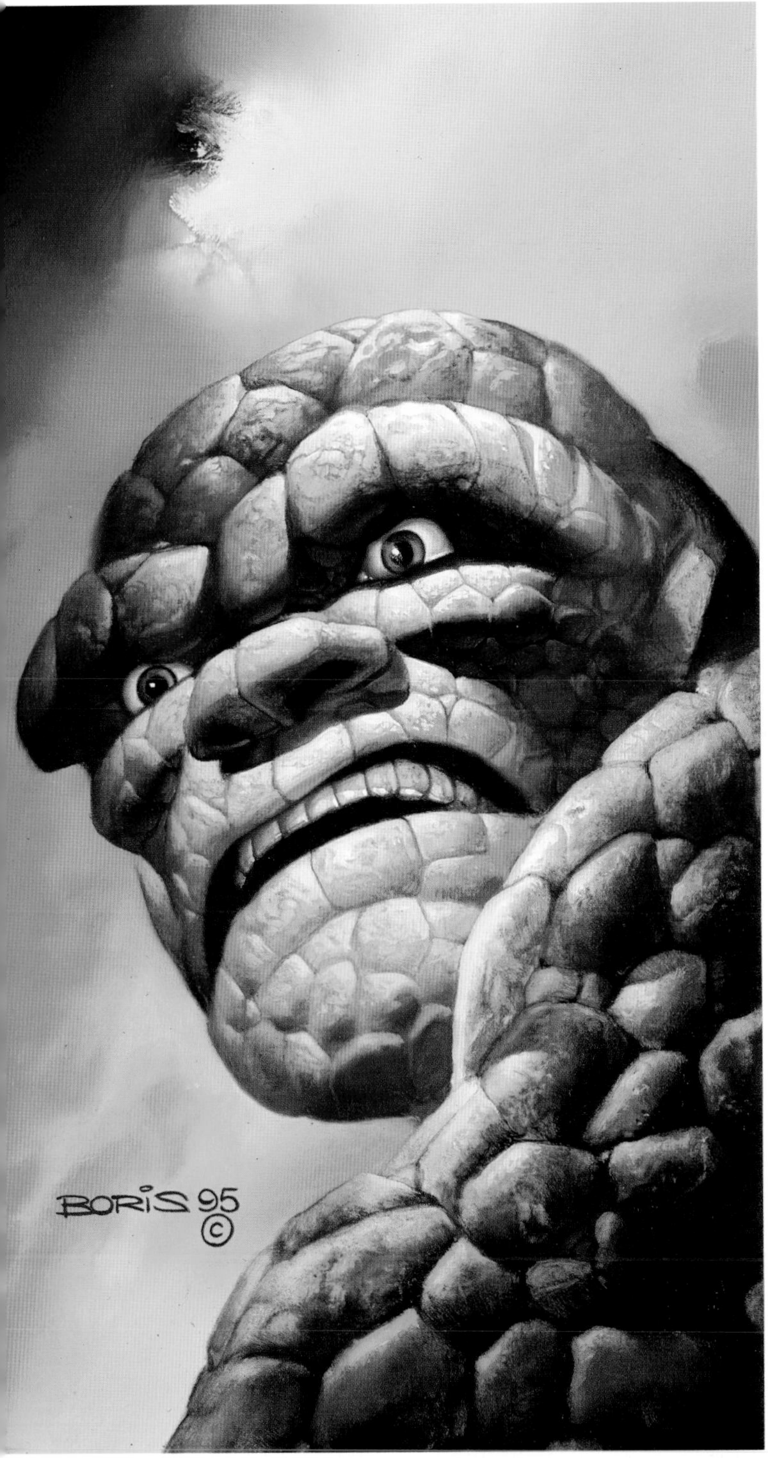
BORIS 95 ©

(below)

DR DOOM

1996, Boris

Trading Card. Fleer Publishing Co.

One of the Fantastic Four's more persistent opponents.

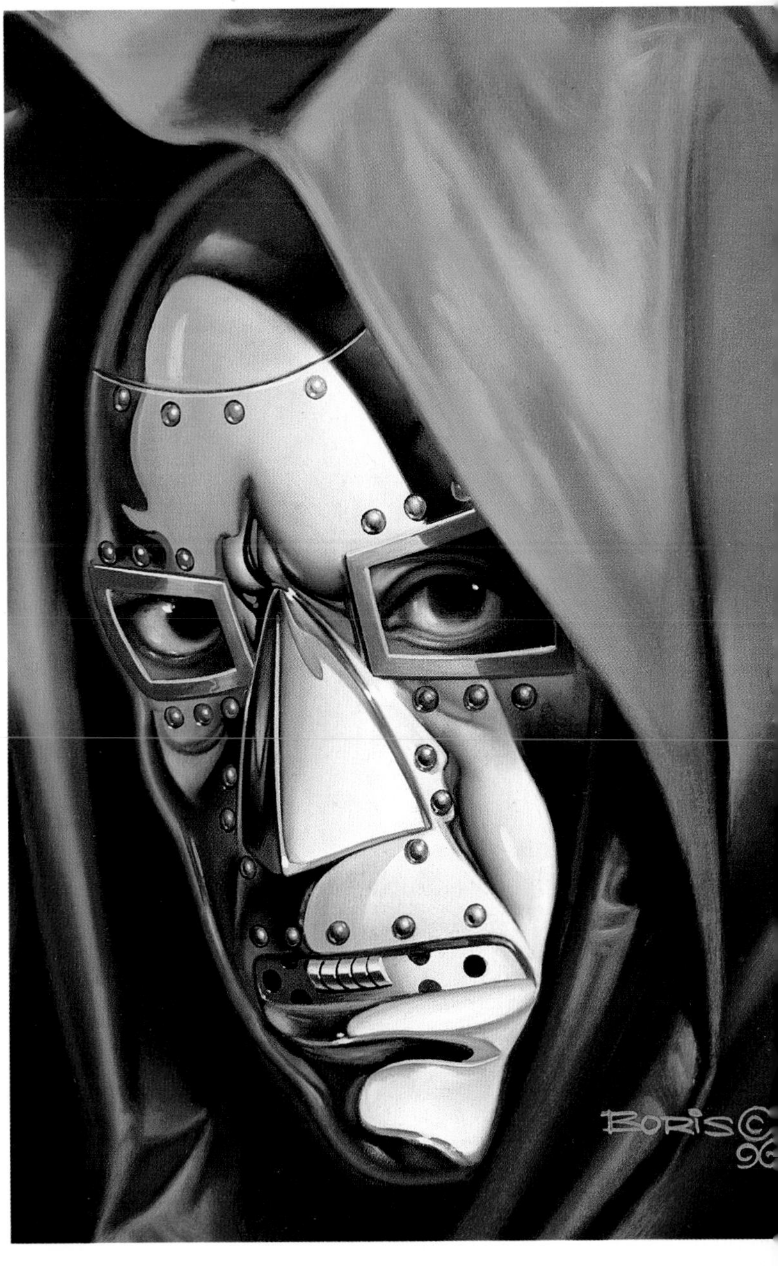
BORIS © 96

(above)

THING

1995, Boris

Trading Card. Fleer Publishing Co.

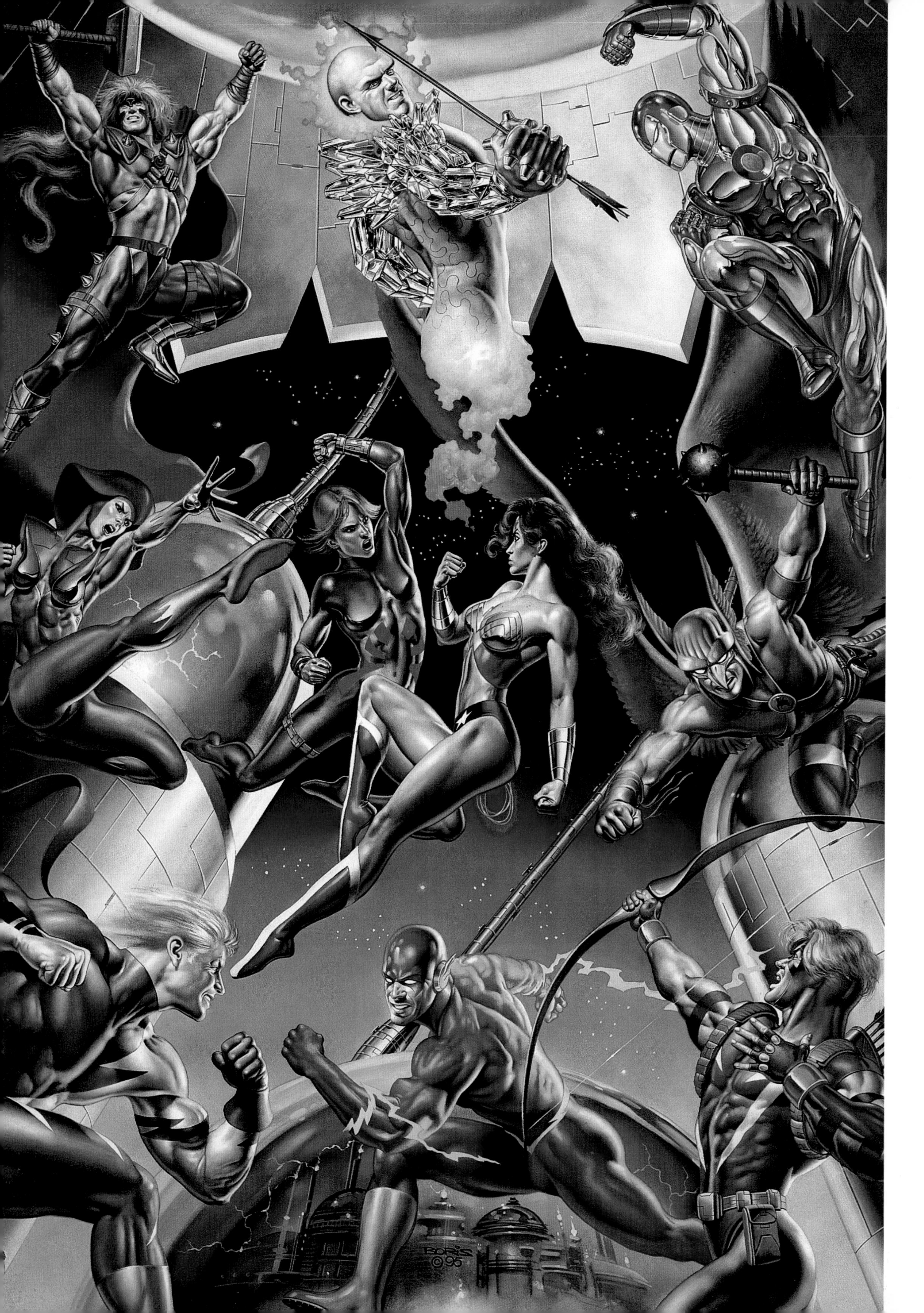
BORIS
©95

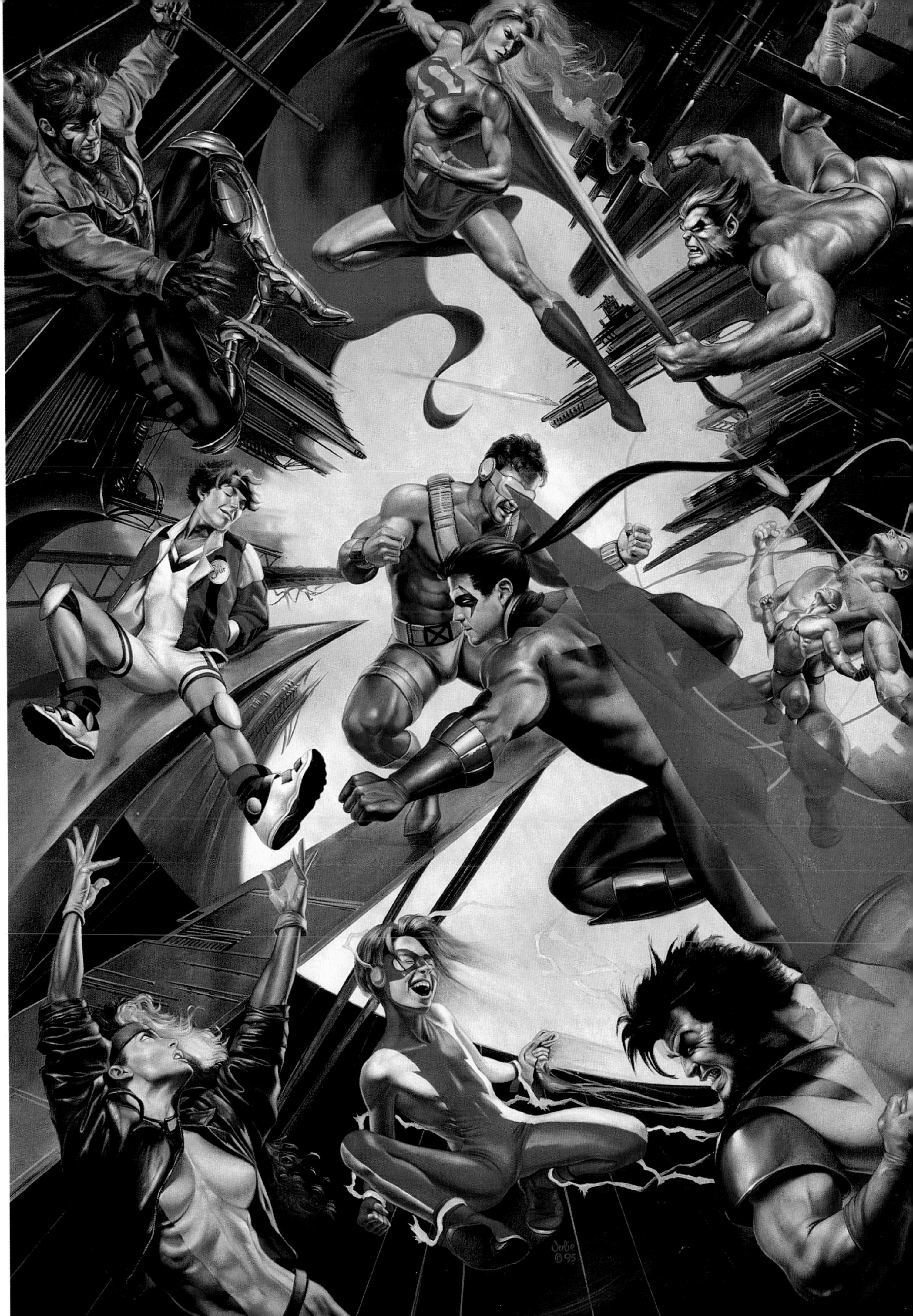

(page 78)

MARVEL / DC TEAMUP 1

1995, Boris

Trading Cards. Fleer Publishing Co.

TM & © 1995 DC Comics / 1999 Marvel

Characters, Inc.

All rights reserved.

As the two largest comic publishers, Marvel and DC have defined the whole genre between them over the past 50 years. They are supposedly rivals and each has followers that hate and despise the other, but secretly they know they're on the same side. Occasionally they even recognize it with collaborations like this, pooling their separate superheroes for some joint venture. These two pictures were designed to be split up into nine separate trading cards that fans could collect and piece together.

(page 79)

MARVEL / DC TEAMUP 2

1995, Julie

Trading Cards. Fleer Publishing Co.

TM & © 1995 DC Comics / 1999 Marvel

Characters, Inc.

All rights reserved.

(above)

THE FLASH

1994, Boris

Trading Card.

TM & © 1994 DC Comics

All rights reserved.

Currently DC have invited Stan Lee, Marvel's leading light and probably the single greatest comic innovator ever, to create an alternate universe of his own starring their characters. In 12 issues he'll rewrite the origins and characters of Batman, Superman, Wonder Woman and many others, working with some of the best artists from both Marvel and DC. By the time you read this it may already have happened, but just now all comic fans are agog at what Lee will come up with. Apparently the venture is something he has often toyed with purely as a fun idea that seemed unlikely ever to happen.

(right)

CAPTAIN ATOM

1994, Julie

Trading Card.

TM & © 1994 DC Comics

All rights reserved.

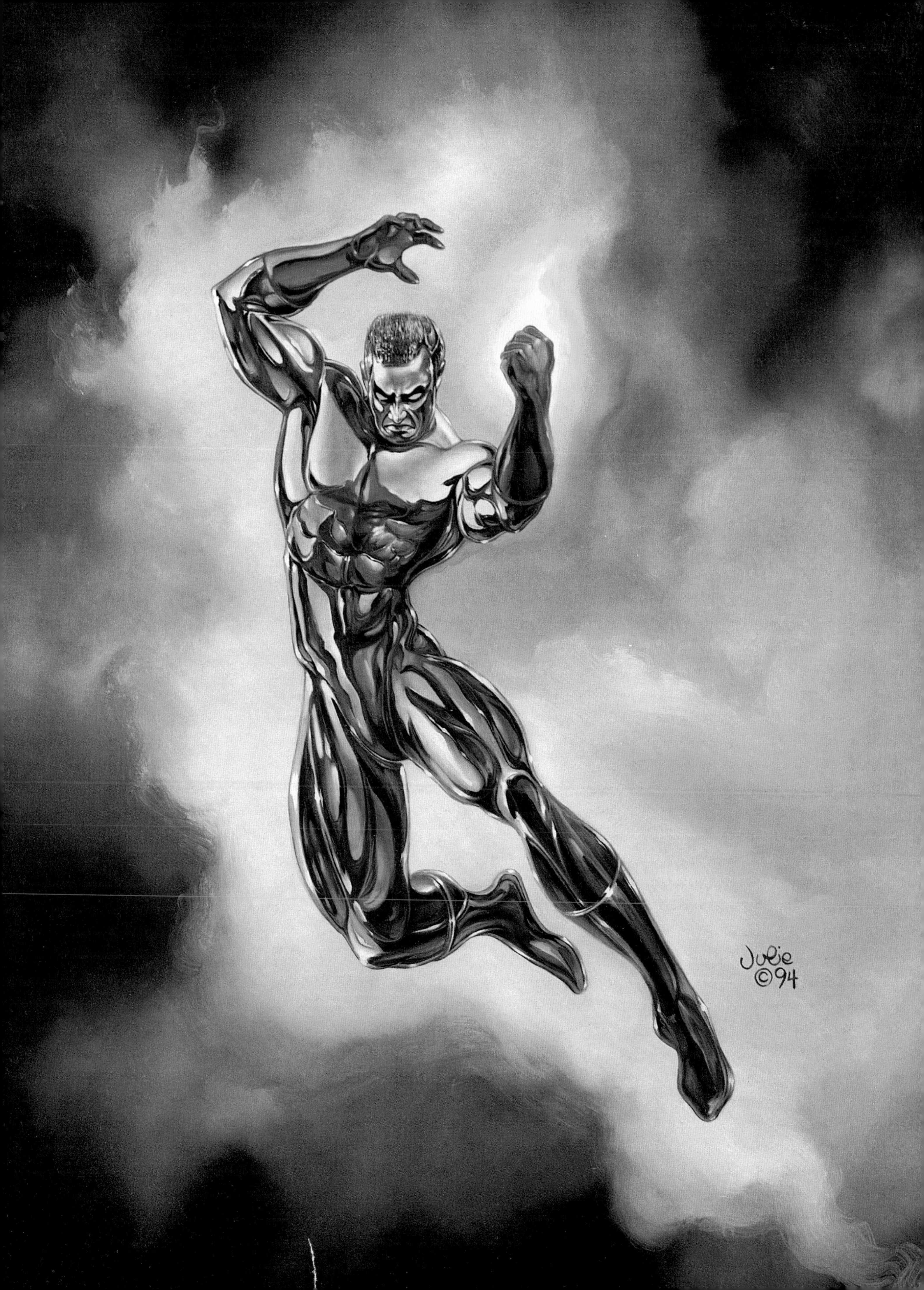
Julie
©94

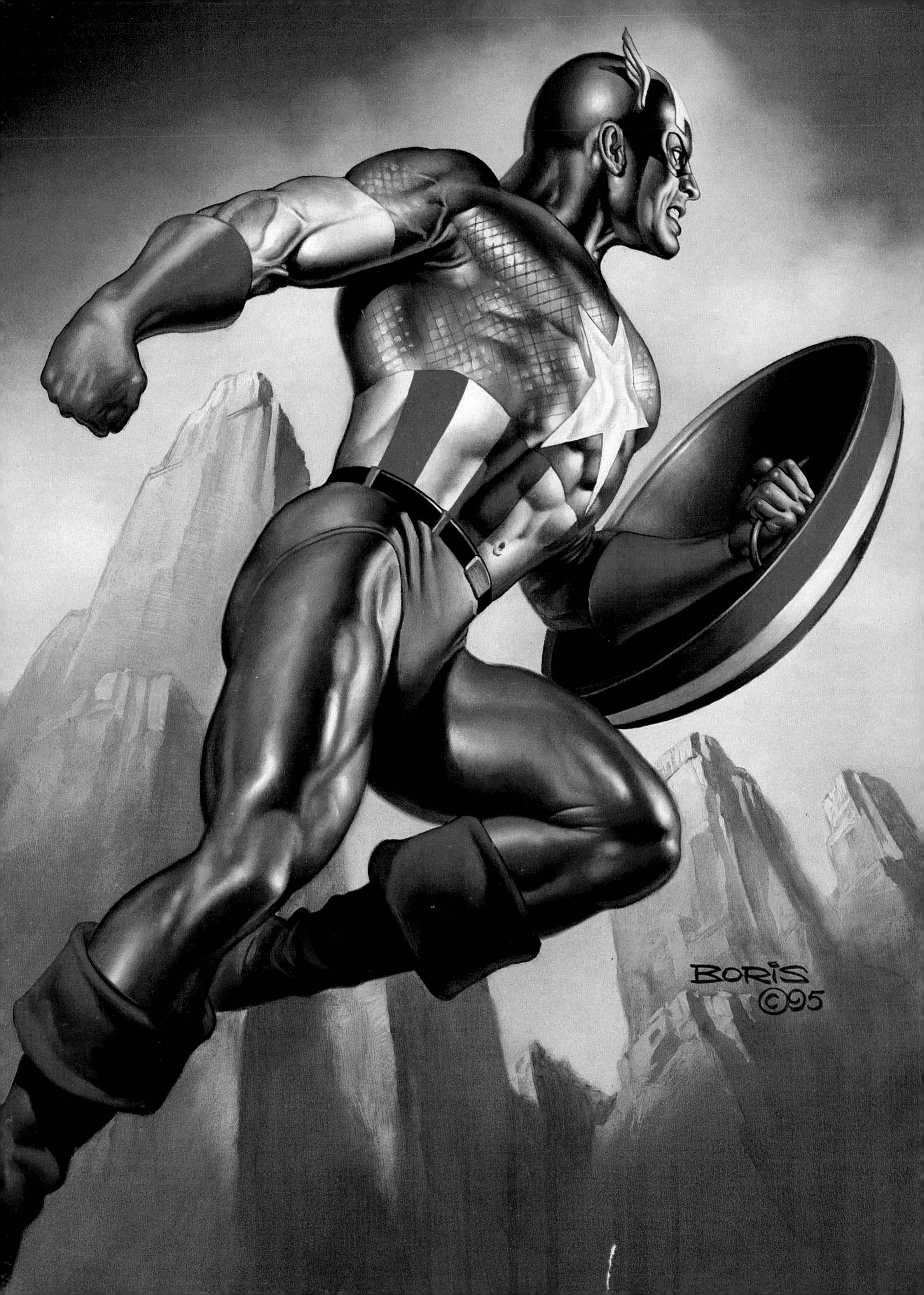
BORIS
©95

Avengers

Captain America was originally Steve Rogers, an aspiring New York artist, who in 1940 was appalled by what the Nazis were doing in Europe. He tried to enlist in the army but, having always been sickly, totally failed to pass the fitness tests. However his eagerness was rewarded by recruitment into a top-secret government program called Operation Rebirth. After many months of preparation he was injected with a Super-Soldier drug followed by special radiation treatment that transformed his puny physique into a tireless powerhouse.

The Nazis, however, caught wind of the project and, terrified at the prospect of facing an army of superheroes, wiped out everyone involved so that the secret of the process was lost. Steve Rogers alone survived. Donning the costume and name of Captain America, he went into battle as the champion of freedom and democracy. His chief enemy was Red Skull, the incarnate force of evil behind the Nazi machine.

While training for his mission, Rogers meets Bucky Barnes who uncovers his secret and becomes his partner. Together they battle through the war, helping thwart evil on countless occasions, but finally they are caught in a booby trap. Bucky is killed in the explosion and Steve Rogers hurled into the icy wastes of the far North. There he remained frozen in a state of suspended animation for decades.

Meanwhile several others took on the Captain America role. Rogers' immediate successor was William Nasland, who was killed shortly after the war while preventing the assassination of a Congressional candidate named John Kennedy. His place was taken for a few years by Jeff Mace, formerly Patriot of the Liberty Legion. When he retired in 1950 the title remained vacant for a few years.

(left)

CAPTAIN AMERICA

1995, Boris
Trading Card. Fleer Publishing Co.
TM & © 1995 Marvel Characters, Inc.
All rights reserved.
Captain America is one of the more fascinating Marvel characters. Conceived as an anti-Nazi comic champion during the Second World War, his tangled career offers an interesting angle on how many Americans have perceived themselves and their place in the world over the past 60 years.

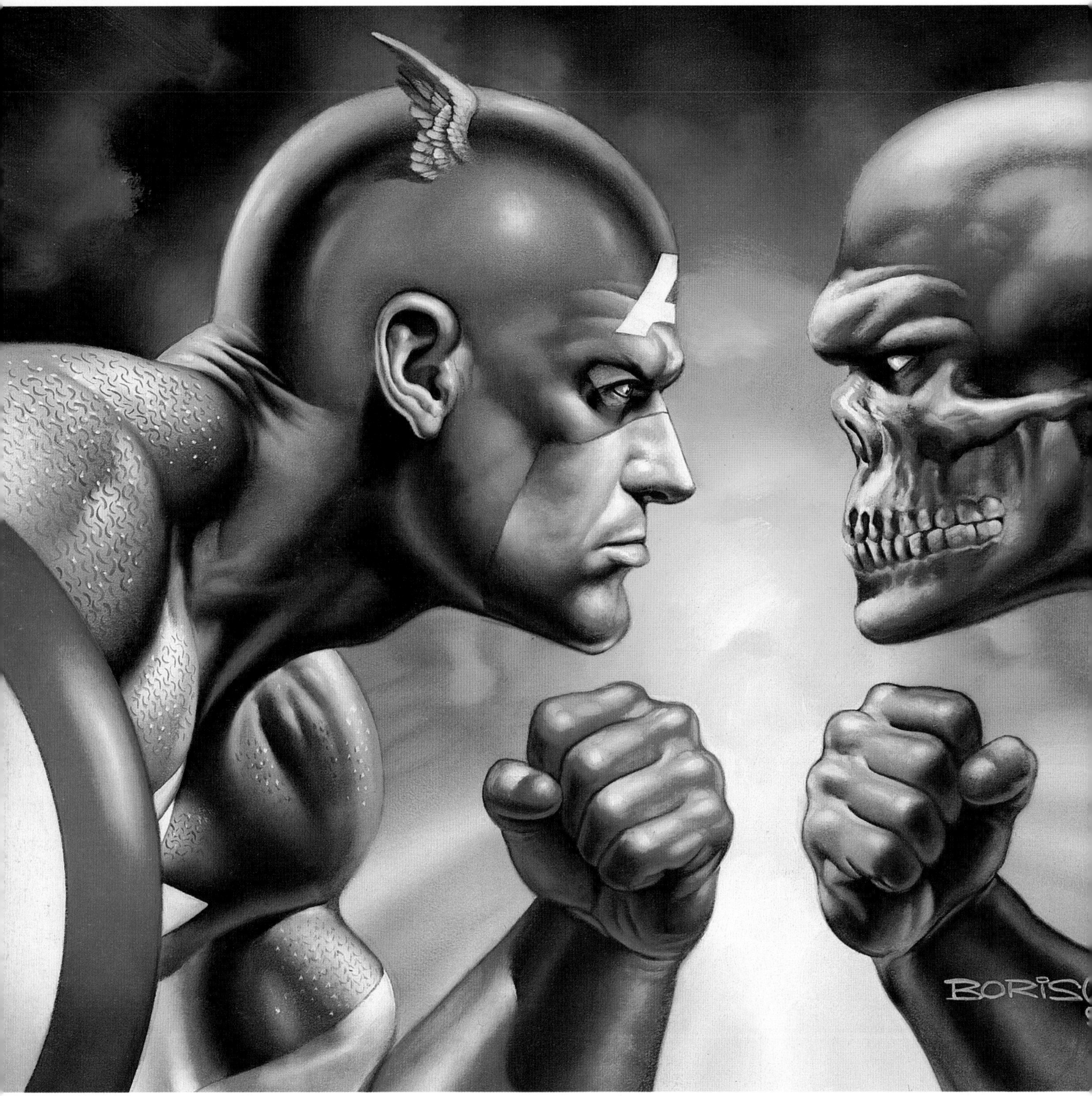
BORIS

Then came a long break until the 60s during which the original Steve Rogers remained frozen in his block of Arctic ice. Finally, however, it fell into the sea and melted. Rogers revived and was found by the Avengers, whose company he joined. When the original Avengers retired, Captain America formed a new team with the reformed villains Hawkeye (though he was only an accidental baddie), Scarlet Witch, and Quicksilver. His old enemy, Red Skull, also had a fresh lease of life and in various guises has needed constant thwarting ever since.

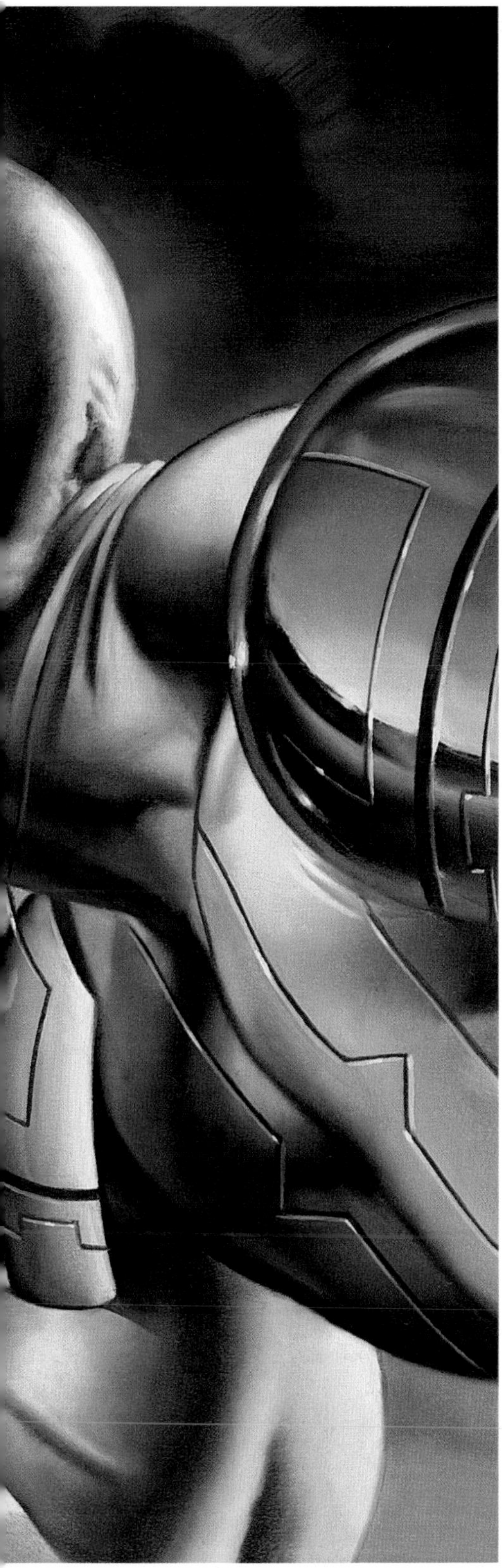

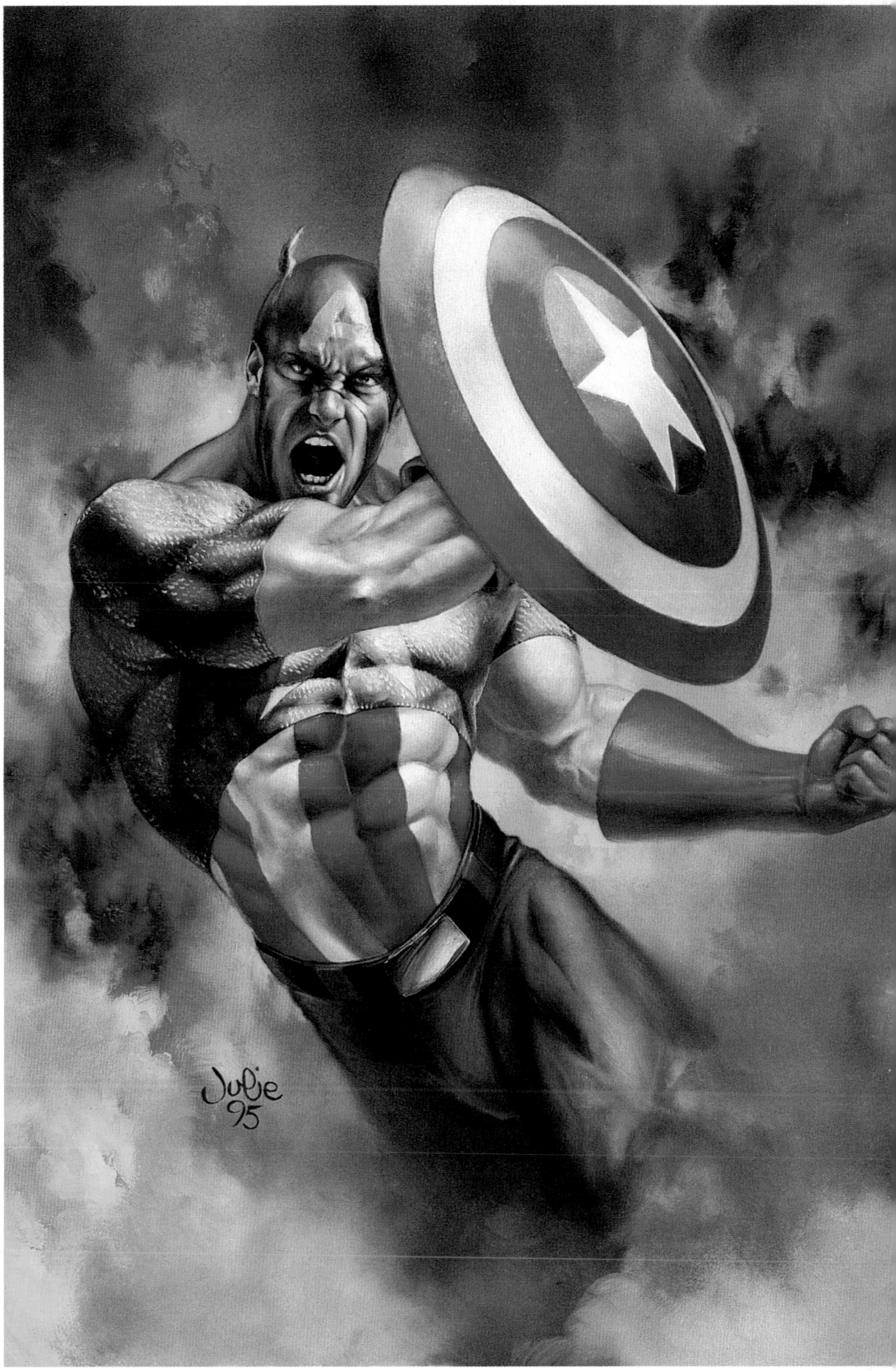
Julie
95

(left)

CAPTAIN AMERICA & RED SKULL

1996, Boris

Trading Card. Fleer Publishing Co.

(above)

CAPTAIN AMERICA

1995, Julie

Trading Card. Fleer Publishing Co.

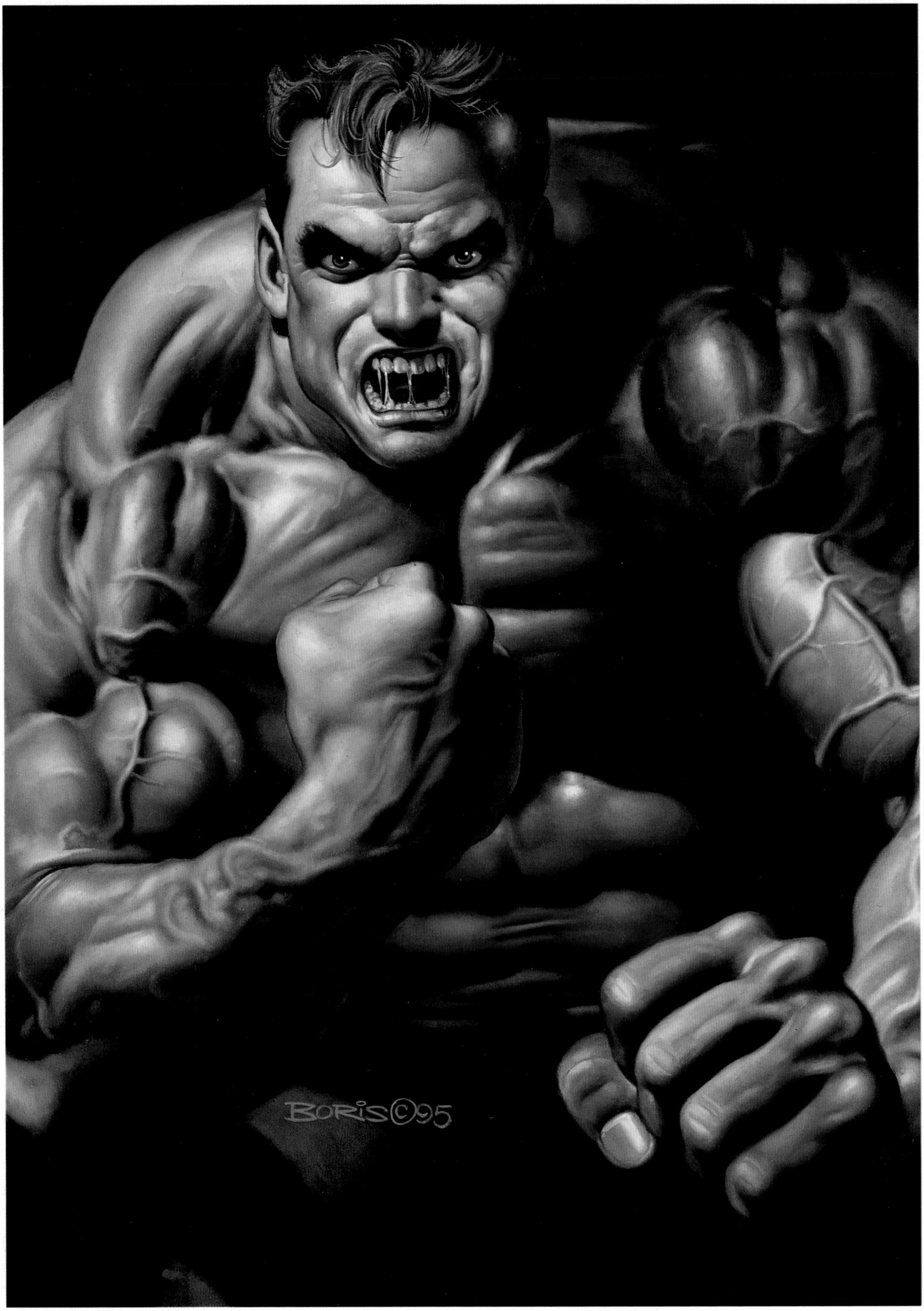
BORIS©95

The Hulk is one of the best-loved creations of the legendary team of Stan Lee and Jack Kirby. He was not an immediate success though. When the Hulk was first launched in his own comic back in 1962, it only managed six issues before being axed. Thereafter he just made cameo appearances in other comics and these were what really generated interest in the character; to the point where in 1968 he was relaunched as the Incredible Hulk in his own comic once again, and has not really looked back since.

In the mind of the general public the Hulk's fame peaked in the early 80s with the runaway success of the TV series. Between 1977 and 1982 over 80 episodes were filmed and they appealed to all kinds of people that normally take no interest in comics. The wider audience has moved on but the Hulk remains as popular as ever with Marvel readers.

(above)
THINKING HULK
1996, Boris
Trading Card. Fleer Publishing Co.
TM & © 1996 Marvel Characters, Inc.
All rights reserved.

(left)
HULK 1
1995, Boris
Trading Card. Fleer Publishing Co.
TM & © 1995 Marvel Characters, Inc.
All rights reserved.

(right)
RAGING HULK
1996, Boris
Trading Card. Fleer Publishing Co.
TM & © 1996 Marvel Characters, Inc.
All rights reserved.

The Hulk's attraction is that we all feel like him at times and would love to turn into a big green monster and trash everything in sight. That his rages often achieve some good once the dust has settled is also part of it. We can all relate to that. We may not like losing our temper but sometimes there's simply no other choice!

(right)
SHE HULK
1996, Julie
Trading Card. Fleer Publishing Co.
Bruce Banner's cousin comes to share his strength and power to mutate when he's forced to give her a transfusion of his blood to save her life. She has more control over her form than her cousin and is usually She Hulk by choice. She grew up in California but moved to the East Coast to join the Avengers.

(left)
GREY HULK
1996, Julie
Trading Card. Fleer Publishing Co.

(right)
HULK 2
1995, Julie
Trading Card. Fleer Publishing Co.

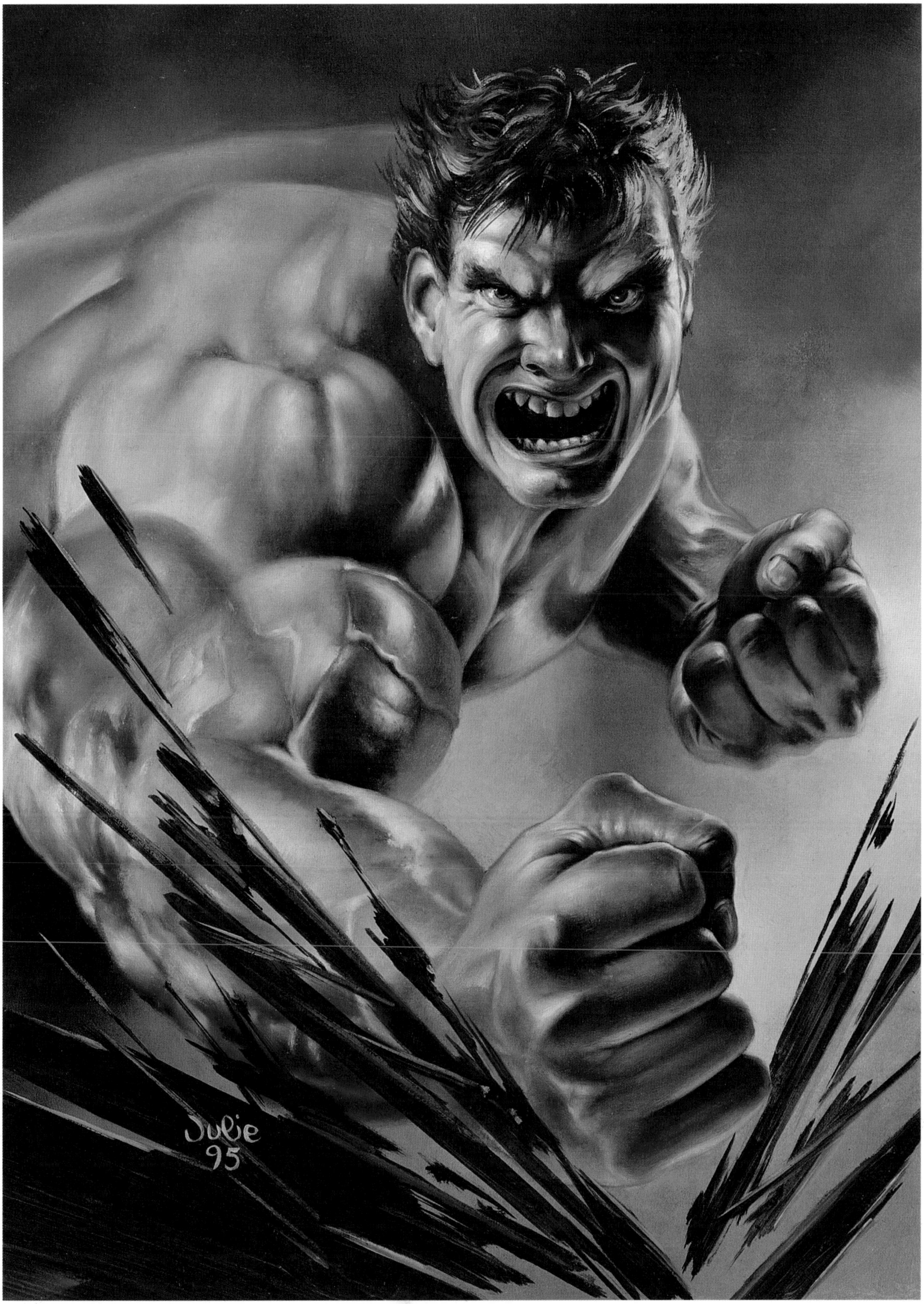
Julie
95

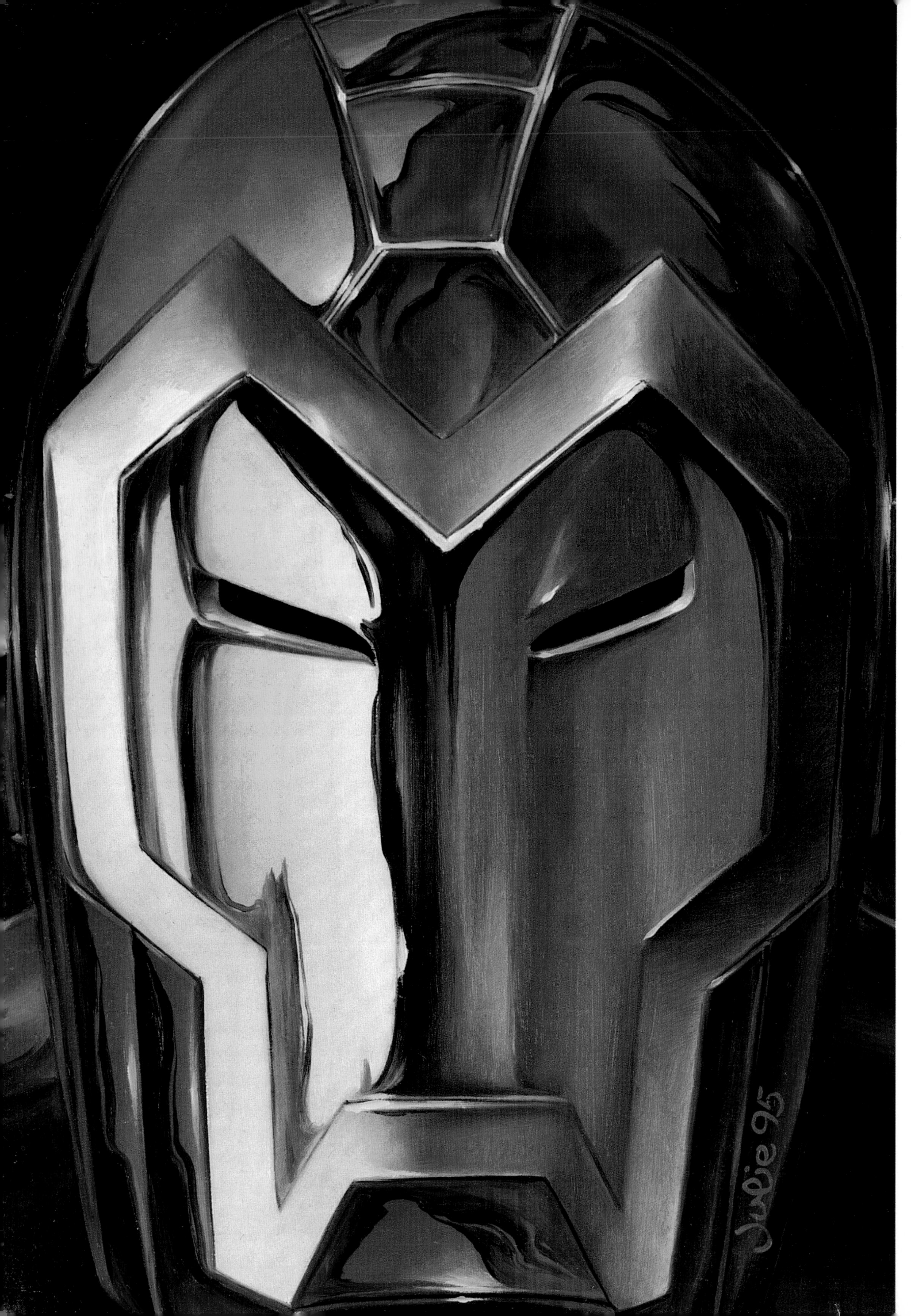
Julie 95

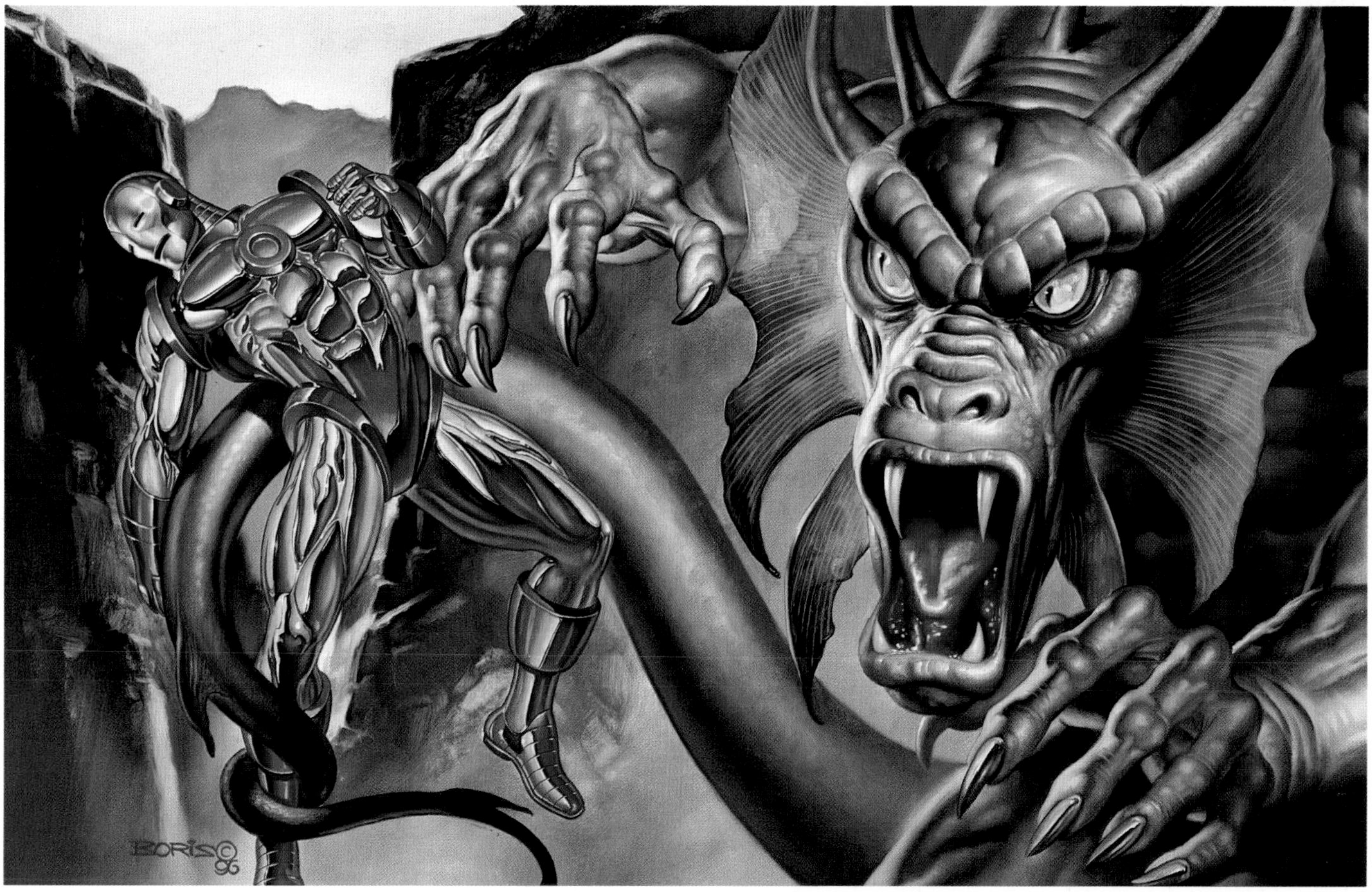
BORIS© 96

(above)

IRON MAN VS FIN FANG FOOM

1996, Boris

Trading Card. Fleer Publishing Co.

(left)

IRON MAN 2

1995, Julie

Trading Card. Fleer Publishing Co.

(right)

IRON MAN 1

1993, Julie

Trading Card. Fleer Publishing Co.

Iron Man's other identity is Tony Stark, an inventor. All his superpowers come from his armour, which has evolved to this red and gold version.

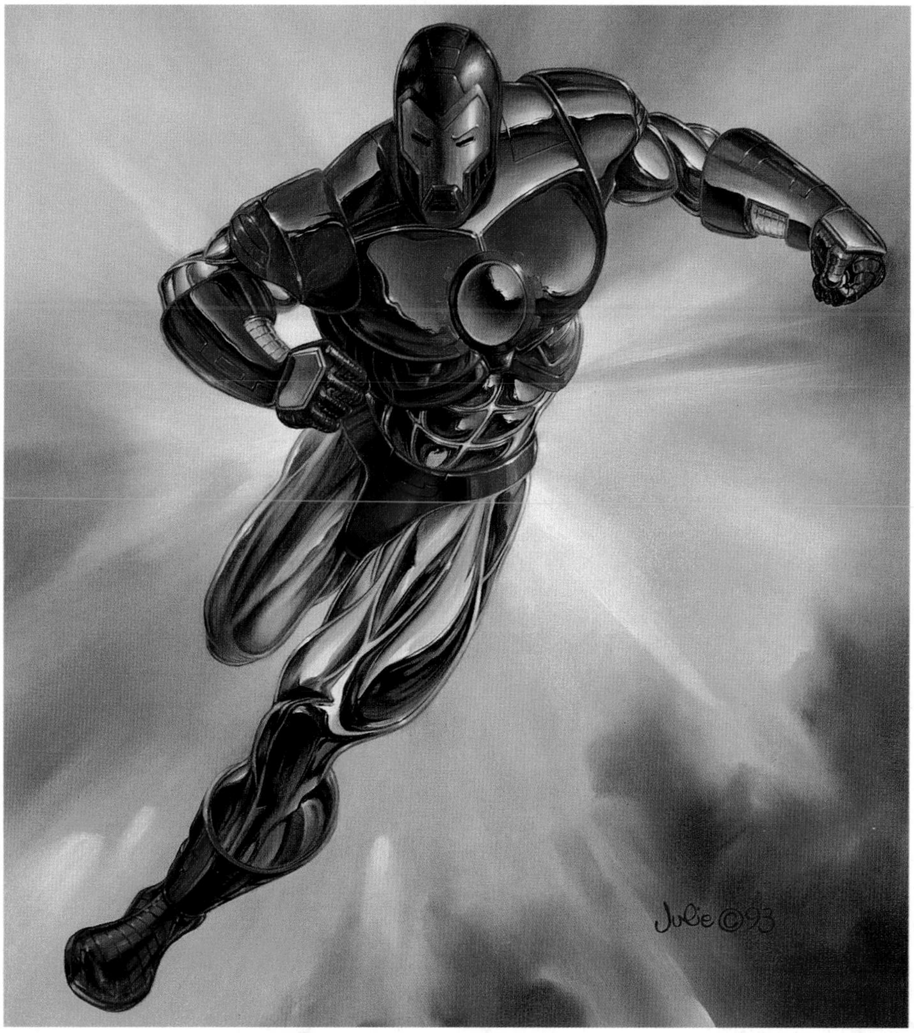
Julie ©93

(left)
GIANT MAN

1996, Julie

Trading Card. Fleer Publishing Co.

TM & © 1996 Marvel Characters, Inc.

All rights reserved.

(right)
YELLOW JACKET

1996, Boris

Trading Card. Fleer Publishing Co.

TM & © 1996 Marvel Characters, Inc.

All rights reserved.

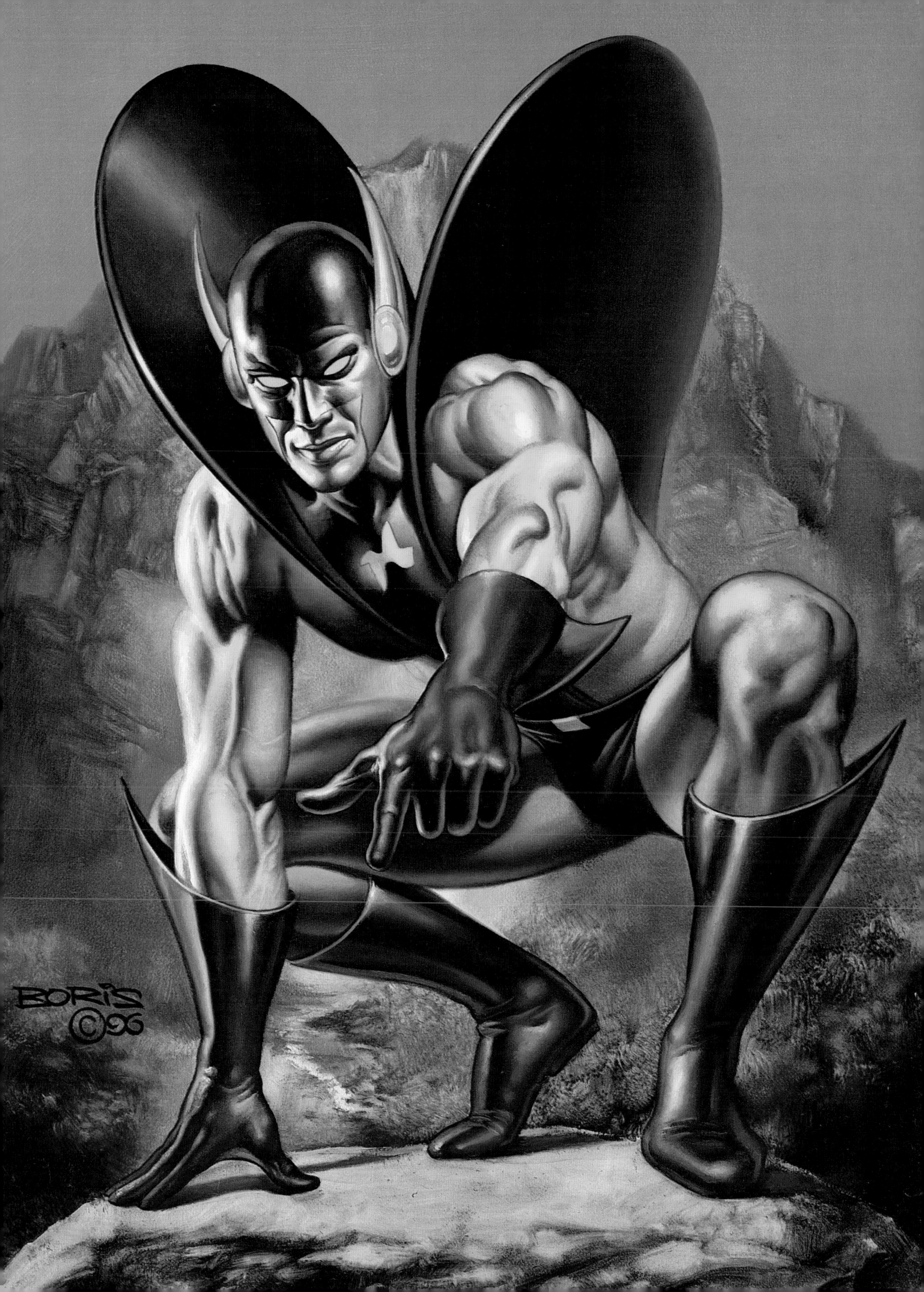
BORIS
©96

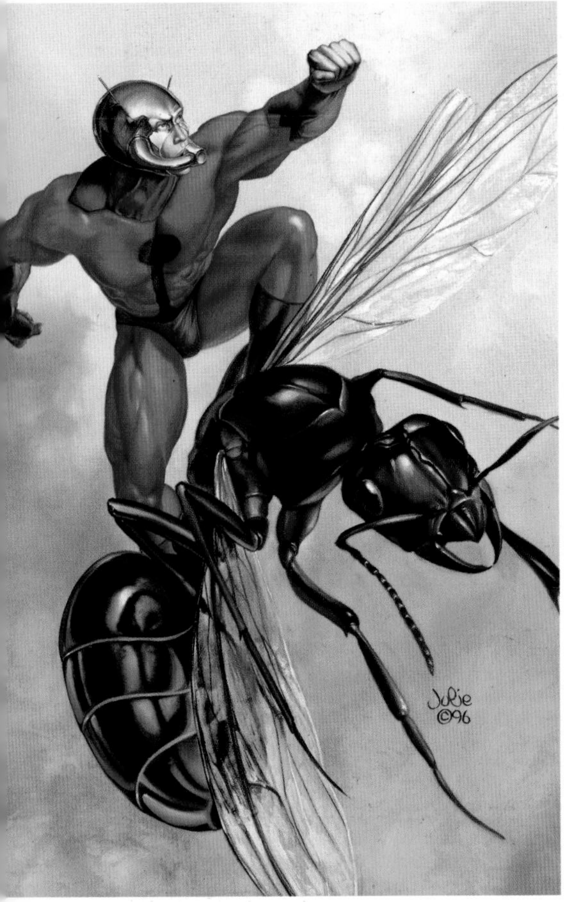
Julie
©96

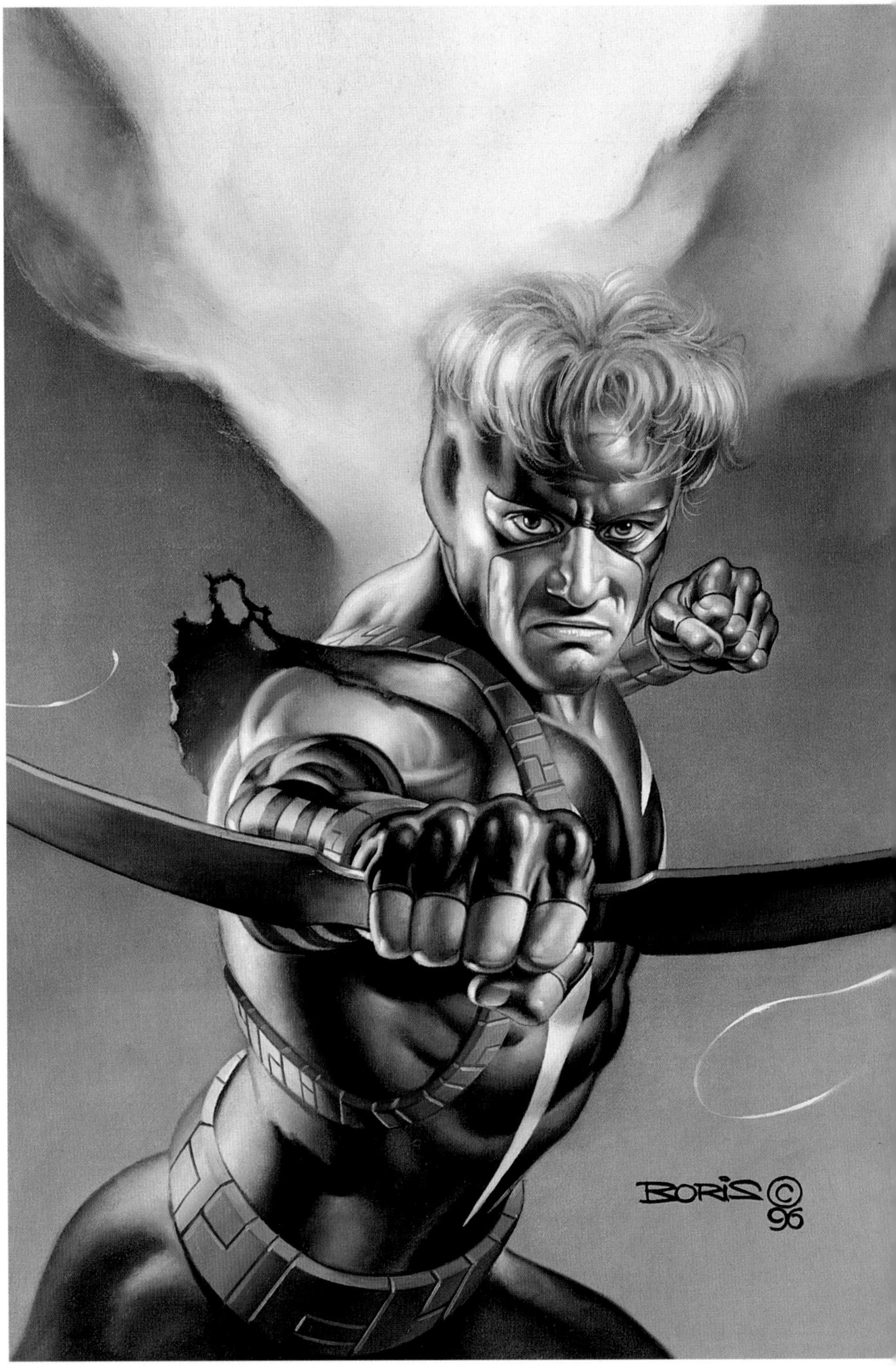
BORIS ©
96

(above)

ANTMAN

1996, Julie

Trading Card. Fleer Publishing Co.

(right)

HAWKEYE

1996, Boris

Trading Card. Fleer Publishing Co.

Clint Barton's parents died when he was eight years old. He and his brother later ran away from their state orphanage in order to join a circus. In time Clint became Hawkeye the Marksman and was inspired by Iron Man's example to don costume and fight crime. By accident, his first adventures threw him on the wrong side of the law, but once the initial misunderstanding was cleared up he was invited to join the Avengers.

(far right)

SCARLET WITCH

1995, Julie

Trading Card. Fleer Publishing Co.

Twin sister of Quicksilver and daughter of the evil Magneto, Wanda the Scarlet Witch has a talent for altering probability and making unlikely things happen. Her 'hex-bolts' can alter the consistency of matter, disrupt circuitry, start fires, deflect moving objects and so on. For a time she and her brother were forced to join Magneto's Evil Mutants but they defected to the Avengers.

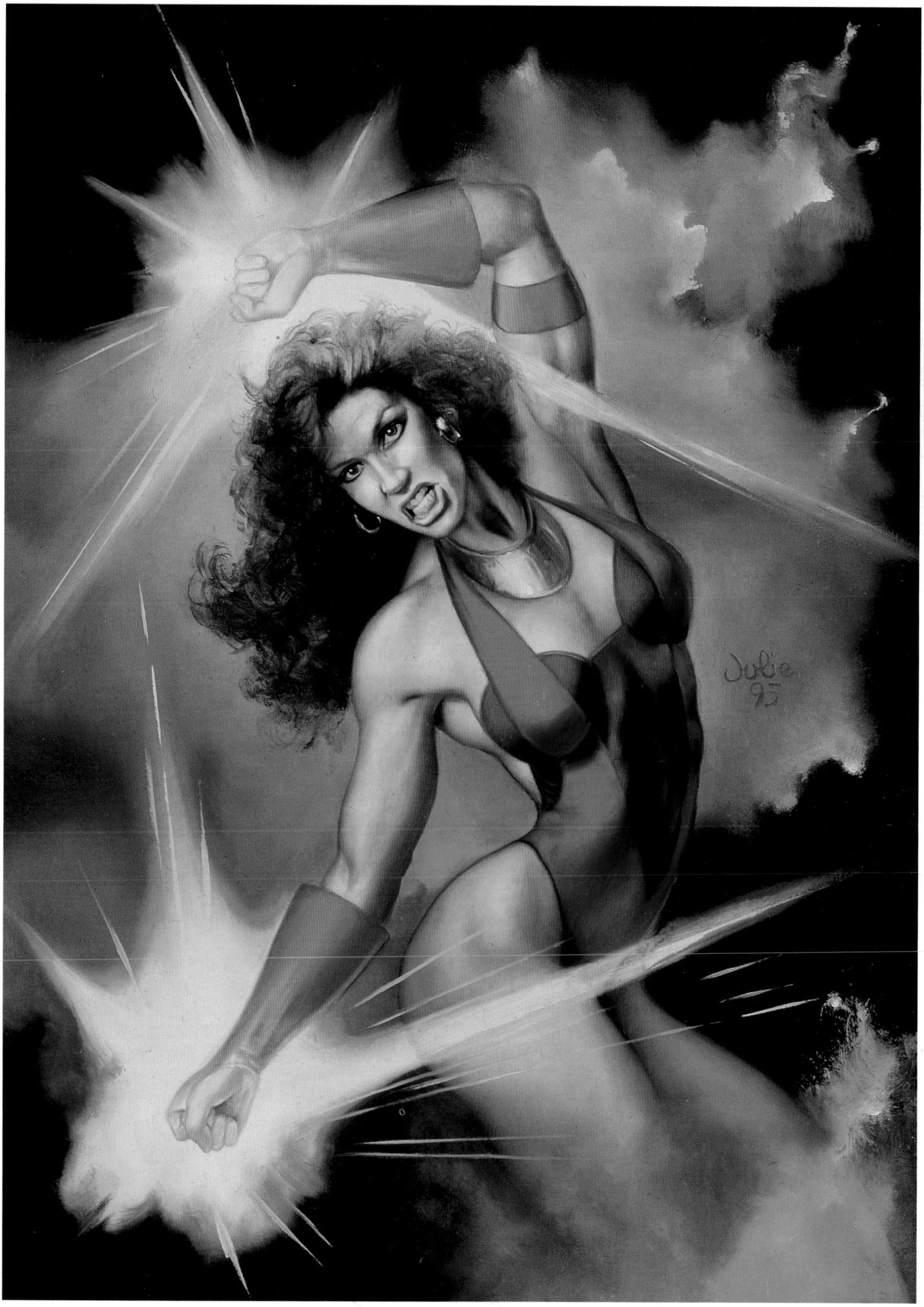
Julie
95

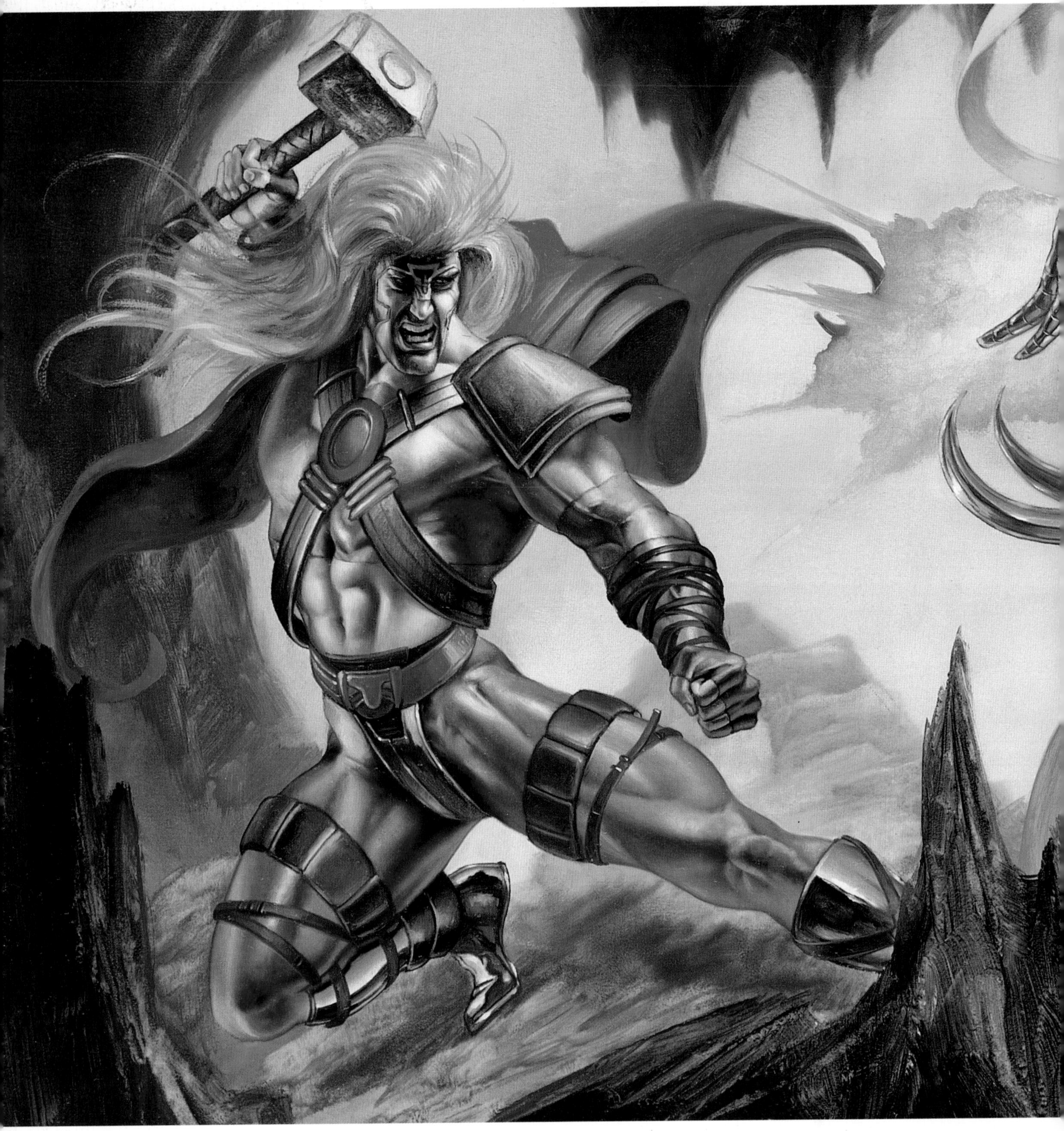

(above)

THOR VS LOKI

1996, Julie

Trading Cards. Fleer Publishing Co.

A twin set of cards designed to fit together. According to Marvel mythology, Thor and his evil twin Loki are the very same as the gods worshipped by the ancient Scandinavians. For various reasons they retired and withdrew from Earth. Then later Odin, to teach his son Thor a lesson in humility, had him incarnated on Earth as the mild and lame Dr Ronald Blake. When the time came for him to learn his true identity, Odin engineered Blake a

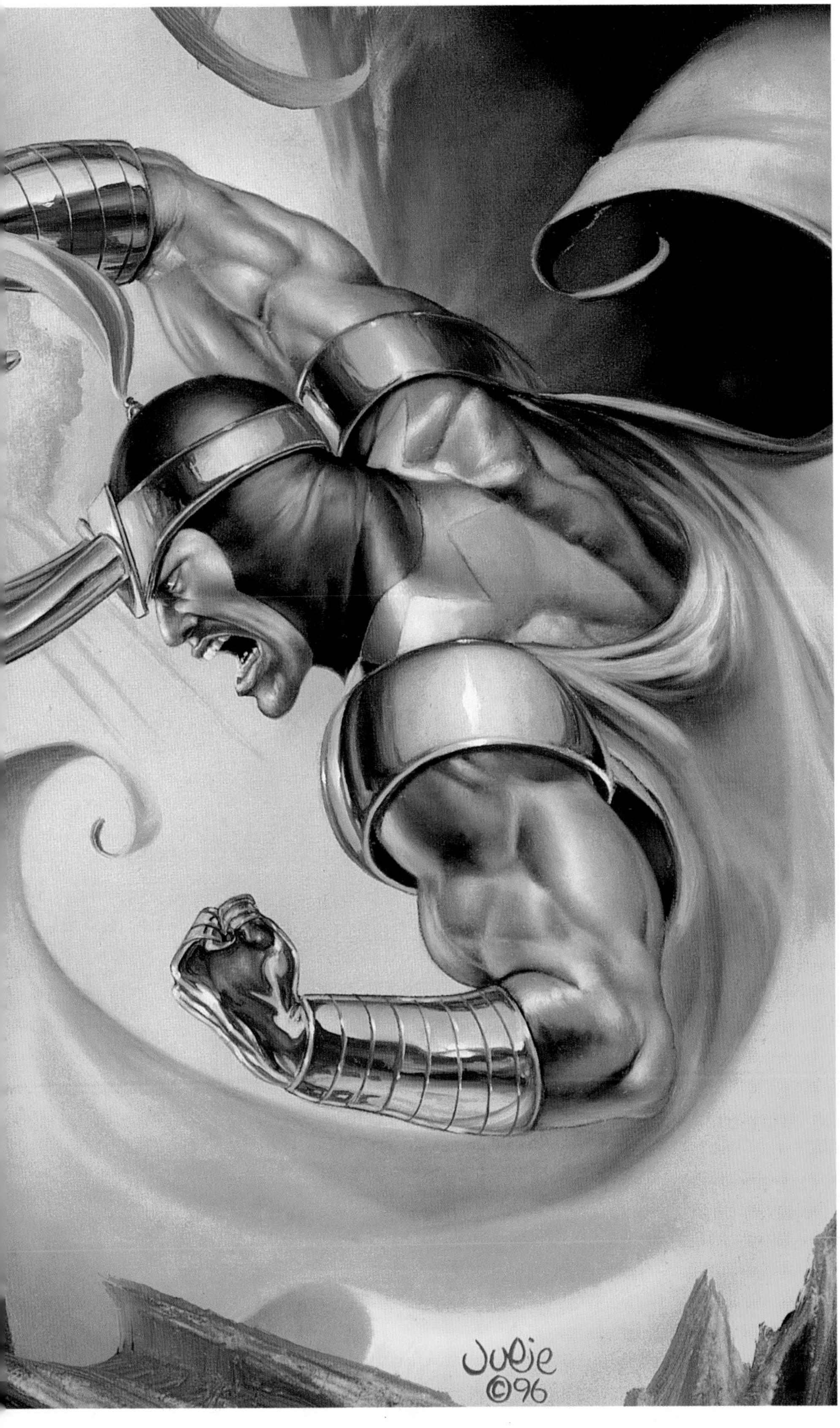

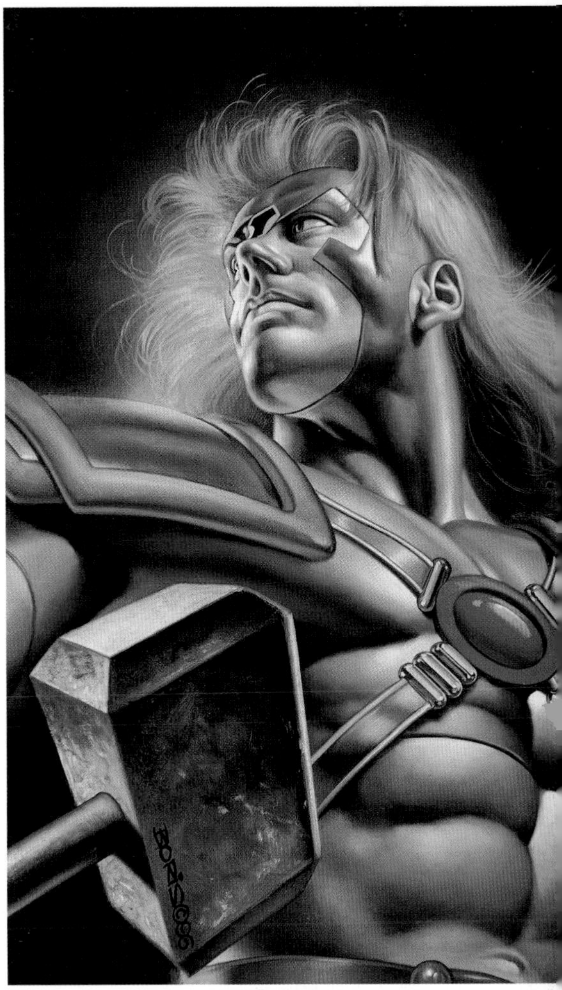

(above)

THOR

1996, Boris

Trading Card. Fleer Publishing Co.

TM & © 1996 Marvel Characters, Inc.

All rights reserved.

holiday in Norway where 'chance' led him to the very cave in which he had been first born aeons before. He finds a gnarled branch lying there, and when he strikes it on the ground all is revealed in a blinding flash. The branch becomes his ancient mystical hammer Mjolnir, and he regains his full powers. He later joins the Avengers in their wars against evil.

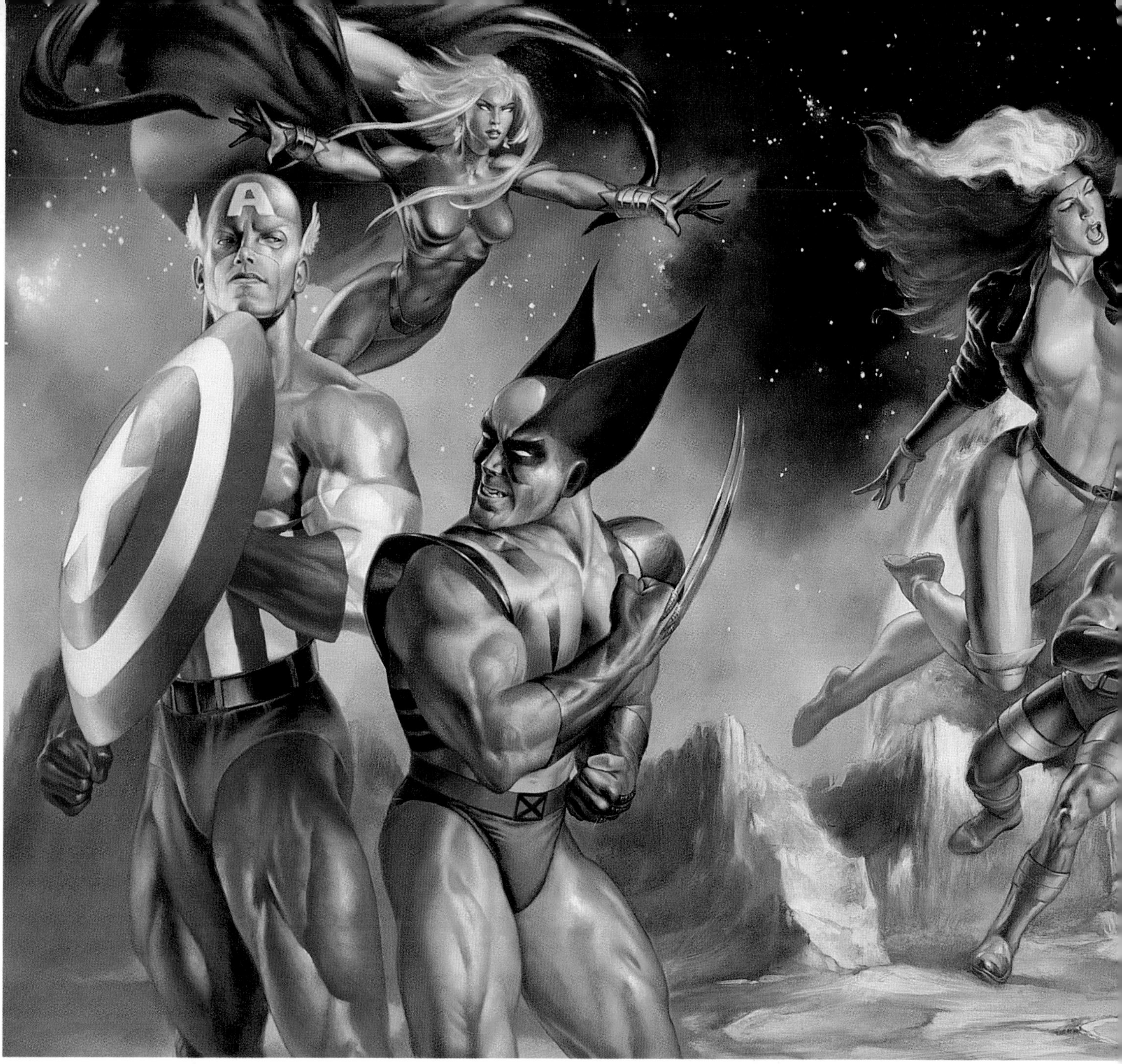

(above)

X-MEN AND AVENGERS

1998, Julie

Cover. Byron Preiss Multimedia

Three cards each featuring three characters and designed to connect up. Bringing different teams together occasionally is a good way to refresh them in the readers' eyes and perhaps draw in fans from rival groups. Occasionally it also leads to the characters changing their allegiance. The Avengers have always been a very fluid group. Their present line-up is about as stable as it has ever been but Quicksilver, for one, often goes off on his own adventures and joins other teams.

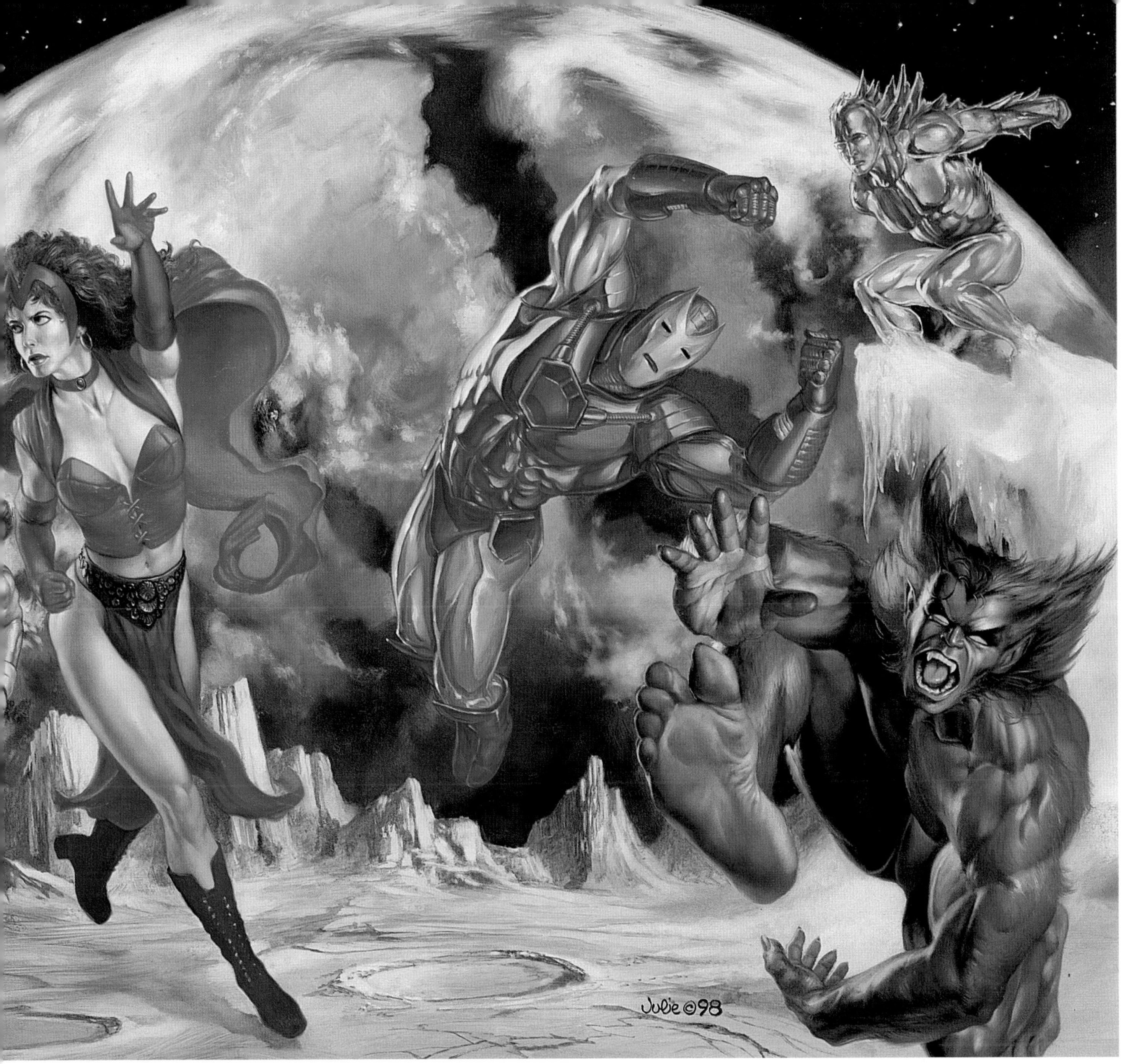
Julie ©98

(right)

QUICKSILVER

1996, Boris

Trading Card. Fleer Publishing Co.

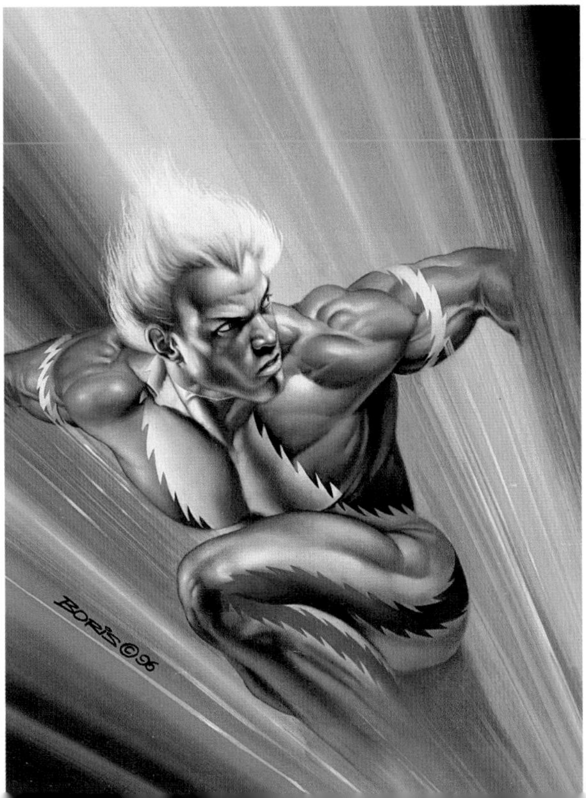
BORIS©96

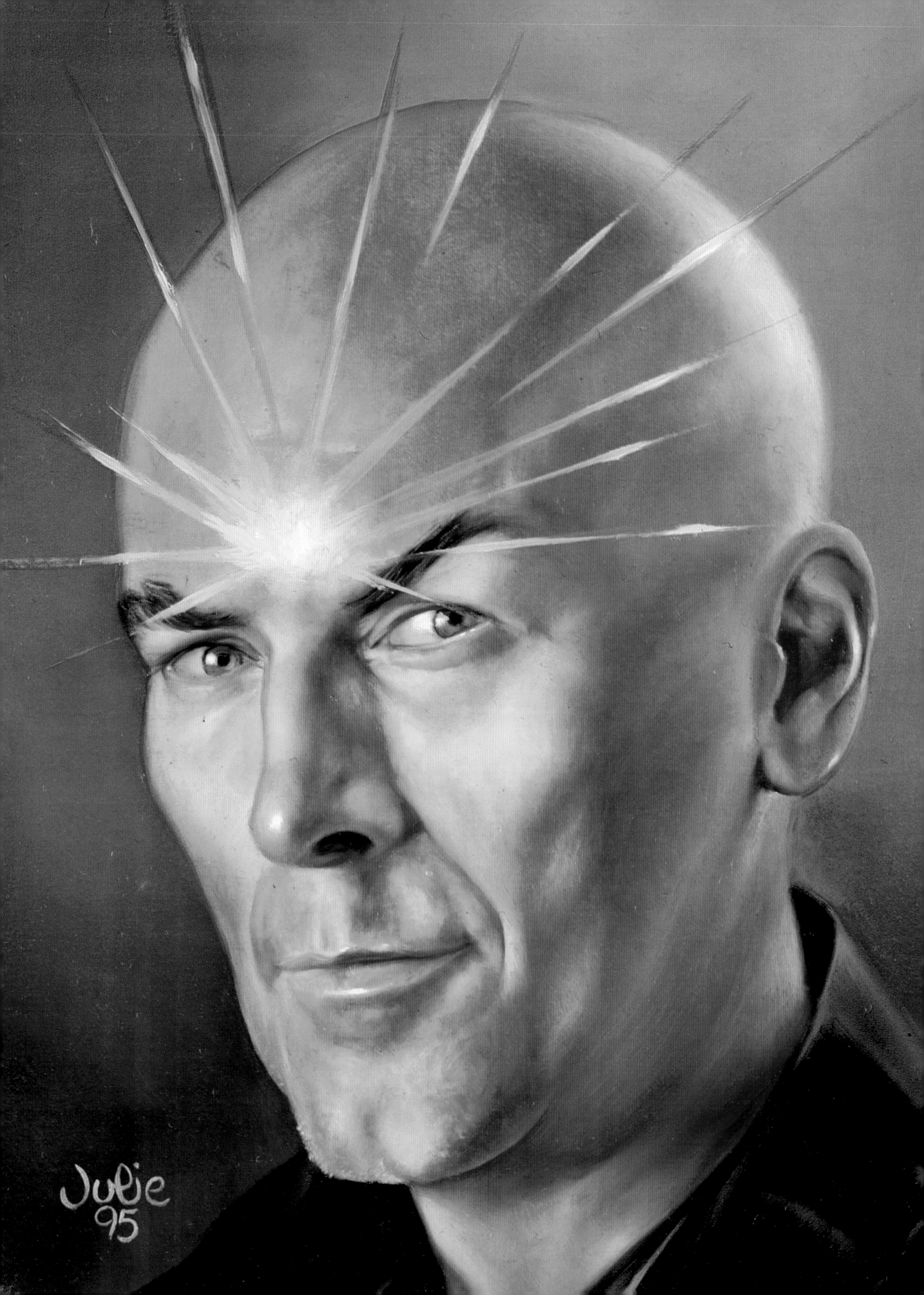
Julie
95

X-MEN

The translation of comics to the big screen has always been a bit hit-and-miss. The shining successes are of course Superman, Spiderman, Flash Gordon (perhaps) and Batman, which, like the Hulk on TV, managed to reach far beyond the usual superhero audience. Others, for no obvious reason, simply fail to make much of an impression.

At the time of writing this book a film of the X-Men is in production by 20th Century Fox and it will be interesting to see how it fares. What is fairly certain is that it will please the legions of X-Men fans, but whether it will crash the barriers to wider appreciation is what everyone at the studios would give their right arms to know now. The choice of Patrick Stewart (Captain Jean Luc Picard from *Star Trek*) and Ian McKellan in the starring roles of Professor X and his arch enemy Magneto is promising. Also the director Brian Singer (*The Usual Suspects, Apt Pupil*), screenwriter Christopher McQuarrie (who won an Oscar for *The Usual Suspects*) and everyone else involved have strings of hit films to their credit, but still you can never quite tell. That's the thrill of any kind of creative adventure. There are some things about which it is only possible to be wise after the event.

The X-Men are possibly the most successful Marvel comic team ever, with over 400 million titles sold over the four decades of their career. Their founder, leader and guiding light is Professor X, Francis Charles Xavier. Apart from being an intellectual genius he is the most powerful telepath in the Marvel universe, and is able to enter other people's minds to erase their memories if need be. He is the X-Men's father figure, particularly with Cyclops, with whom he often has an uneasy father-son rivalry, one that Freud would most certainly relish.

(left)

PROFESSOR X

1995, Julie
Trading Card. Fleer Publishing Co.

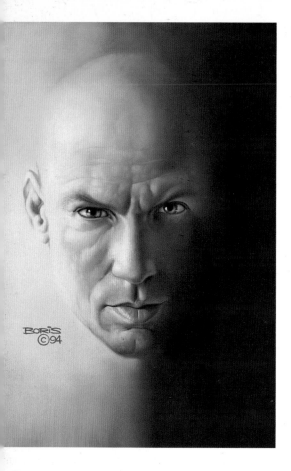

(above)

PROFESSOR X

1994, Boris

Trading Card. Fleer Publishing Co.

TM & © 1994 Marvel Characters, Inc.

All rights reserved.

Xavier was crippled early in his superhero career during a clash with the alien Lucifer and has since operated from his famous wheelchair. For a while he abandoned the X-Men to go and live in space with Lilandra, the Shiar Empress. She cloned him a new body, but back on Earth he was quickly disabled again by the Shadow King.

(above right)

COLOSSUS

1993, Julie

Trading Card. Fleer Publishing Co.

TM & © 1993 Marvel Characters, Inc.

All rights reserved.

Originally called Piotr Nikolaievitch Rasputin, Colossus was recruited from Siberia by Professor X, along with Wolverine and others, in the second wave of X-Men. They were needed to rescue the original team from the sentient island Krakoa that had trapped them.

(right)

CYCLOPS 1

1994, Boris

Trading Card. Fleer Publishing Co.

TM & © 1994 Marvel Characters, Inc.

All rights reserved.

Cyclops was born Scott Summers and was the first mutant invited by Xavier to join the X-Men. His marriage to Jean Grey (Marvel Girl, later Phoenix) is one of the few examples of marital staying power in the Marvel universe and together they are the effective leaders of the X-Men. The others in the original team were Beast (Henry McCoy), Iceman (Robert Drake) and Angel (Warren Worthington III). Scott Summers discovered his powers by accident. As a teenager he developed headaches for which the only cure seemed to be ruby quartz glasses. He found these could channel a crimson optic blast by accidentally discharging one at some machinery being lowered from a tall building. As it crashed towards the innocent bystanders below, he fired another blast that disintegrated it.

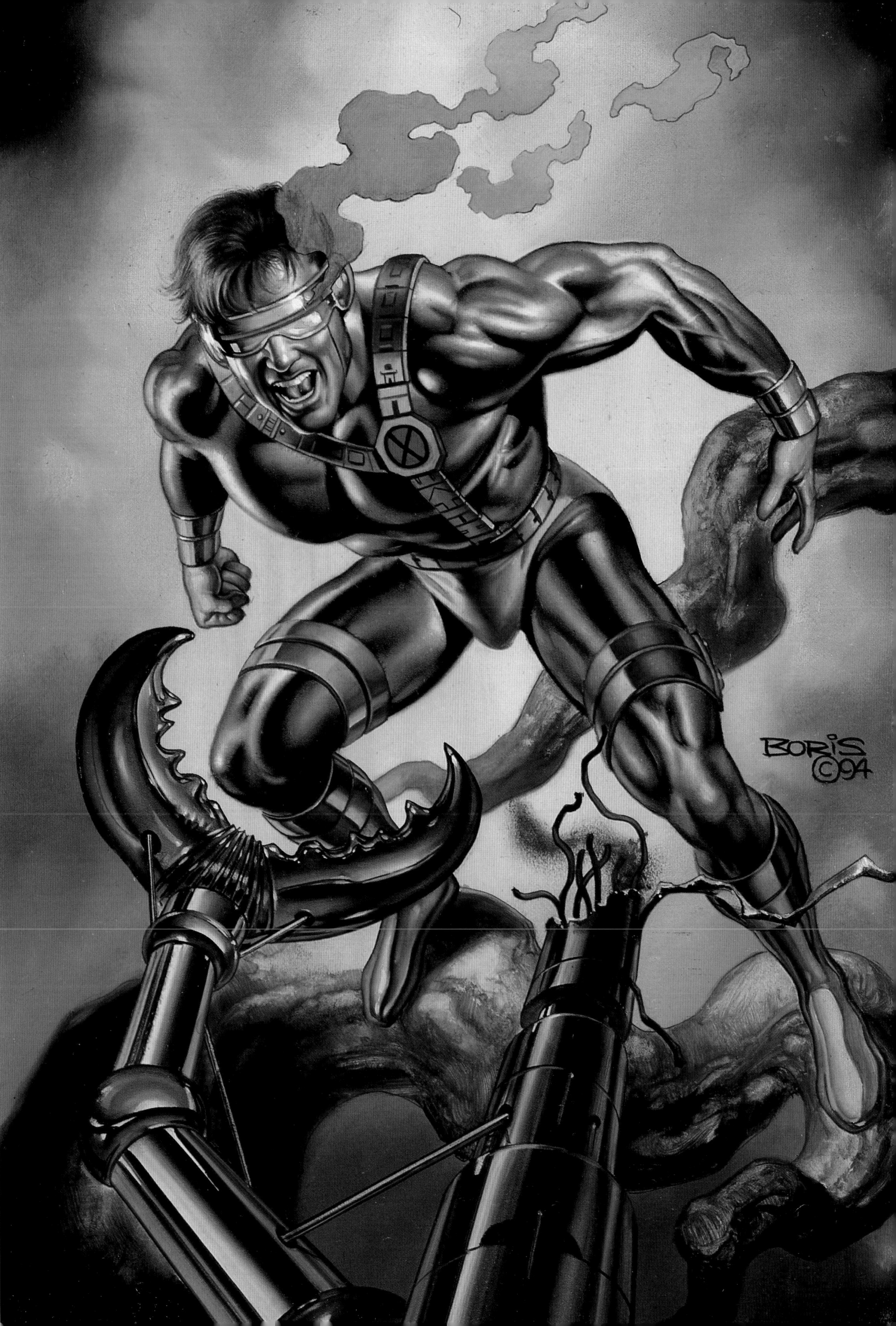
BORIS
©94

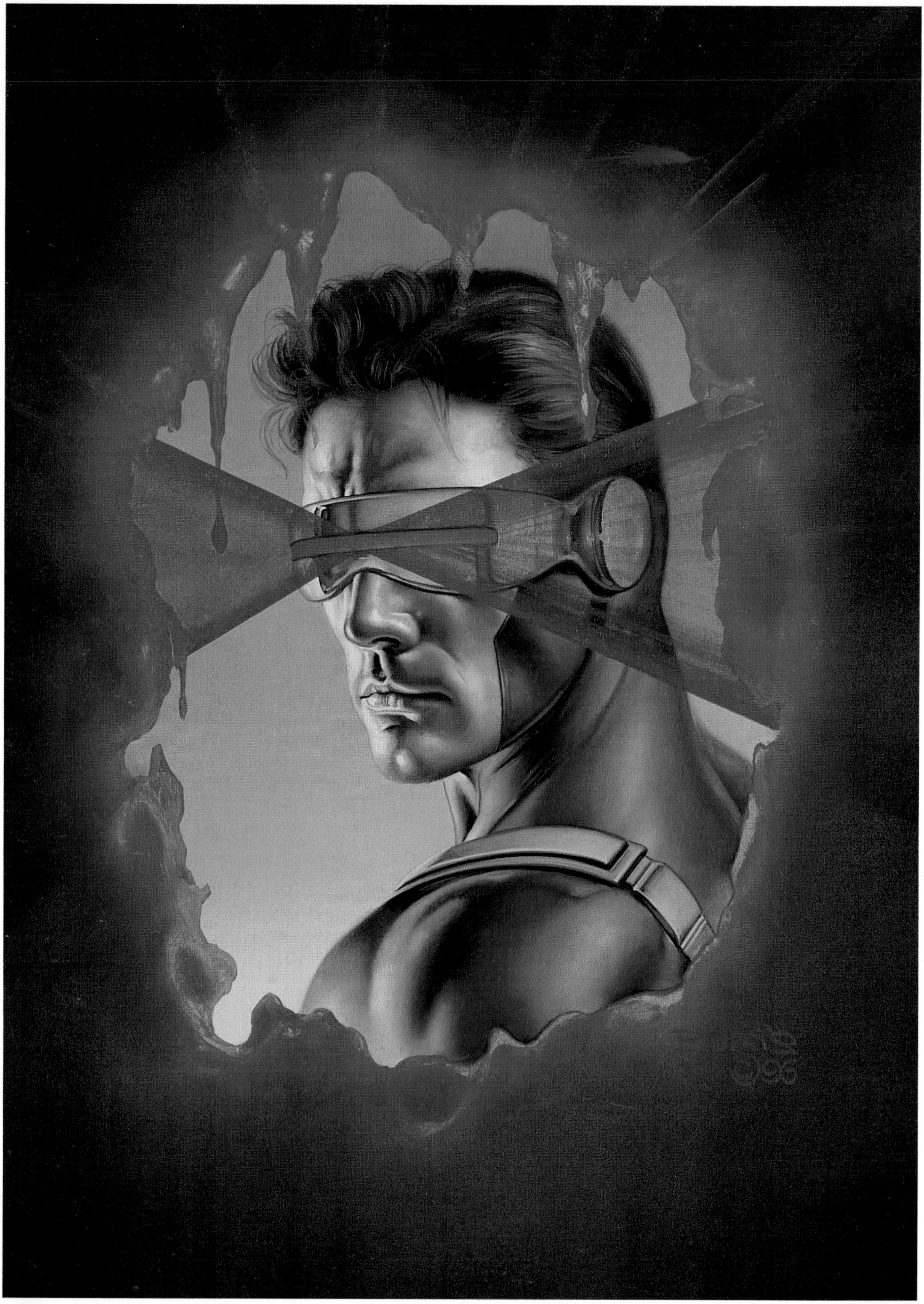

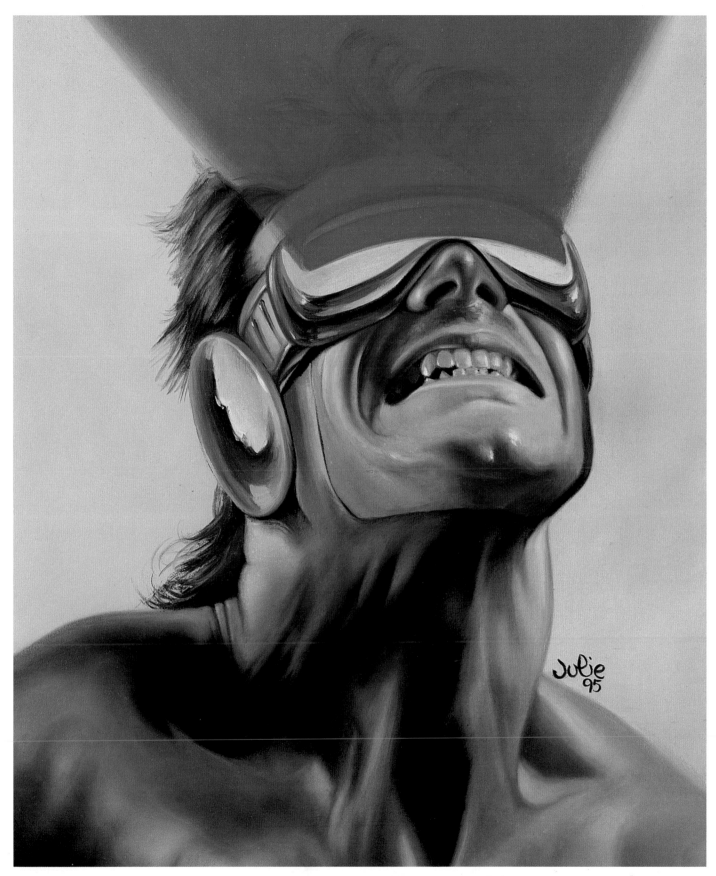

(left)

CYCLOPS 2

1996, Boris

Trading Card. Fleer Publishing Co.

TM & © 1996 Marvel Characters, Inc.

All rights reserved.

(above)

CYCLOPS 3

1995, Julie

Trading Card. Fleer Publishing Co.

TM & © 1993 Marvel Characters, Inc.

All rights reserved.

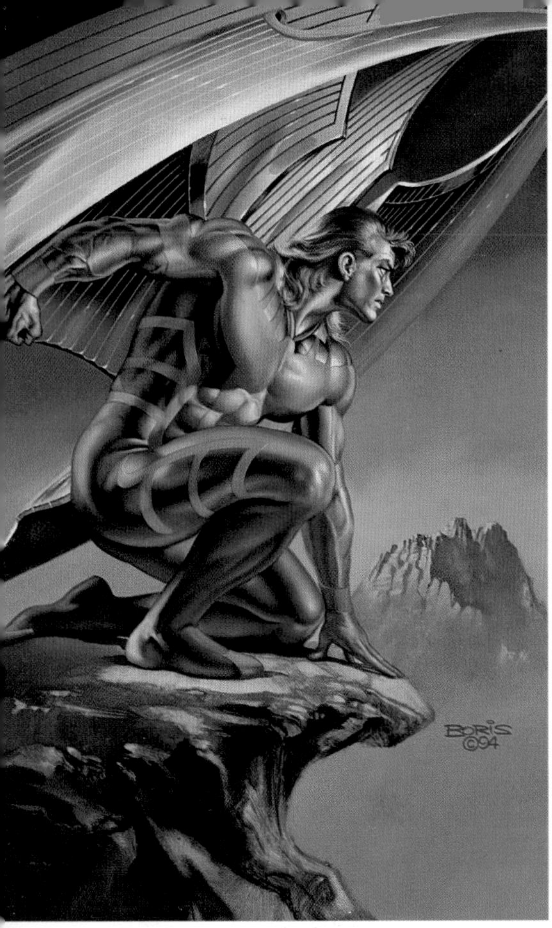
BORIS
©94

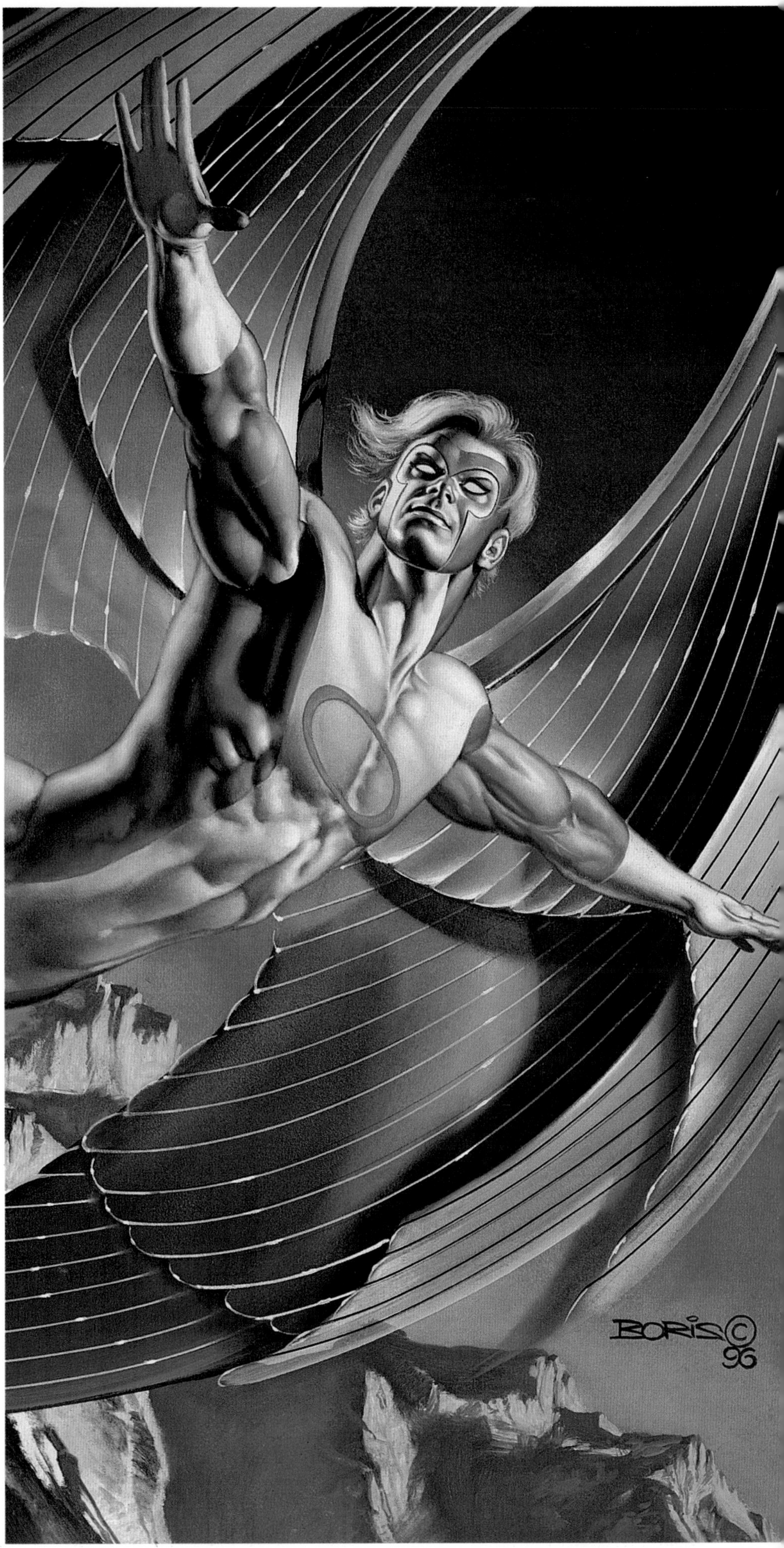
BORIS©
96

(above)

ARCHANGEL

1994, Boris

Trading Card. Fleer Publishing Co.

As Angel, this character was one of the original X-Men. Apocalypse transformed him into Death / Archangel. He has also been known as Avenging Angel and is romantically linked with Psylocke.

(right)

ARCHANGEL 2

1996, Boris

Trading Card. Fleer Publishing Co.

(far right)

ARCHANGEL 3

1996, Julie

Trading Card. Fleer Publishing Co.

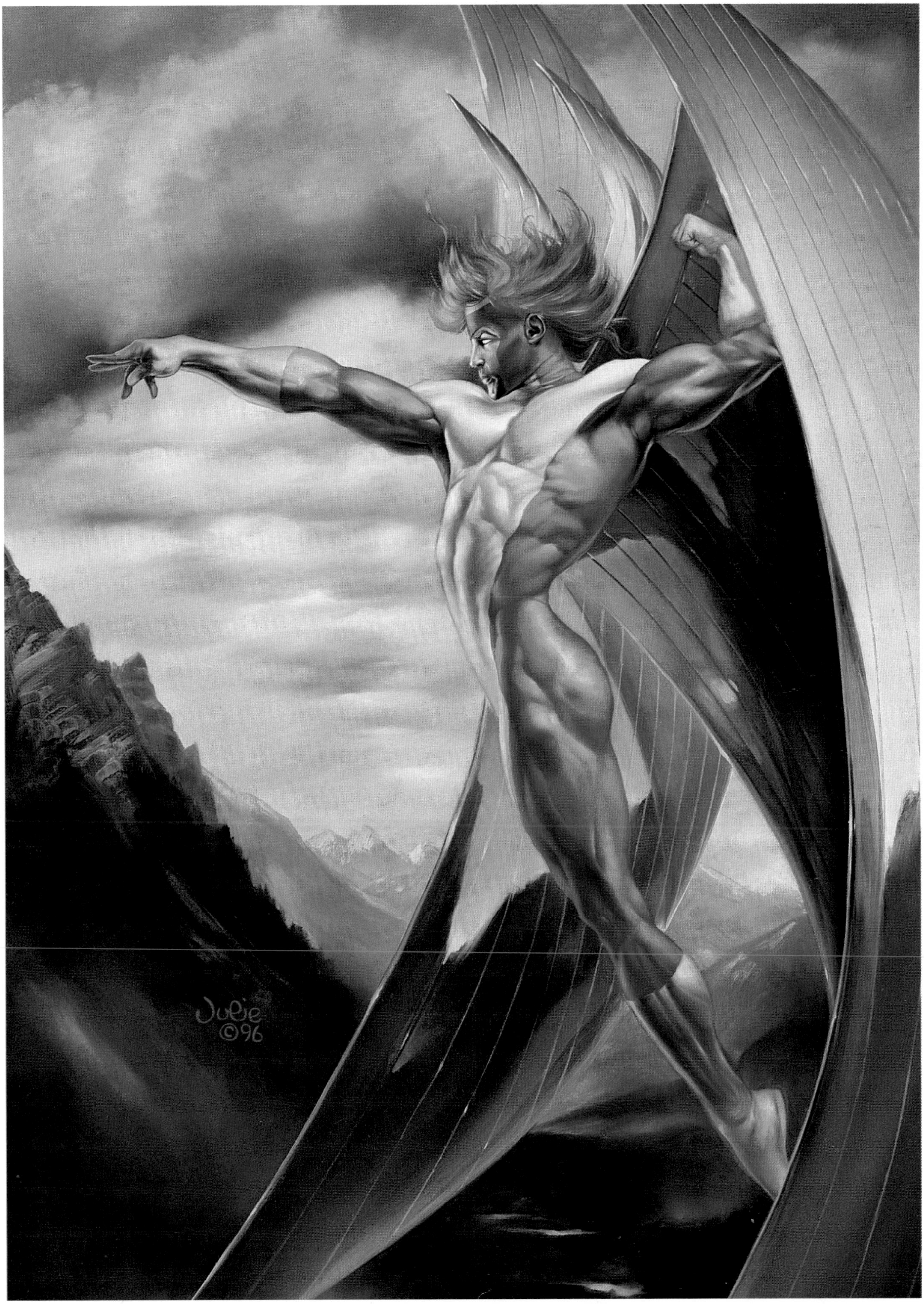
Julie
©96

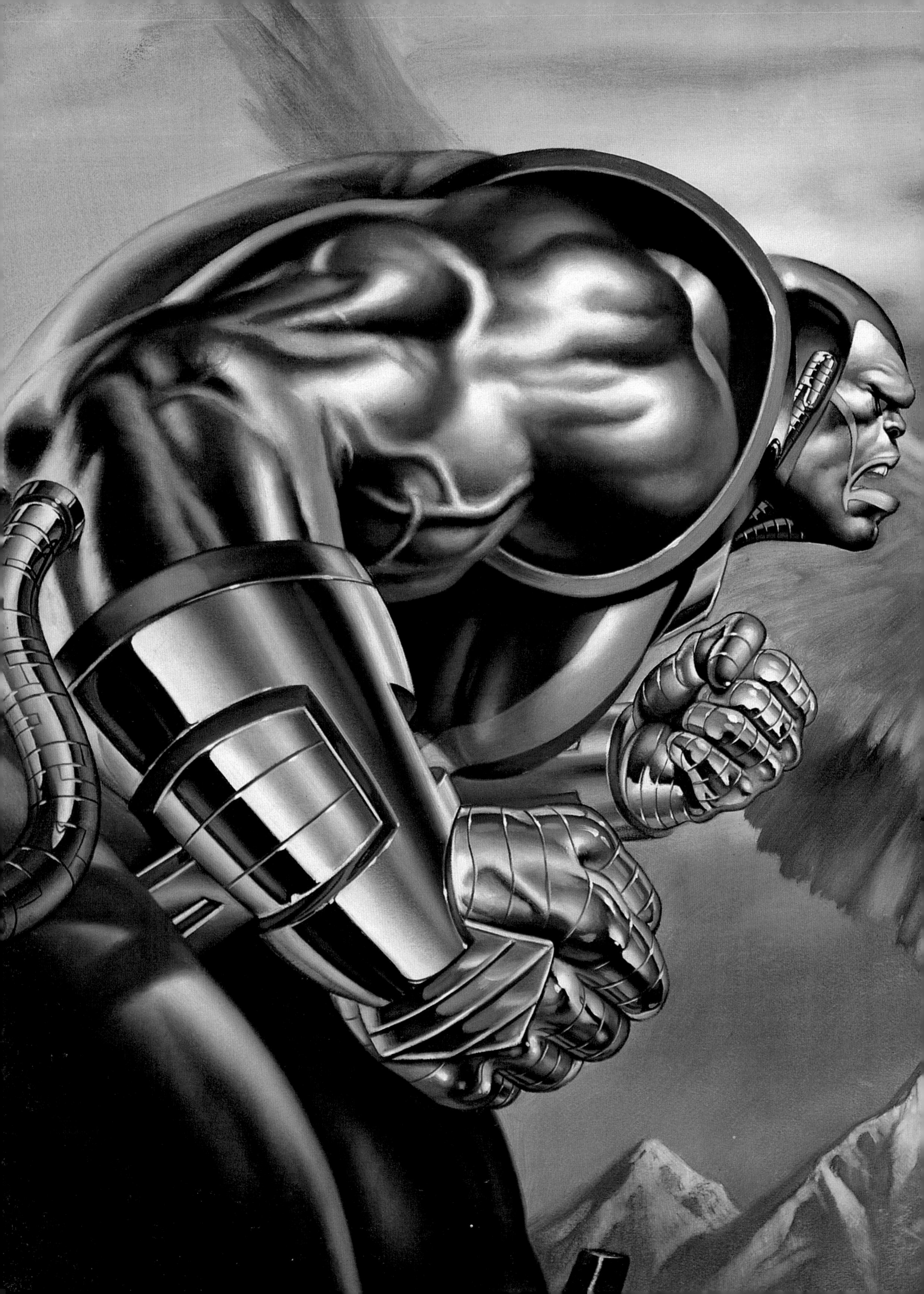

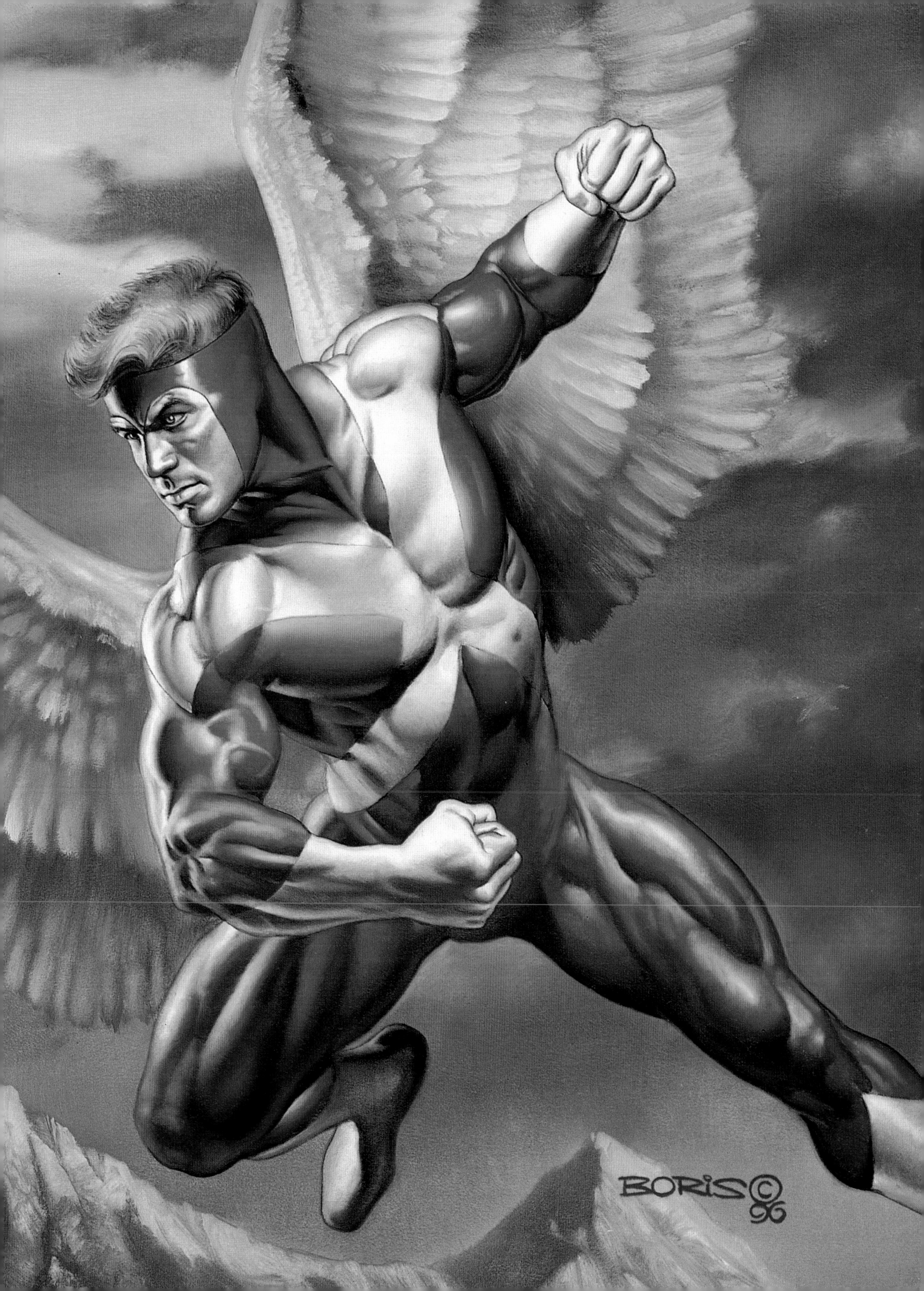
BORIS©
96

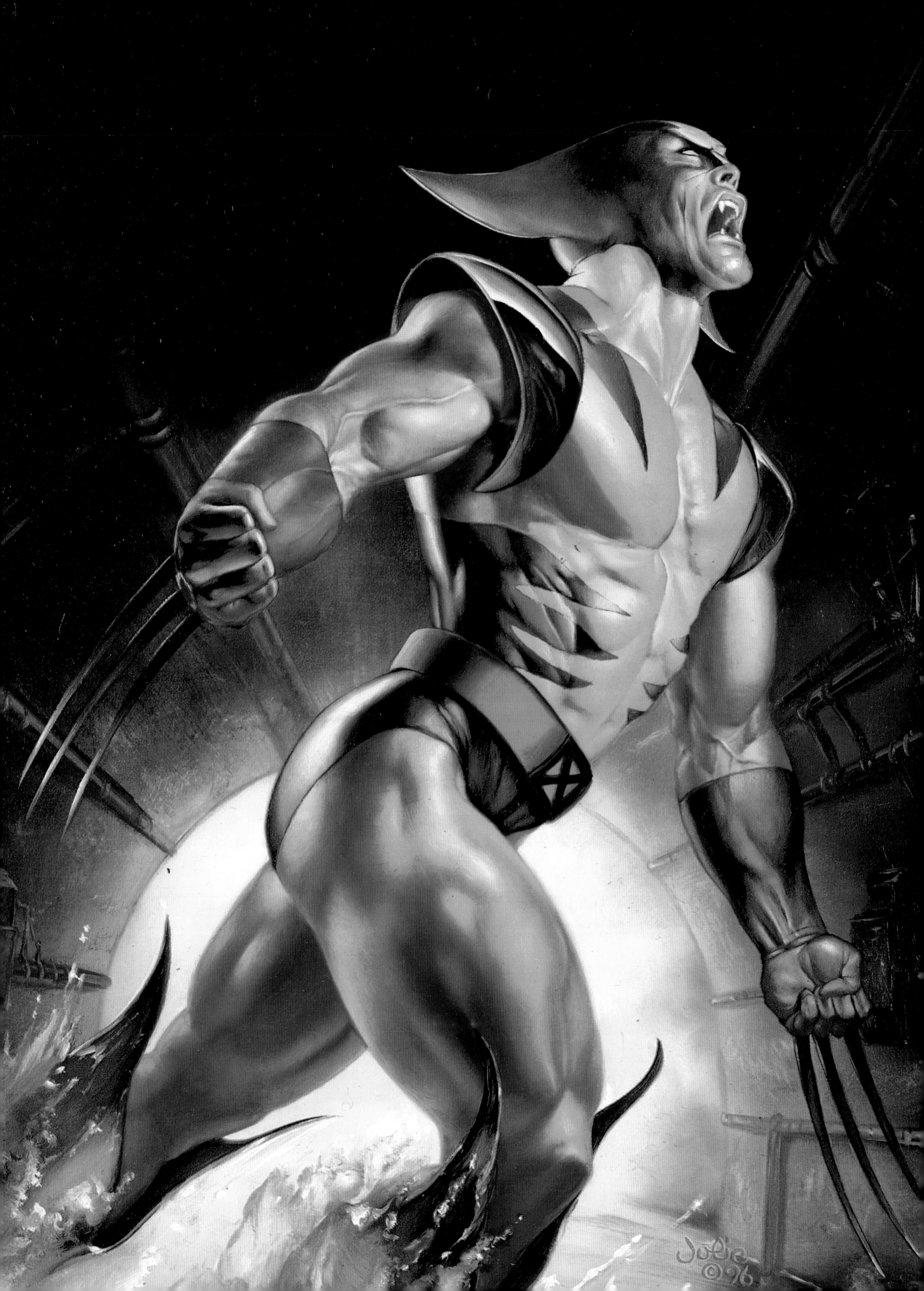
Julie
©96

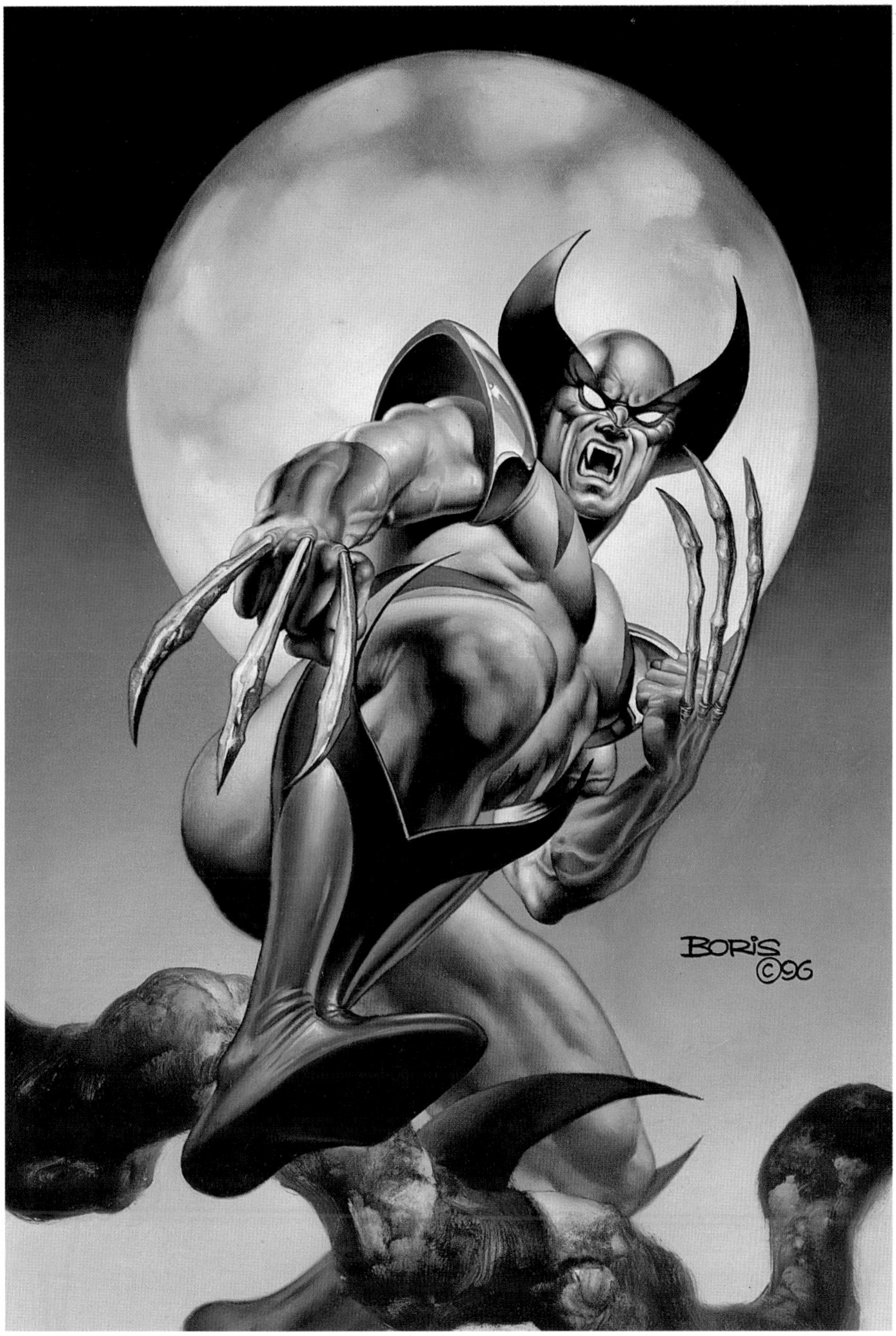
BORIS ©96

(pages 108–109)

APOCALYPSE VS ANGEL

1996, Boris

Trading Card. Fleer Publishing Co.

(left)

FULL MOON

1996, Boris

Trading Card. Fleer Publishing Co.

(below)

WOLVERINE AND SHADOWCAT

1996, Boris

Trading Card. Fleer Publishing Co.

Even Wolverine himself is unsure of his origins, since it was found that many of his memories were artificial implants.

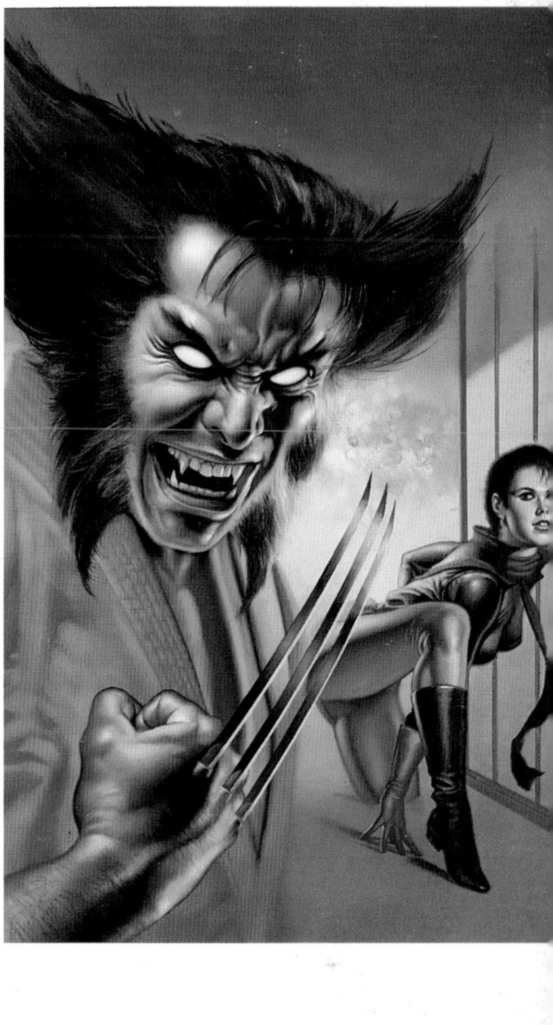

Wolverine has become one of the most popular comic characters of all, often outpolling (and outselling) established favourites like Spiderman and Batman. The fiery-tempered mutant from Canada, armed with unbreakable claws and bones of Adamantium (which are a story in themselves), also has a busy love-life. Just about every heroine in the X-Men's circle has been involved with him at some point, and he has his own comic title just to keep up with his adventures.

(left)

IN THE TUNNEL

1996, Julie

Trading Card. Fleer Publishing Co.

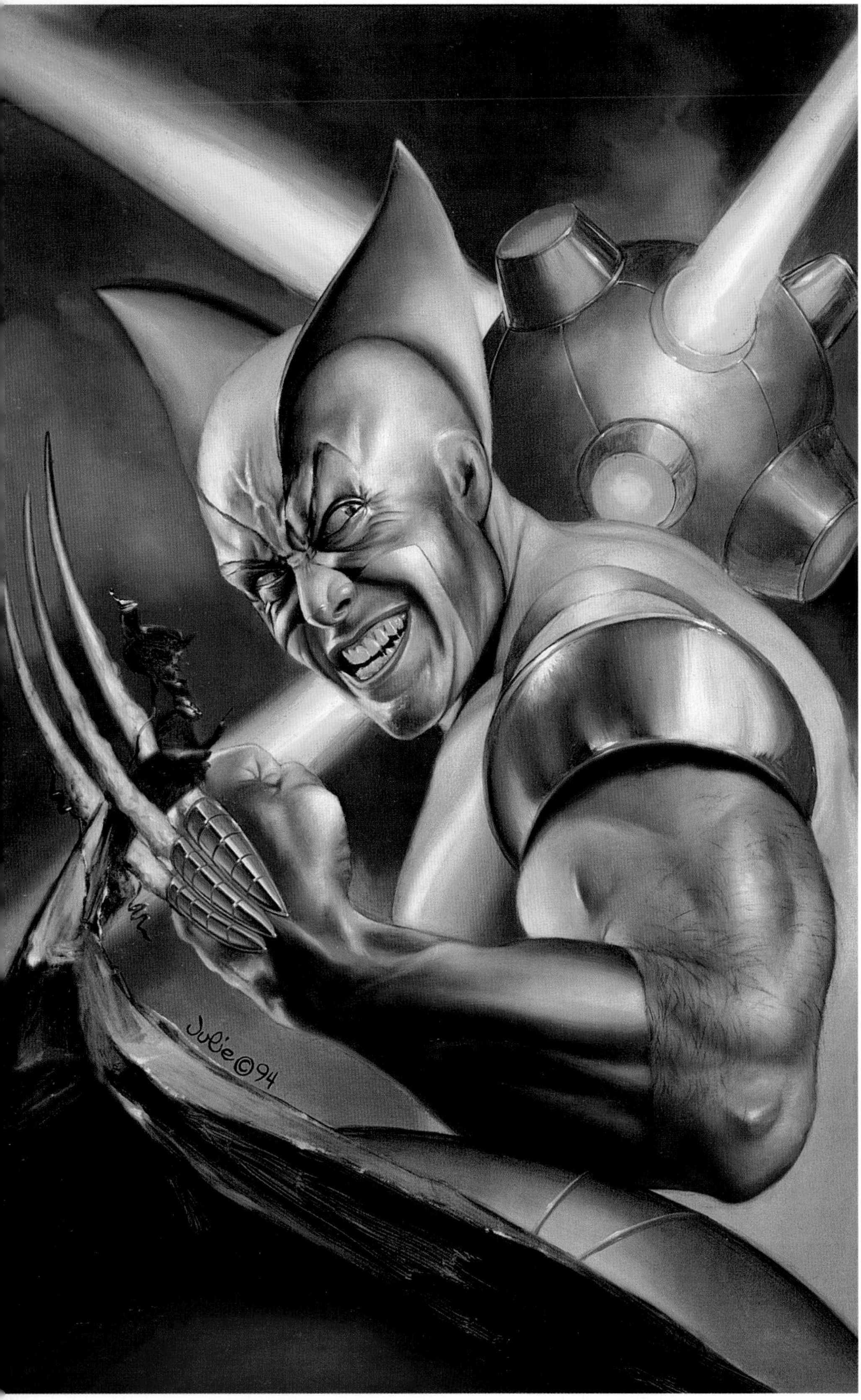
Julie ©94

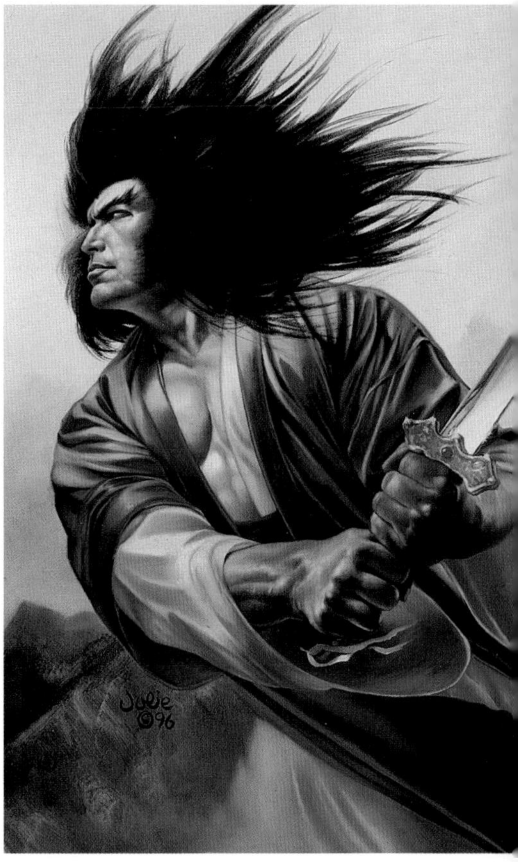
Julie ©96

(above)

LOGAN

1996, Julie

Trading Card. Fleer Publishing Co.

Wolverine off-duty and practising his martial arts. Thanks to a spell in Japan he is master of many varieties.

(left)

WOLVERINE

1994, Julie

Trading Card. Fleer Publishing Co.

(right)

WOLVERINE VS LORD SKINGEN

1996, Julie

Trading Card. Fleer Publishing Co.

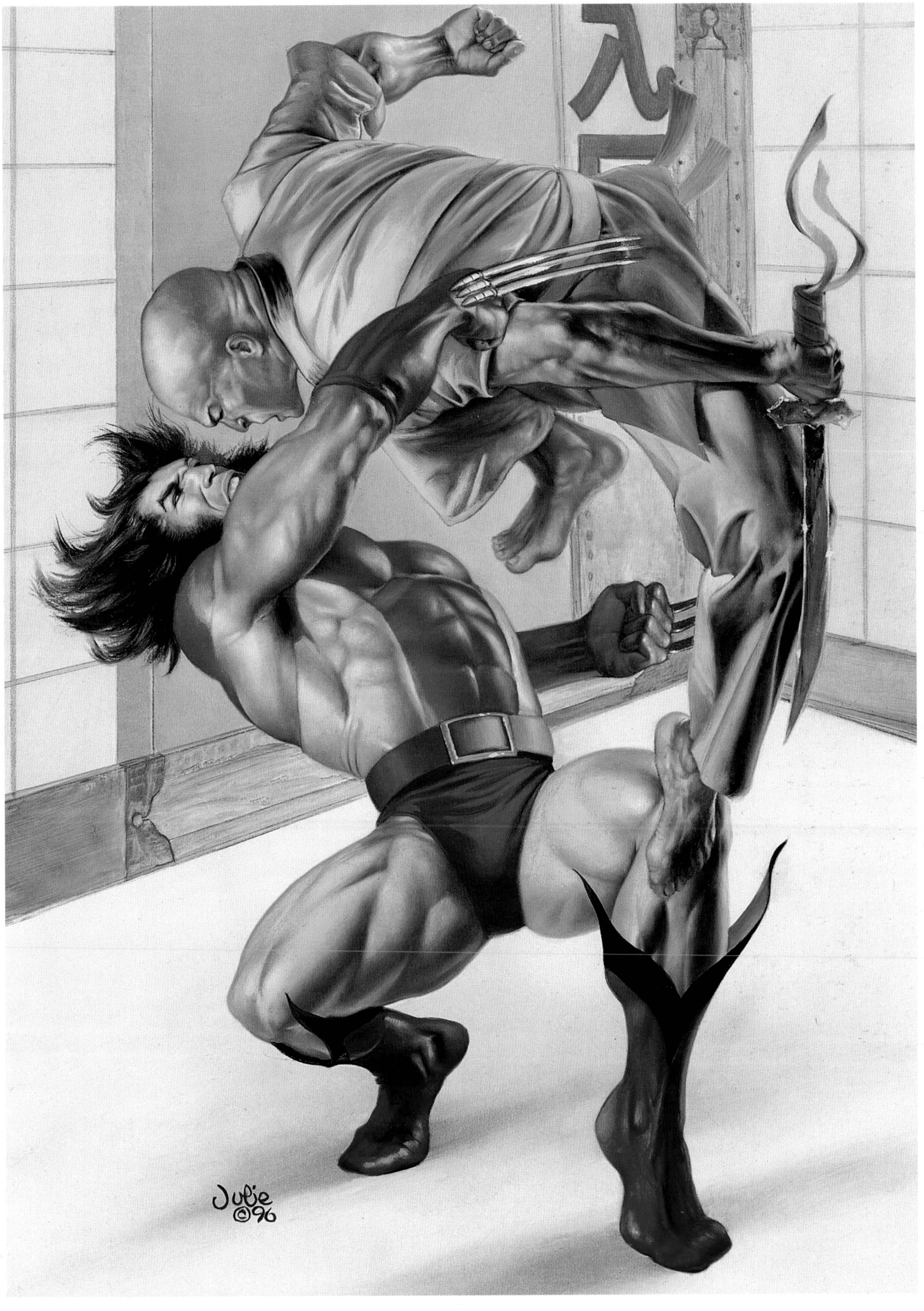
Julie
©96

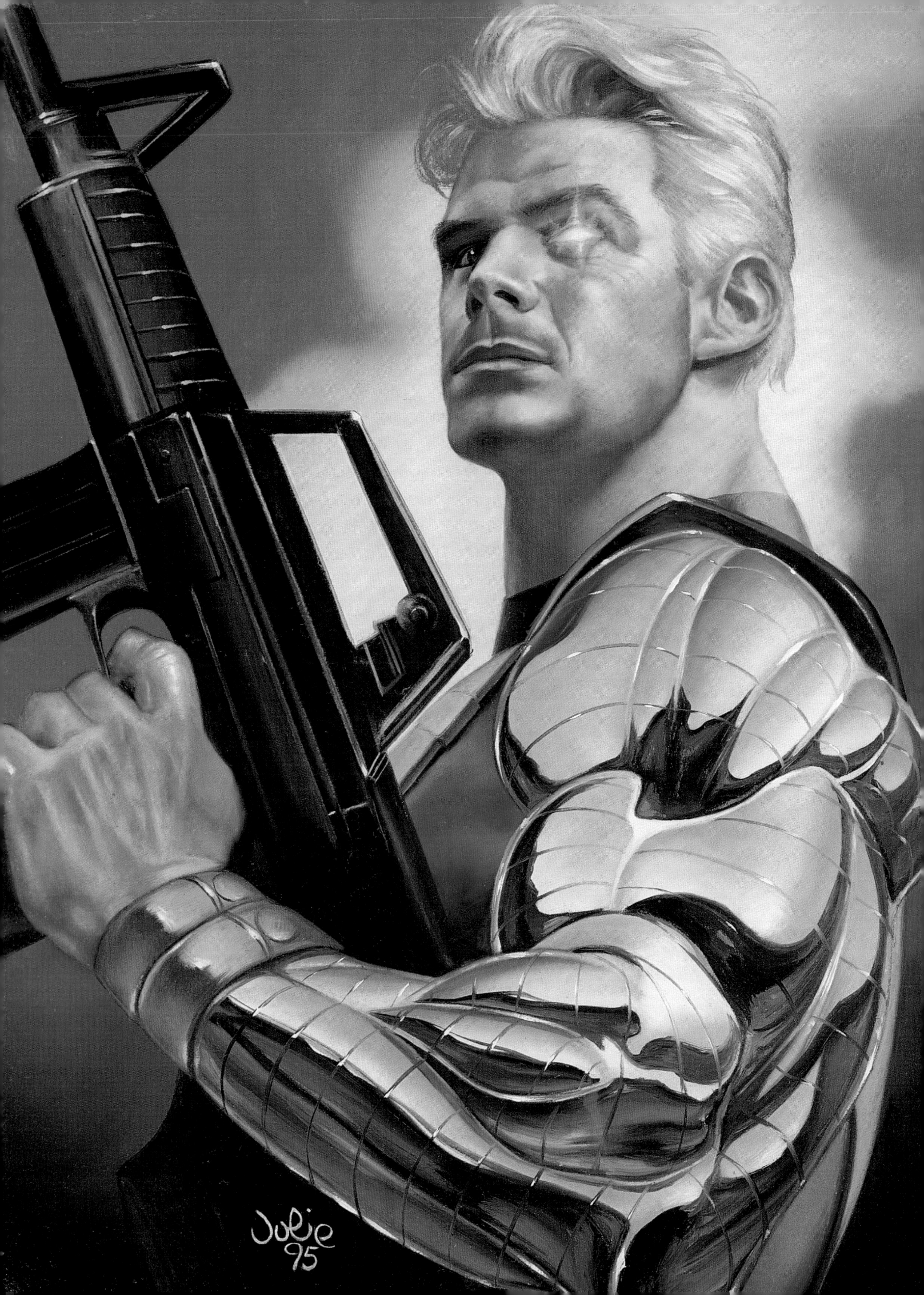
Julie
95

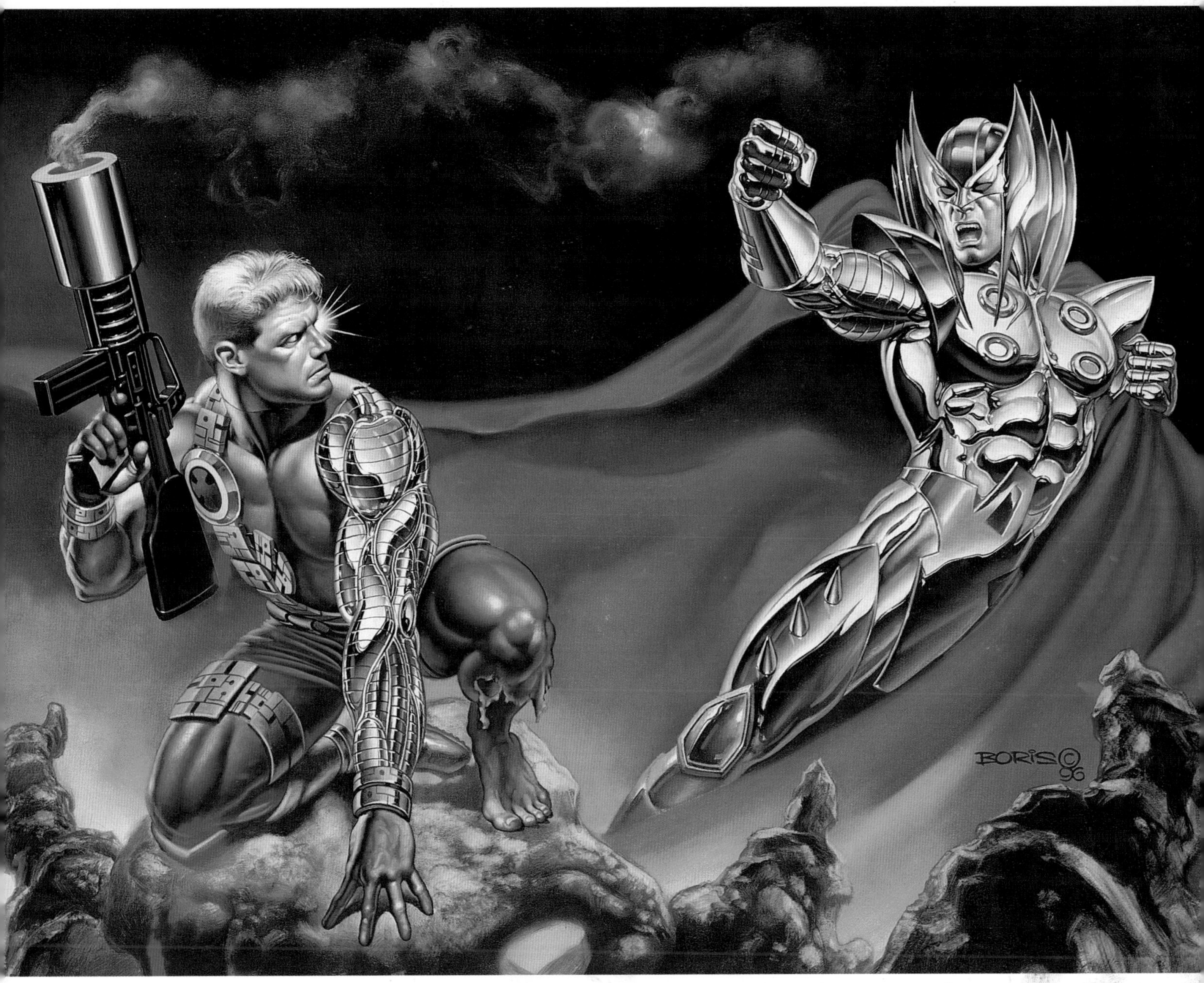
BORIS© 96

(left)

CABLE

1995, Julie

Trading Card. Fleer Publishing Co.

Son of Scott Summers (Cyclops) and Madelyne Prior, Cable is infected with an artificial virus that is slowly consuming his body. Before that happens he is hoping for a final showdown with Apocalypse. His alternate self is Nate Grey, son of Cyclops and Phoenix (Jean Grey). His opposite self is Stryfe, his clone brother.

(above)

CABLE VS STRYFE

1996, Boris

Trading Card. Fleer Publishing Co.

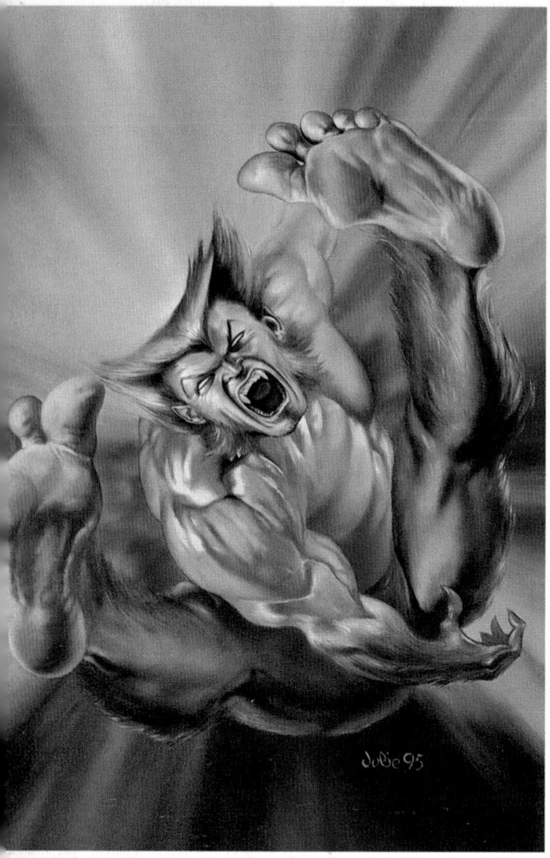

(above)

BEAST

1995, Julie

Trading Card. Fleer Publishing Co.

As Henry McCoy, Beast was one of the original X-Men. He is as clever as he is strong, though not infallible. He acquired his fur through an experiment on himself to enhance his original mutant powers. His appearance is deceptive but the Dark Beast, his alternate self, is every bit as mean as he looks.

(right)

DARK BEAST VS X-MAN

1996, Julie

Trading Card. Fleer Publishing Co.

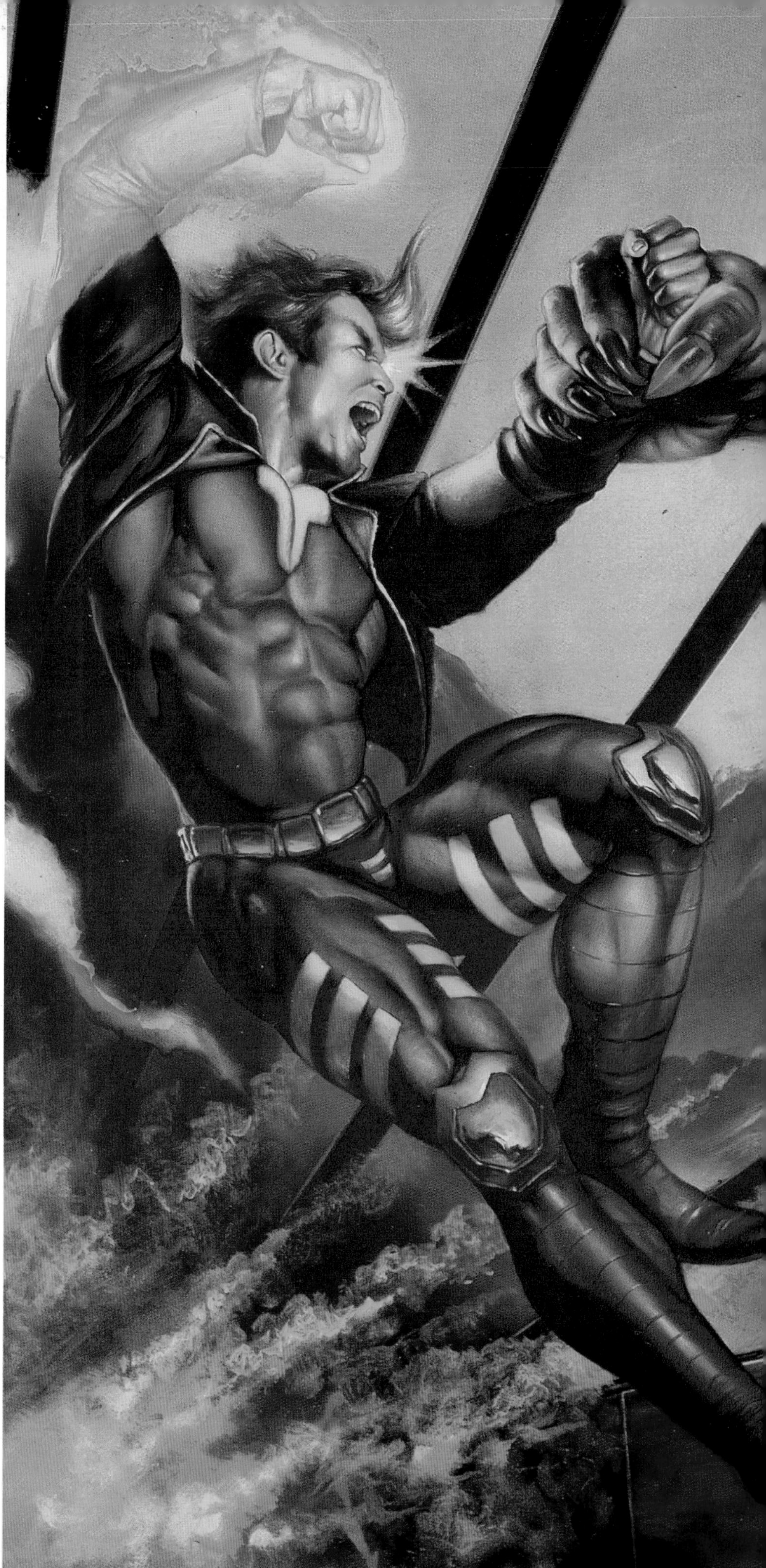

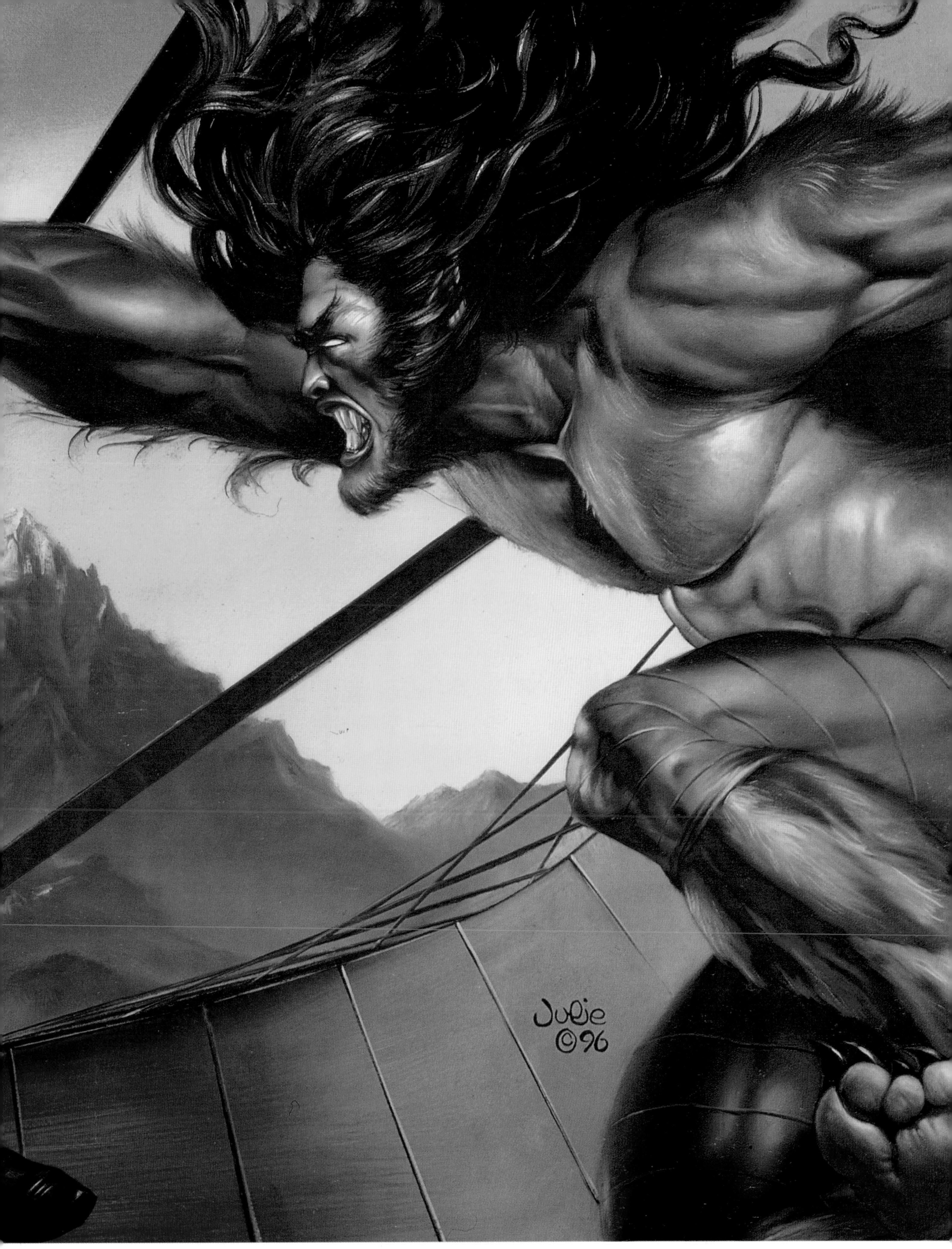
Julie
©96

(right)

GAMBIT

1994, Julie

Trading Card. Fleer Publishing Co.

Explosive playing cards thrown with extreme accuracy are Gambit's trademark weapon. He started as a thief in New Orleans and was recruited into the X-Men by Storm.

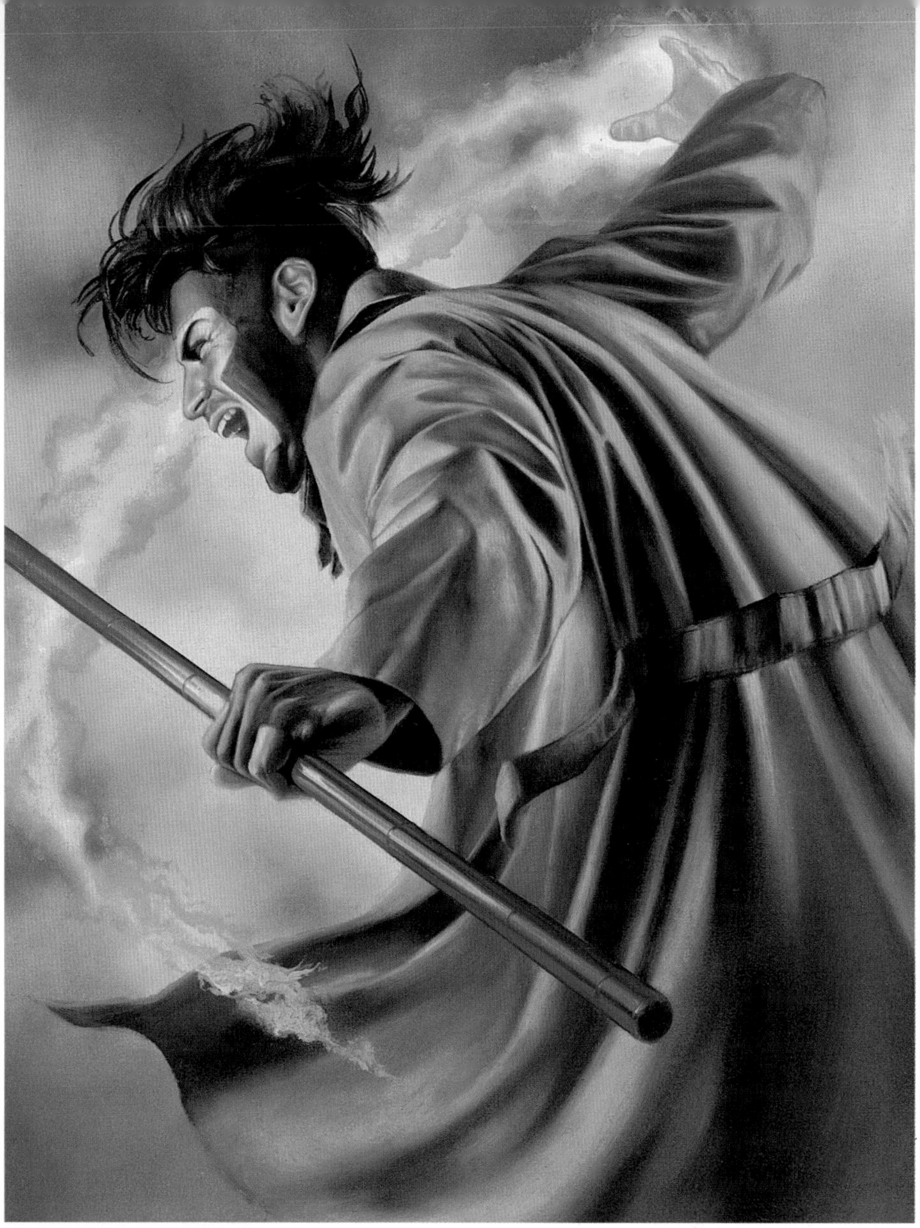

(below)

FORGE

1993, Julie

Trading Card. Fleer Publishing Co.

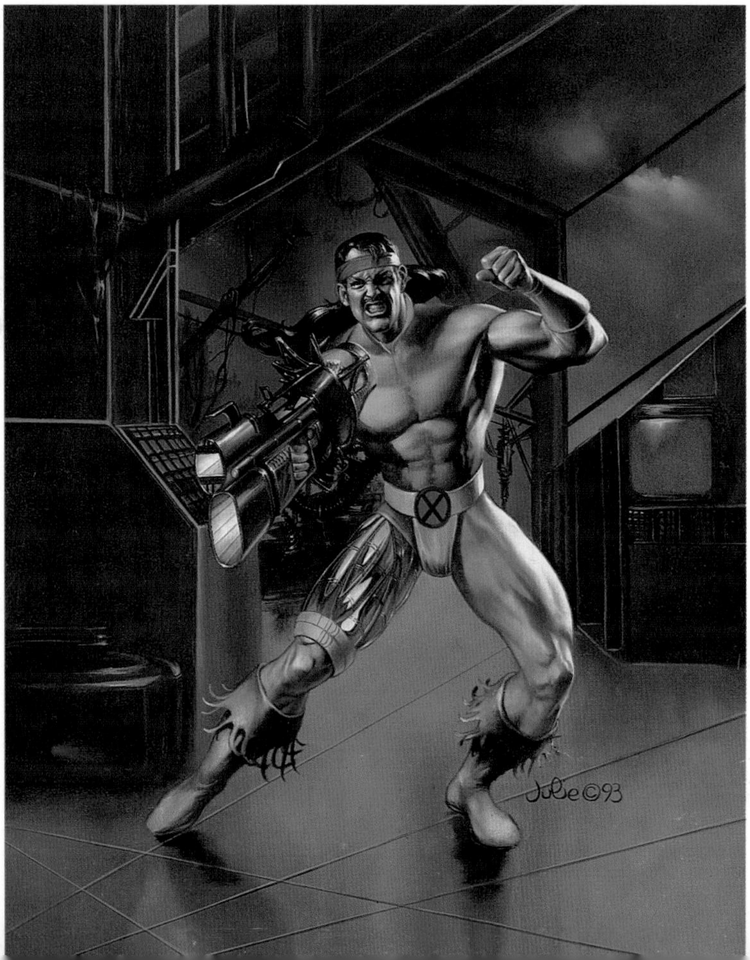
Julie©93

(right)

ICEMAN

1996, Boris

Trading Card. Fleer Publishing Co.

As Robert Drake, Iceman discovered his talent for conjuring up ice when he was a teenager, but kept quiet about it because of the prevailing hostility towards mutants. Then he was forced to use it when he and his girlfriend were attacked by a bully. The local sheriff locked him up for his own safety but Cyclops and Professor X came to his rescue, erasing all memory in the town of what had happened. Thus he became the second X-Man.

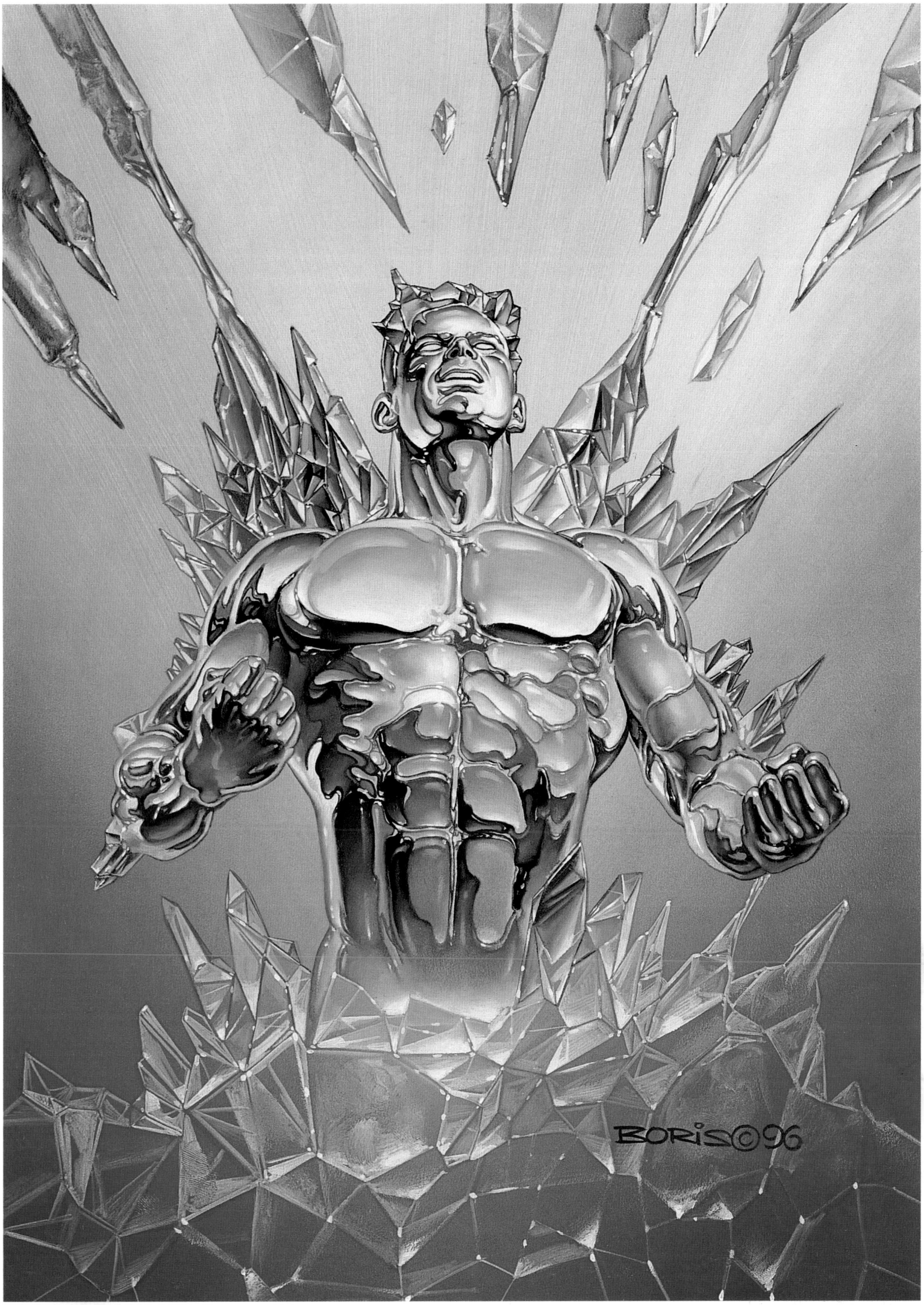
BORIS©96

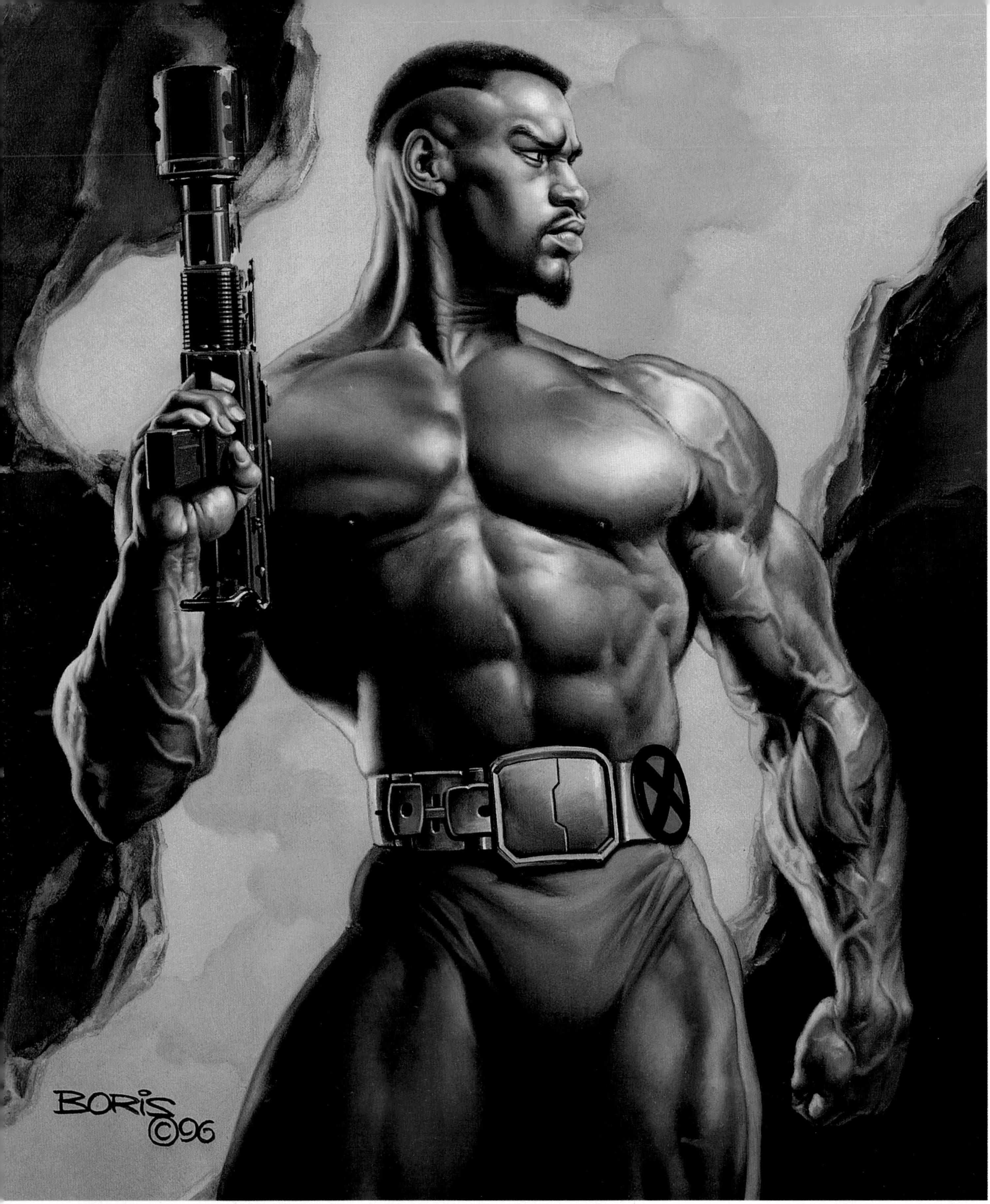
BORIS
©96

(above)

BISHOP

1996, Boris

Trading Card. Fleer Publishing Co.

(right)

BISHOP 2

1994, Boris

Trading Card. Fleer Publishing Co.

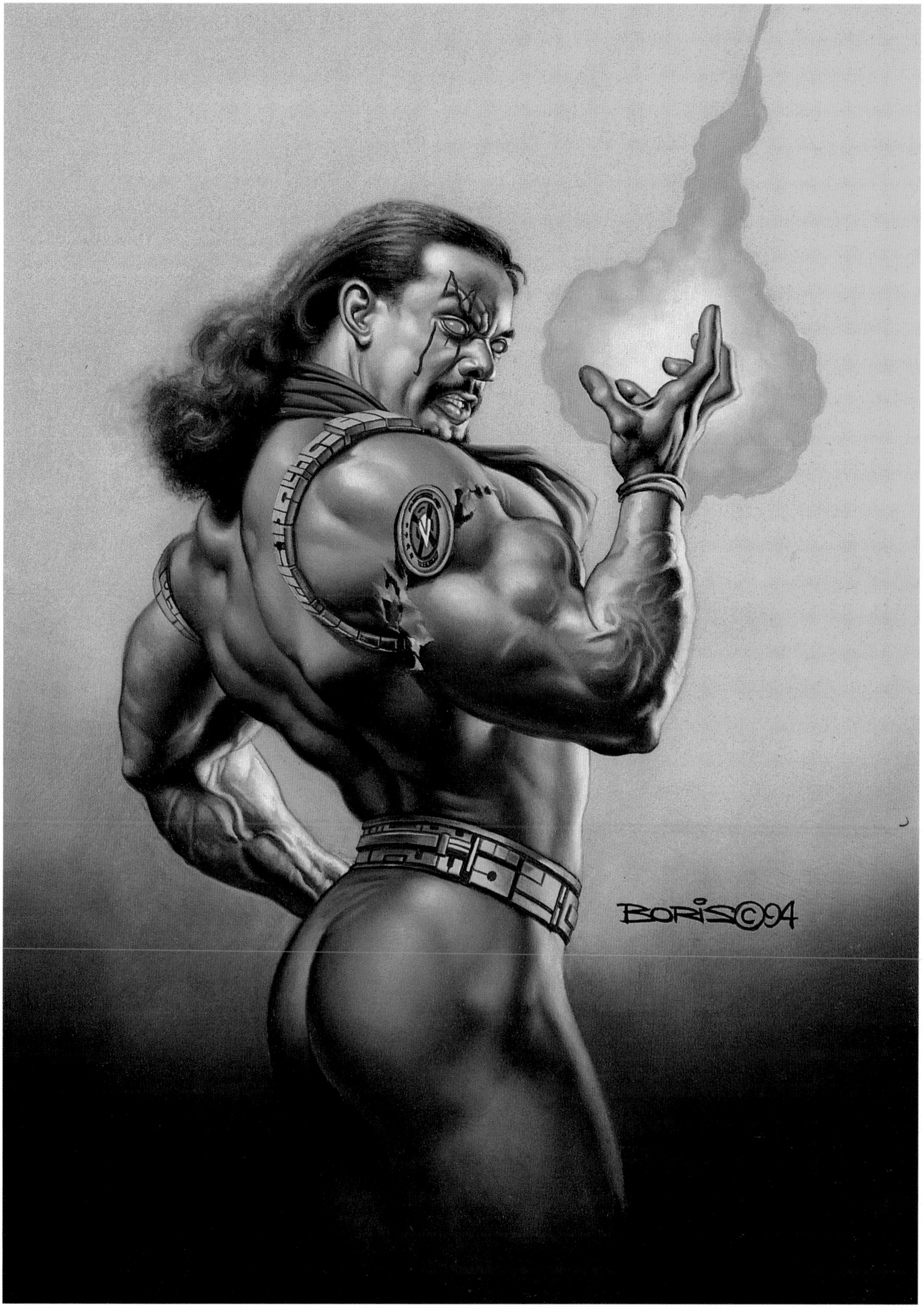
BORIS©94

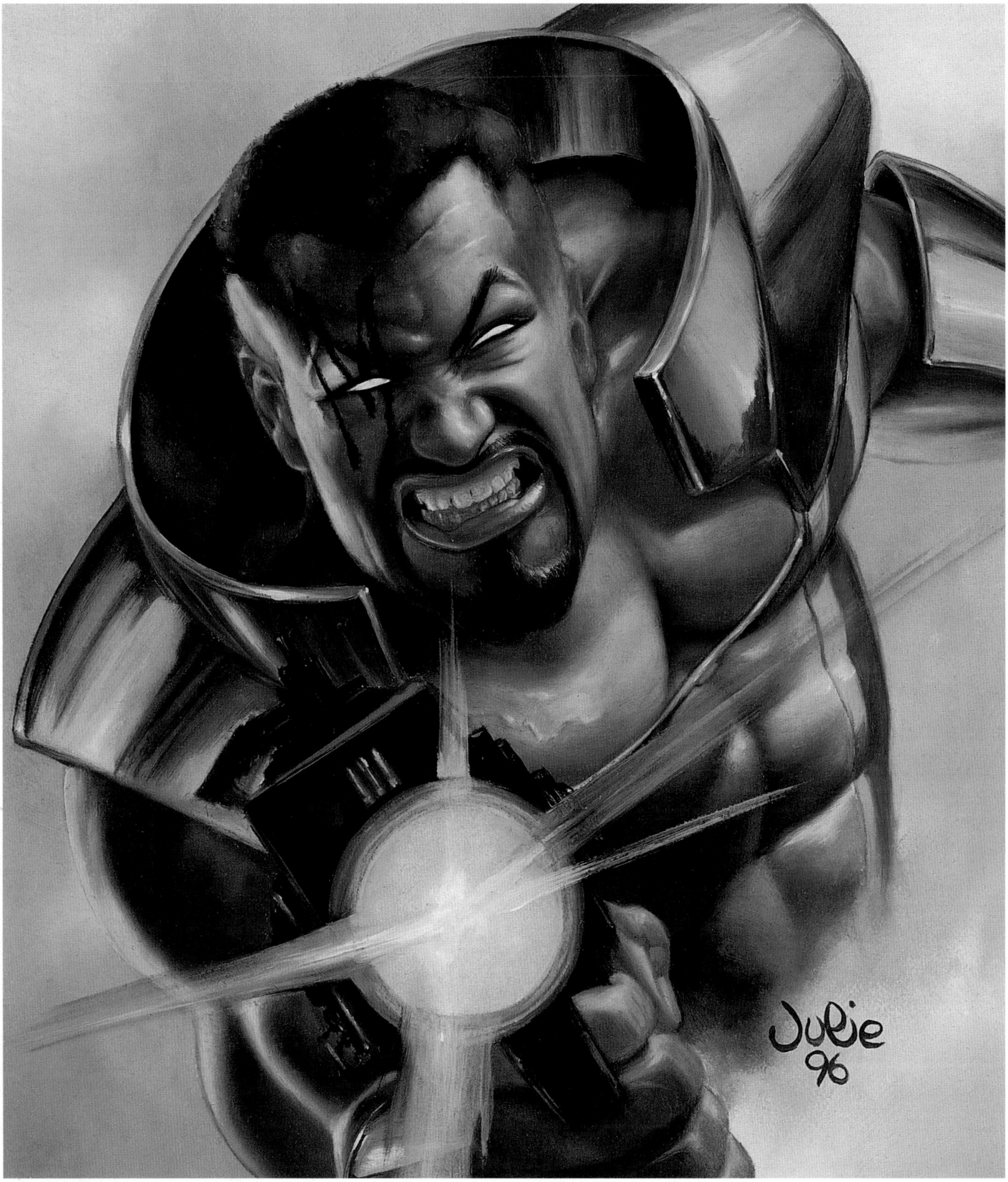
Julie
96

(above)

BLAZING BISHOP

1996, Julie

Trading Card. Fleer Publishing Co.

(right)

ON THE RAMPAGE

1994, Julie

Trading Card. Fleer Publishing Co.

Bishop was born in an alternate future with a totally different history in which the X-Men had been wiped out by a group of robots called the Sentinels. He lands in 'our' time by pursuing the criminal mutant Fitzroy, even knowing he had no chance of getting back.

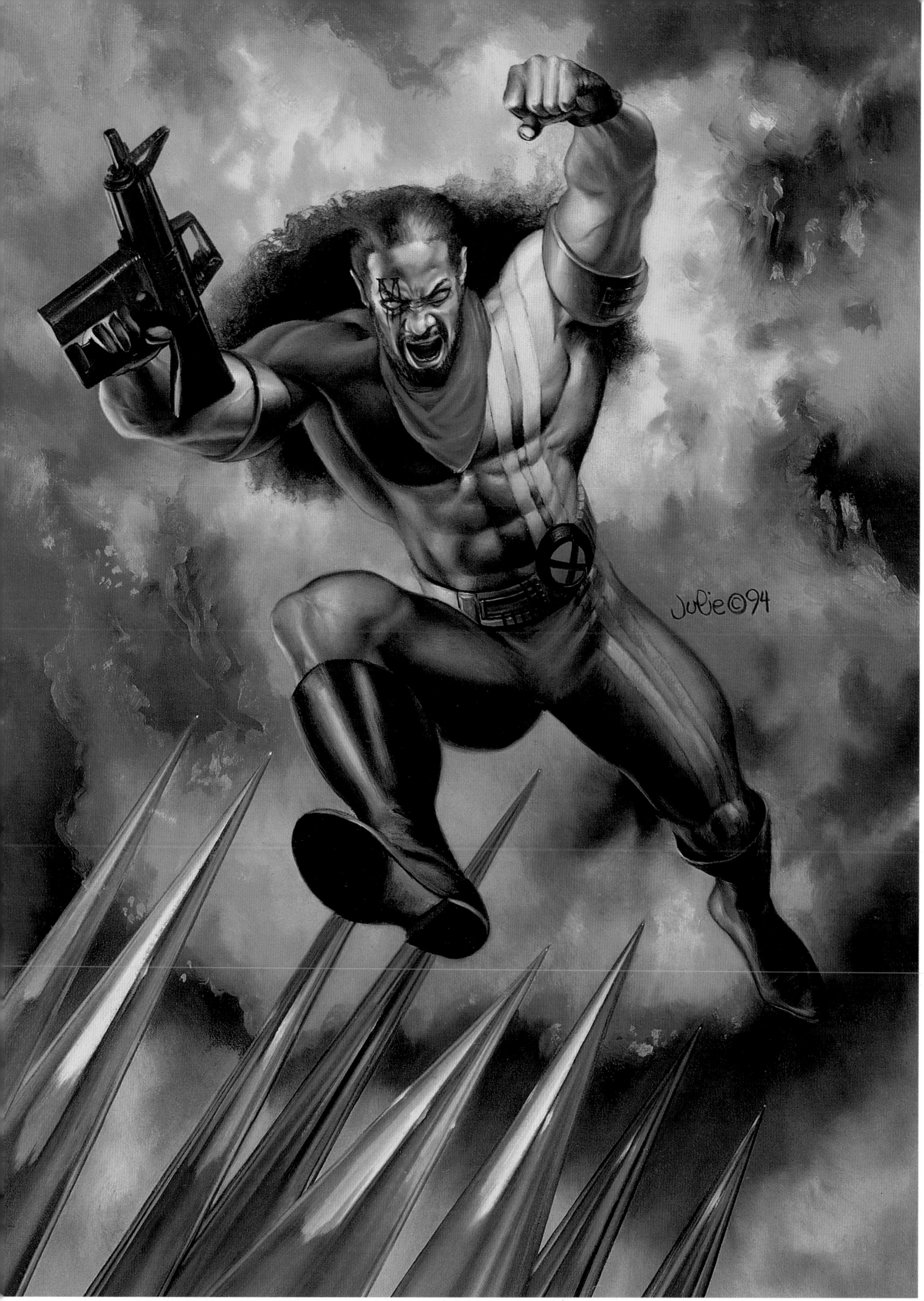
Julie©94

(right)
BANSHEE

1993, Julie
Trading Card. Fleer Publishing Co.
TM & © 1993 Marvel Characters, Inc.
All rights reserved.

Banshee, originally Sean Cassidy from Ireland, gets his name from the shattering sonic blast he can deliver, reminiscent of the famous Irish harbinger of death. With it he can shatter eardrums as easily as windows and it also helps him fly. He became a peacekeeper long before meeting the X-Men but fell into the power of the evil Factor X group. With a bomb fastened to his head he was forced to obey them for a while and the X-Men imagined him an enemy. But after the misunderstanding was cleared up he joined forces with them and now, with Emma Frost, he helps run Professor X's School for Gifted Youngsters. This academy aims to train young mutants to be the next generation of peacekeepers, collectively known as Generation X.

(far right)
GENERATION X

1999, Julie
Cover. Bryon Preiss Multimedia
TM & © 1999 Marvel Characters, Inc.
All rights reserved.

Generation X includes Chamber, Husk, Jubilee, Monet, Penance, Skin and Synch. As with any rising generation they have clashes with their elders and are impatient to be able to do things their own way, but they are basically on the same side.

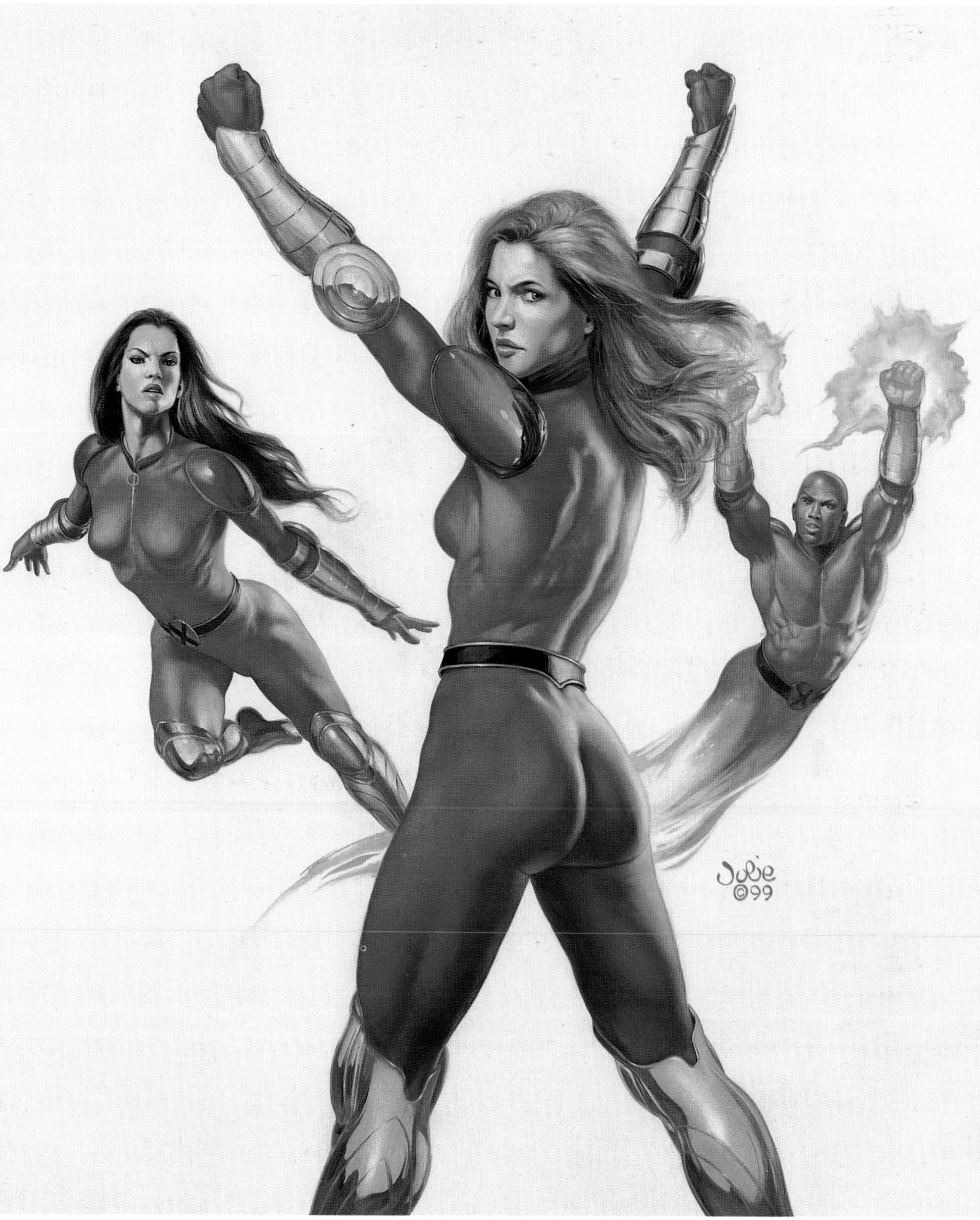
Julie
©99

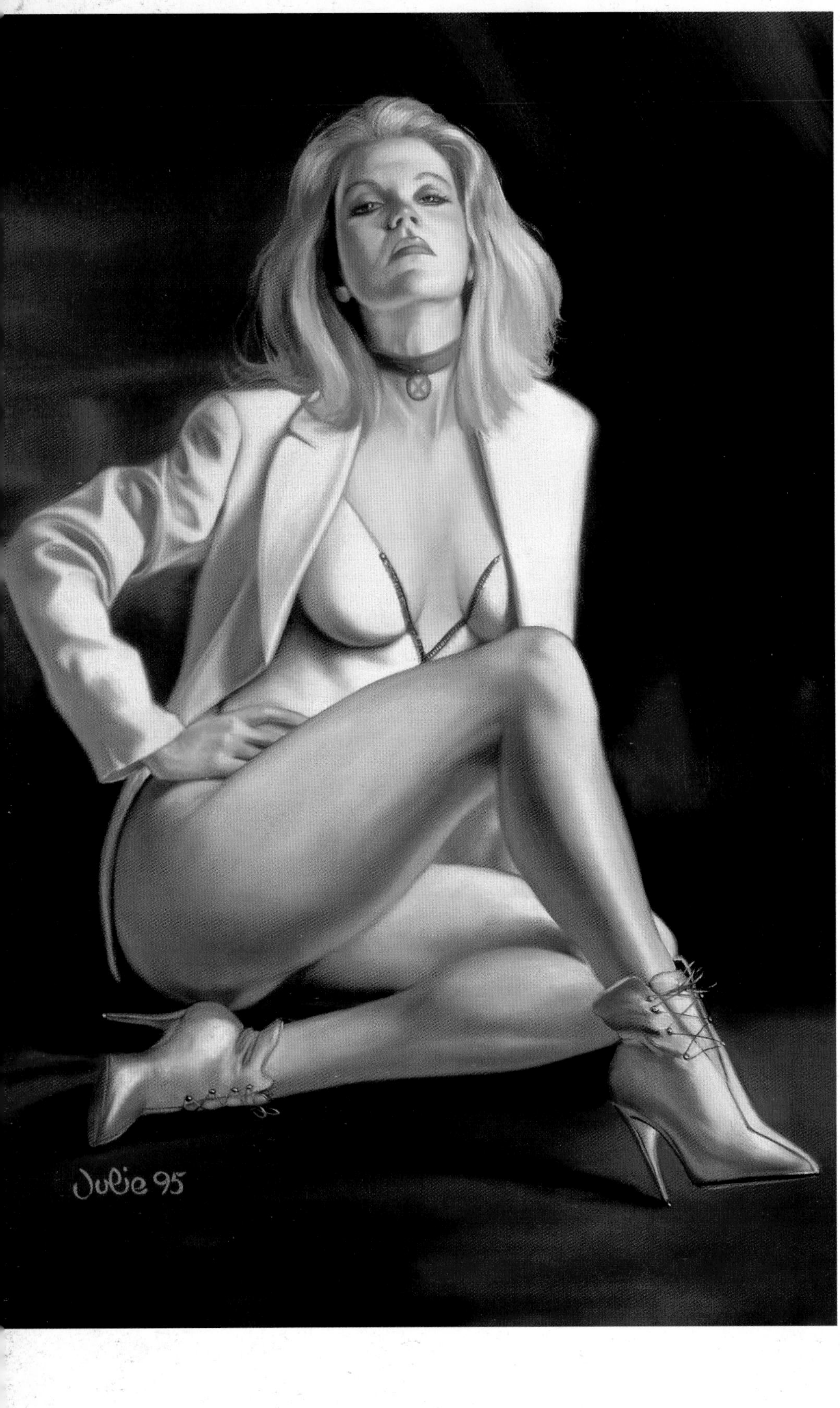
Julie 95

(left)

WHITE QUEEN

1995, Julie

Trading Card. Fleer Publishing Co.

(right)

WHITE QUEEN 2

1994, Julie

Trading Card. Fleer Publishing Co.

Originally Emma Frost, the White Queen, was an enormously powerful telepath with slightly shaky morals who has often not hesitated to use her mind-reading talents to get her own way. Once one of the inner circle of the Hellfire Club (who take their names from chess pieces), she is now a much reformed character dedicated to teaching young mutants how not to behave in the ways she did in her own youth.

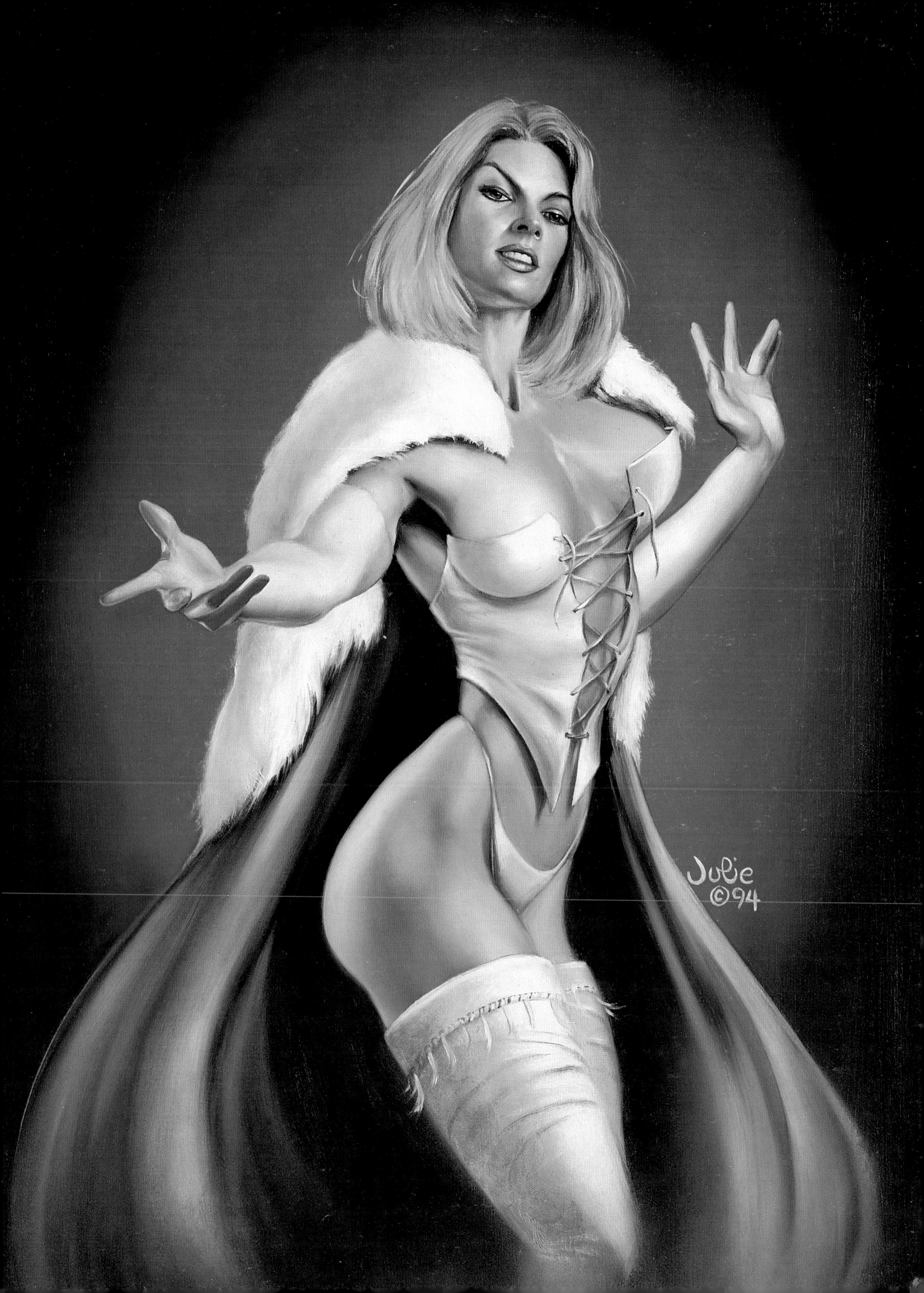
Julie
©94

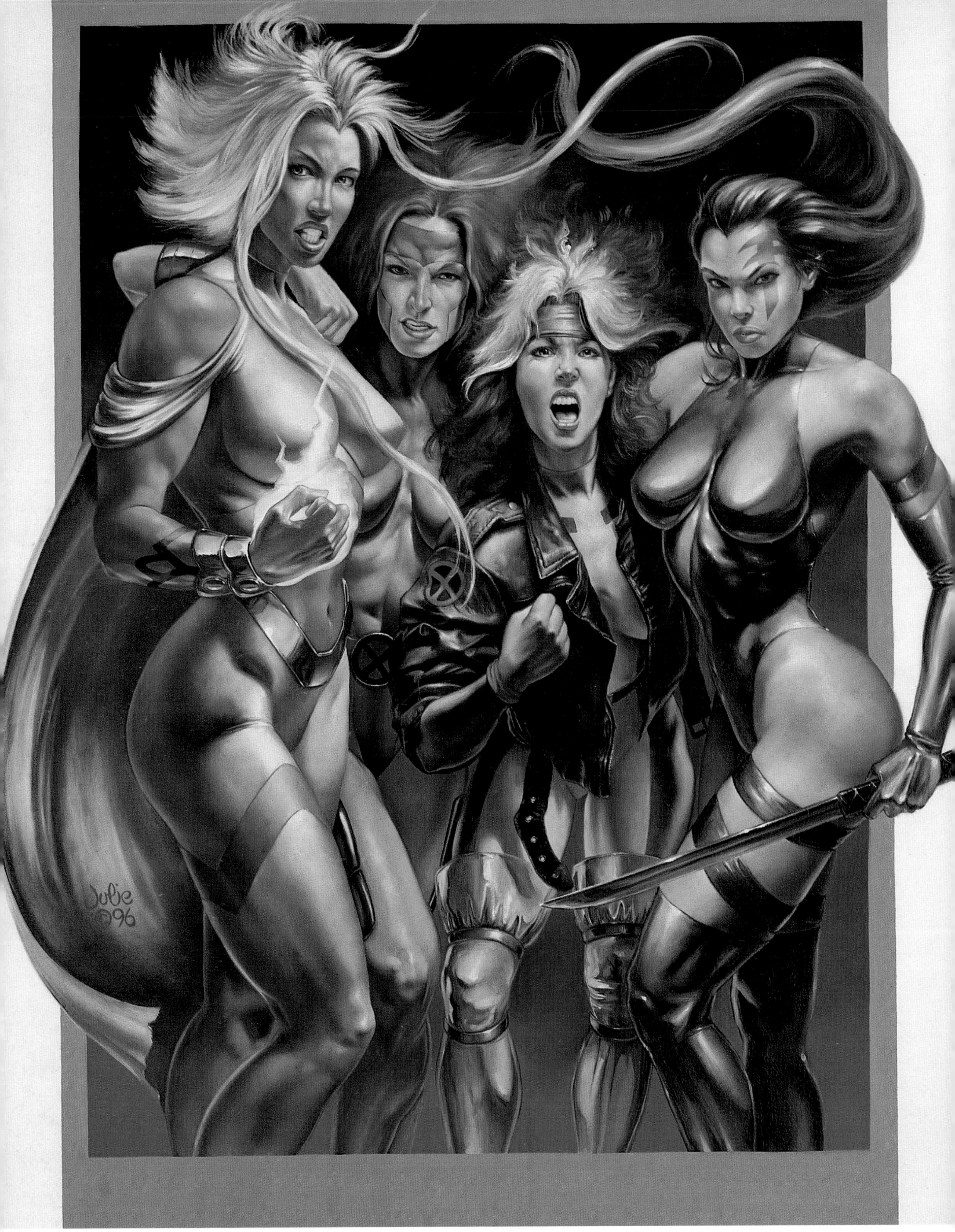
Julie ©96

X-WOMEN

Having spent so much of their time painting fantasy characters who can skip between alternate realities, bend the laws of creation and travel back and forth in time, what are Julie and Boris' own feelings about such matters? If, for instance, they were given a time machine and allowed to choose any three times and places to visit, where would they go?

Boris' answer is a little surprising until one remembers that he plays the violin himself for recreation: 'The one time I really feel I would like to see at first hand is the nineteenth century in order to listen to the great violinists of the age. Because there are no recordings from then, you can only read about how great they were.' Other than that he is simply not interested in time travel, even if it were possible.

Julie: 'The one thing I would want to do is go into the distant, distant past to see how the world was created. It would make me really feel good to understand that. Going into the future, well, there are things I would love to know but it doesn't feel right. If you could go into the future it would change things like the way you think, and that might change the future so it doesn't happen anyway.'

Basically they both very firmly believe that there is a definite system and order to the universe and that if mankind found a way to travel or communicate across time it would only serve to create a complete mess.

So they wouldn't even contemplate using the time machine to spend a day with their favourite artists from the past? Well, Julie could almost be tempted to visit Leonardo da Vinci simply because he was such an amazing person, and possibly more because of his scientific ideas than his art. Boris is doubtful even about this. He feels artists speak best through their work, the actual person can be entirely different: 'If you take any of the really great artists, Michaelangelo, Leonardo, in the end people are just people. It may even bring their art down if you met the person. I really feel that in many ways things are best left as they are.'

(left)
X-WOMEN
1996, Julie
Poster. Marvel Comics

In the Marvel team, males and females alike are called X-Men but we thought it might be a bit of fun to separate them because the females, as in the wider world, often do get overshadowed. Also it saves having one chapter take up half the book. So here you have them, the not so gentler half of the team. In this particular picture: Storm, Jean Grey, Rogue and Psylocke in belligerent mode. This has proved a very popular image and has appeared in a variety of formats.

(right)

ROGUE IN FLIGHT

1994, Julie

Trading Card. Fleer Publishing Co.

Rogue's origins are a mystery, beyond that she grew up in Caldecott County, Mississippi. She knew nothing about her mutant powers until she kissed a teenage boyfriend and had him fall unconscious at her feet. Not only that (which might have been put down to over-excitement) but for a while she was in full possession of his memories and personality. The same thing was repeated every time she touched someone; for as long as they were unconscious she almost became them. In her confusion she allowed herself to be adopted by the terrorist Mystique and later joined her Third Brotherhood of Evil Mutants, foes of the X-Men.

(far right)

ROGUE MISSILES

1994, Boris

Trading Card. Fleer Publishing Co.

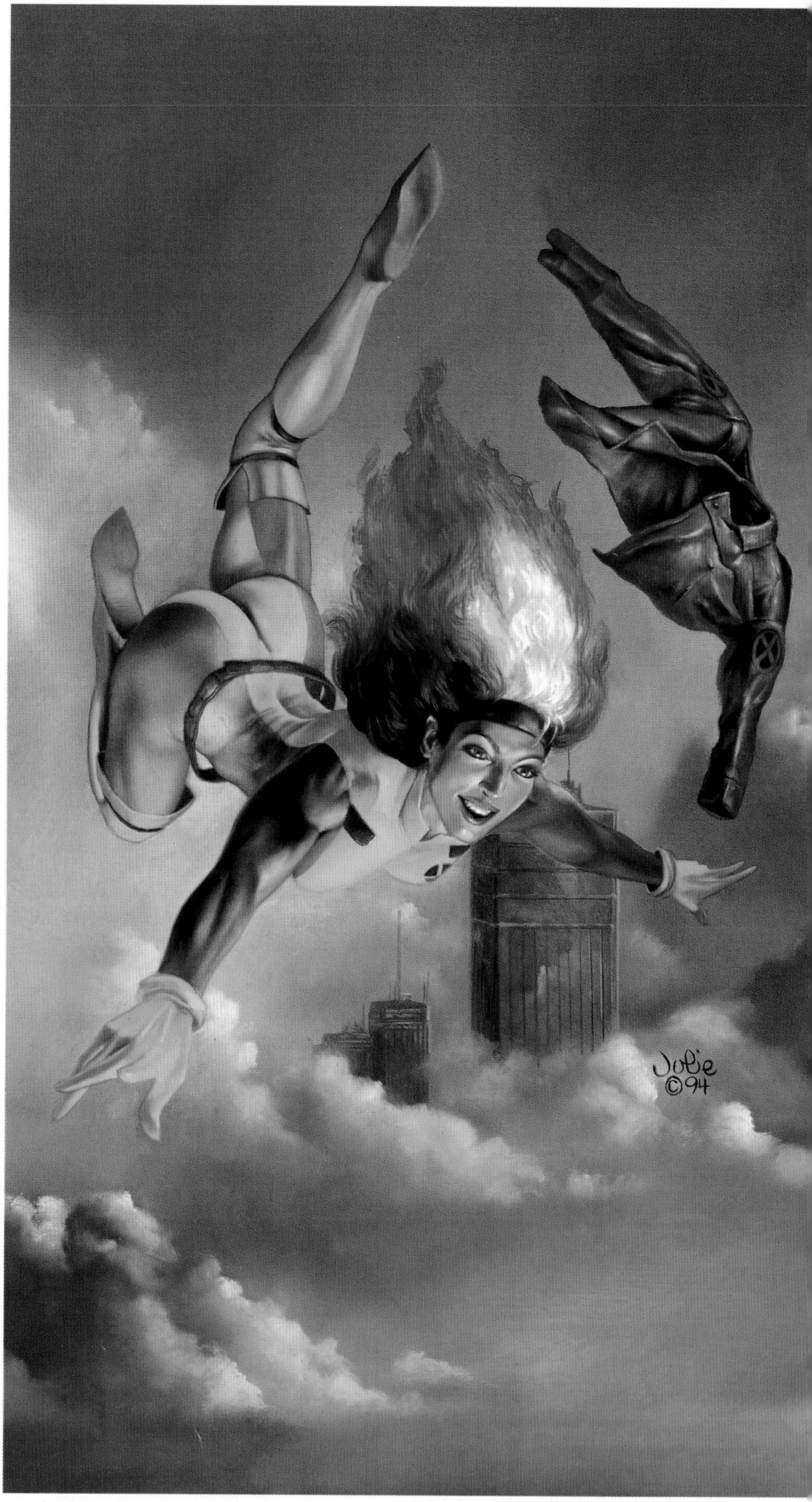
Julie
©94

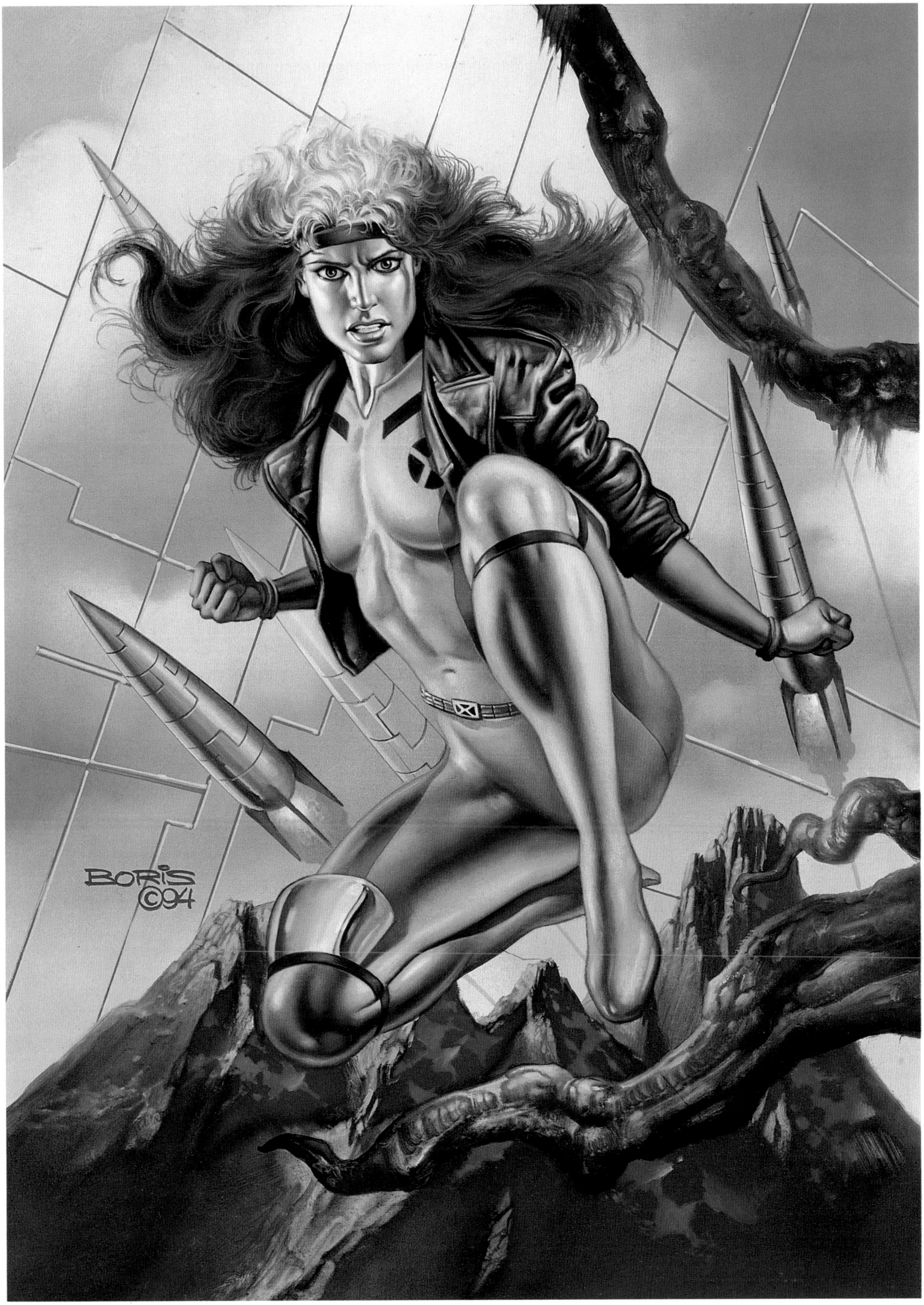
BORIS
©94

(left)
ABOVE THE CITY
1995, Boris
Trading Card. Fleer Publishing Co.
TM & © 1995 Marvel Characters, Inc.
All rights reserved.

During one battle with the X-Men, Rogue absorbed the mind and superpowers of Carol Danvers, the original Ms Marvel. This gave her strength, invulnerability and the power to fly. But for some unknown reason this time the experience was not temporary and ever since she has carried Danvers round inside her as an alter ego who occasionally rises to the surface and takes over. This also caused her to change sides and join her former enemies, though she retains ambivalent feelings for Mystique. Her foster-brother Nightcrawler has also joined the X-Men.

(right)
ROGUE ON THE RUN
1995, Julie
Trading Card. Fleer Publishing Co.
TM & © 1995 Marvel Characters, Inc.
All rights reserved.

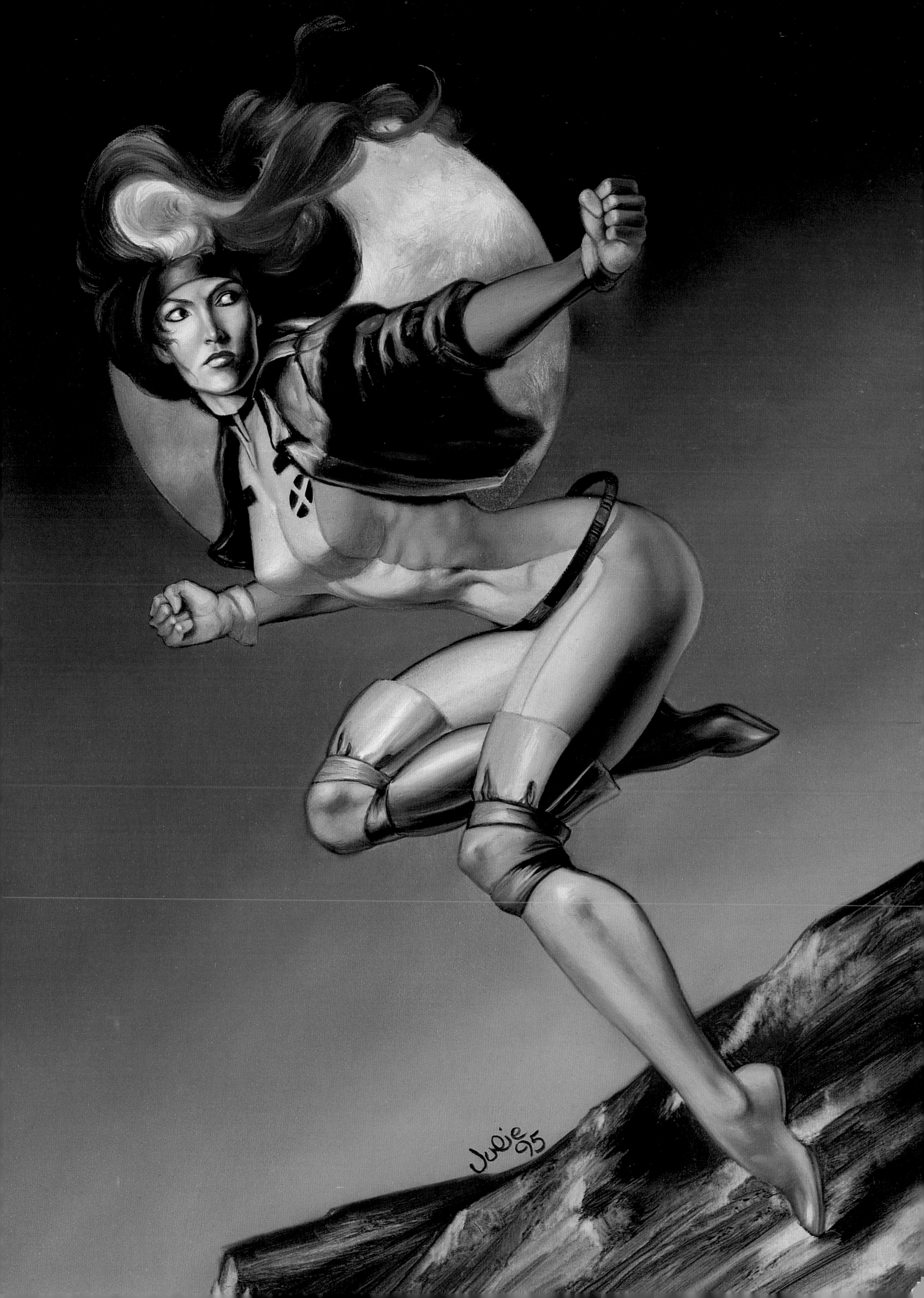
Julie 95

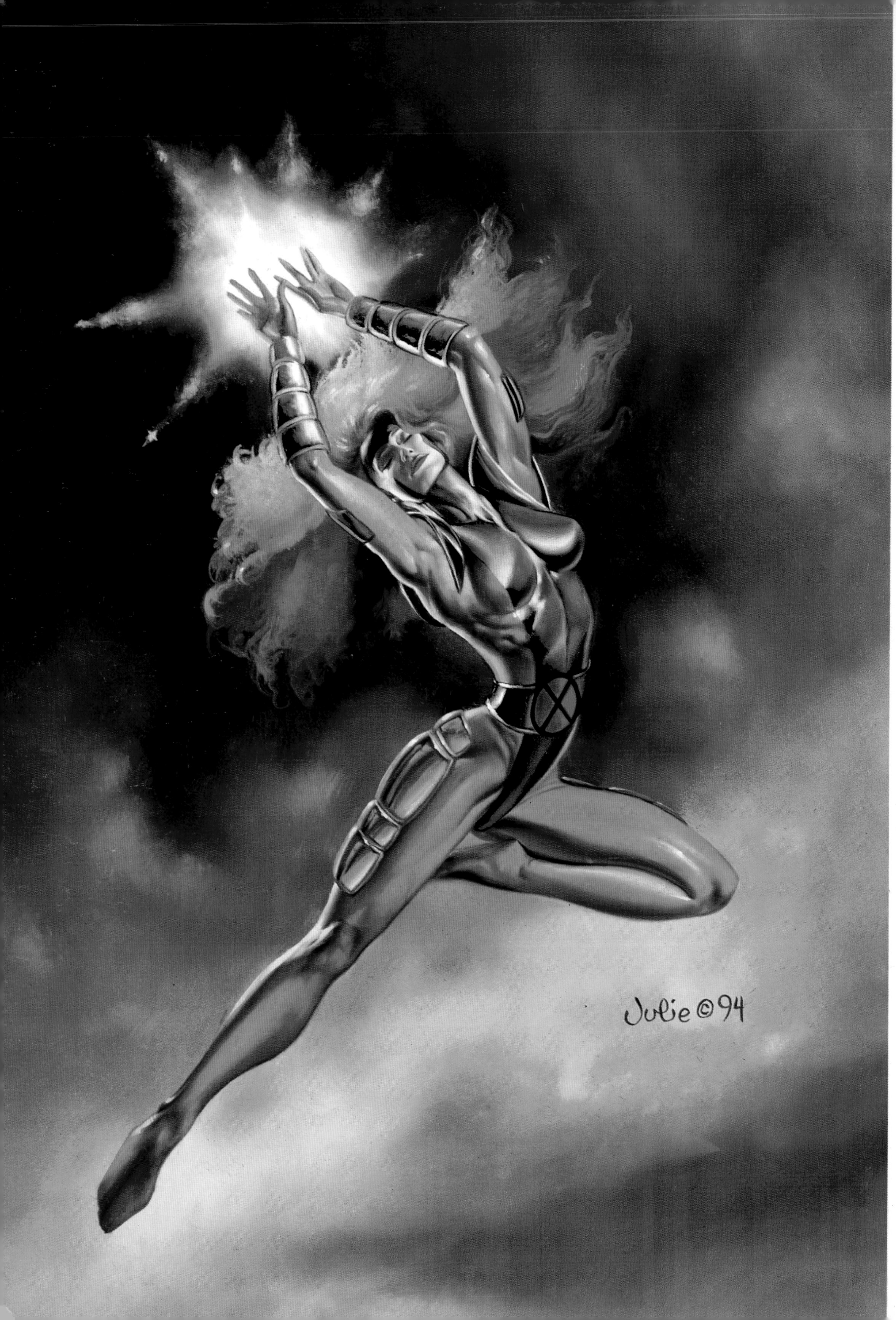
Julie ©94

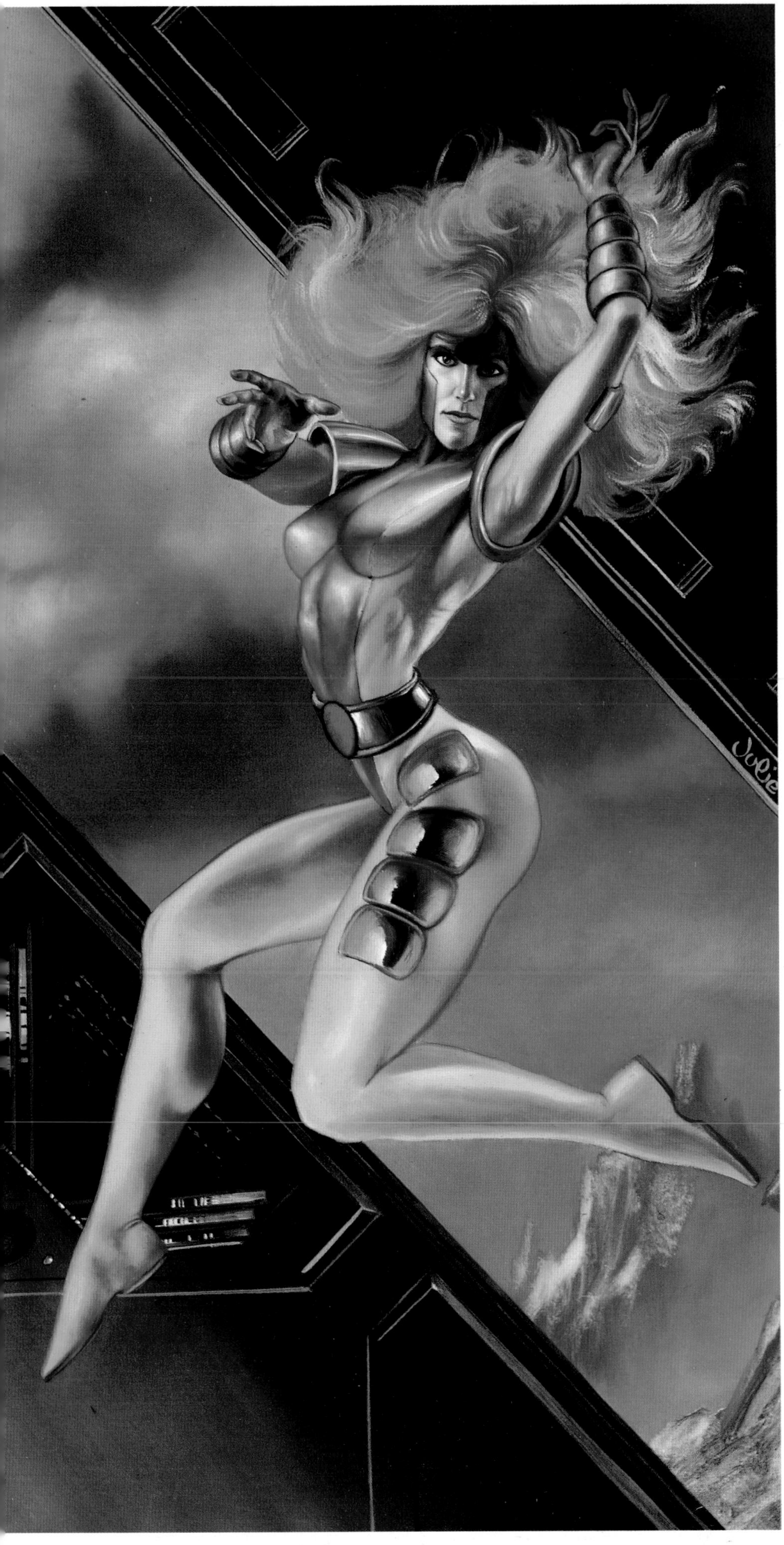
Julie

(far left)

JEAN GREY

1994, Julie

Trading Card. Fleer Publishing Co.

(left)

TELEKINESIS

1995, Julie

Trading Card. Fleer Publishing Co.

Jean Grey discovered her telepathic powers as a child when a friend died in her arms. The shock of sharing the experience of that death was almost too much for her but Professor X taught her how to shield herself from such extreme emotional invasions. Under his care she also learned how to channel this and other powers, such as telekinesis whereby she can make herself and others fly.

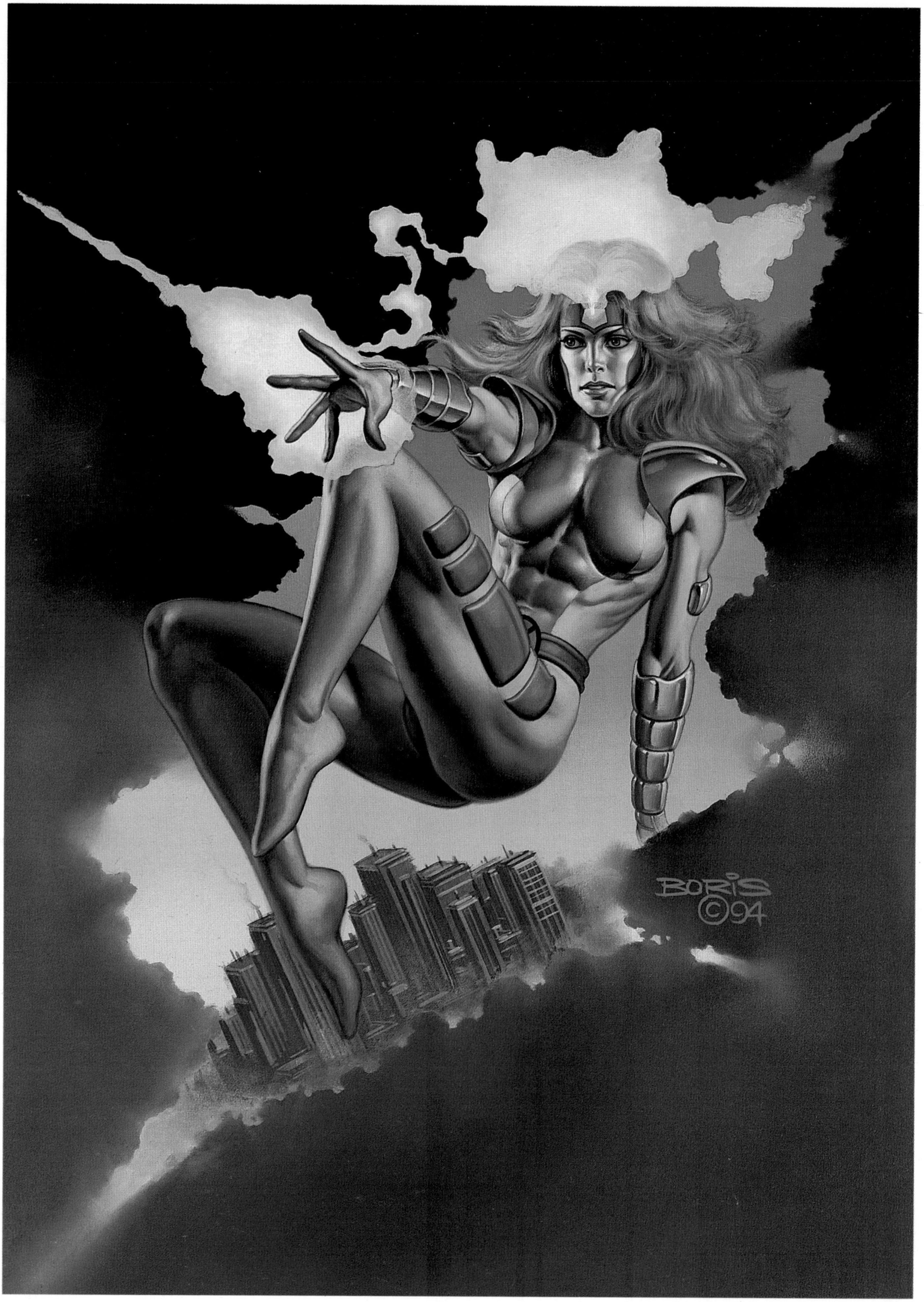
BORIS
©94

(left)

JEAN GREY 2

1994, Boris

Trading Card. Fleer Publishing Co.

(right)

PHOENIX

1994, Julie

Trading Card. Fleer Publishing Co.

As Marvel Girl, Jean Grey joined the first group of X-Men. During one adventure she died, or at least fell into a state of suspended animation. Her place was taken by an impersonal cosmic entity called the Phoenix Force that replicated her appearance and personality so exactly that even her closest friends were fooled into believing she had merely acquired new powers. Calling herself Phoenix, this being absorbed part of the real Jean Grey's personality into itself. When it later went mad and threatened to destroy the whole universe, this part of Jean surfaced and saved the day by taking charge and committing suicide. The real Jean Grey then revived and assumed the name Phoenix herself.

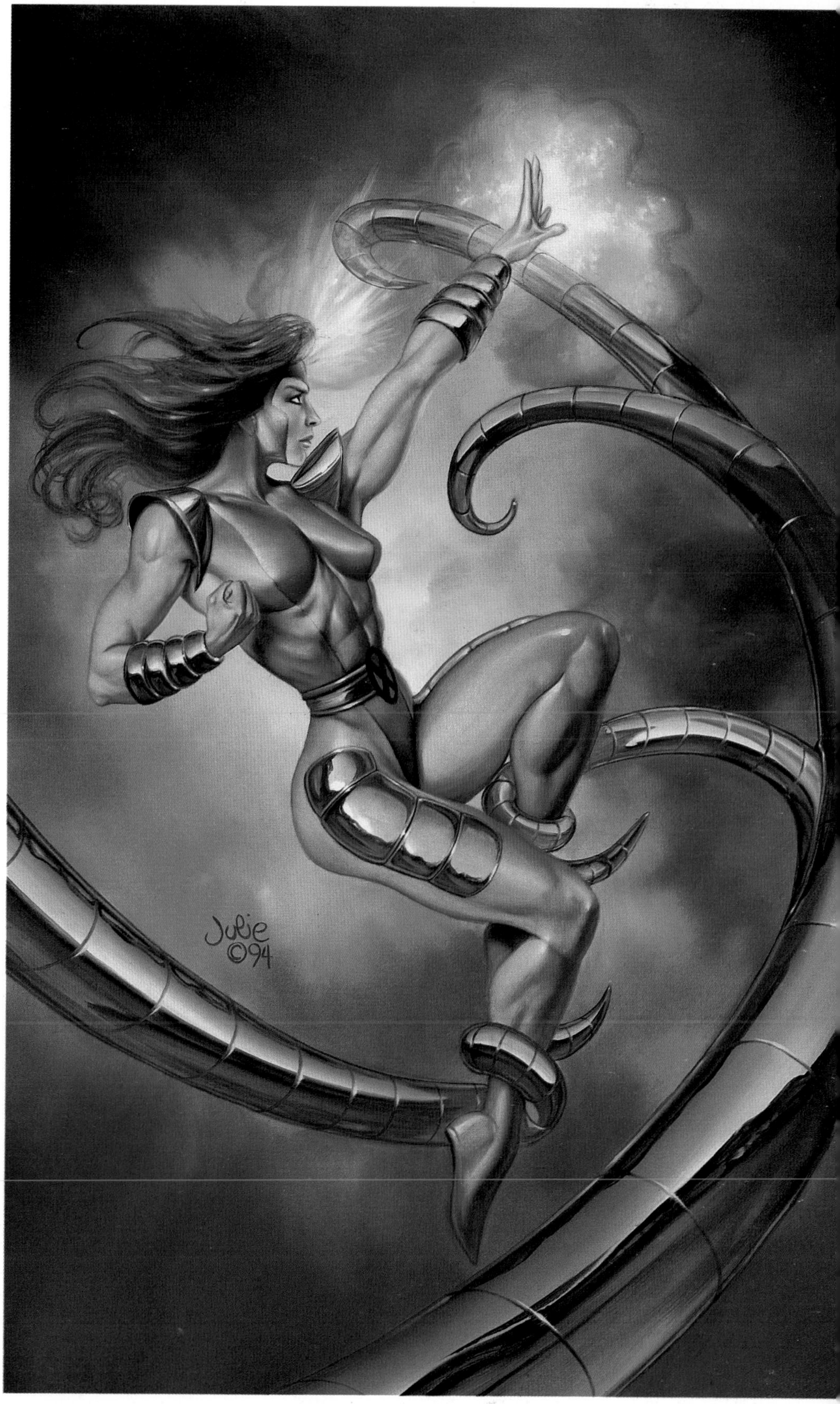
Julie
©94

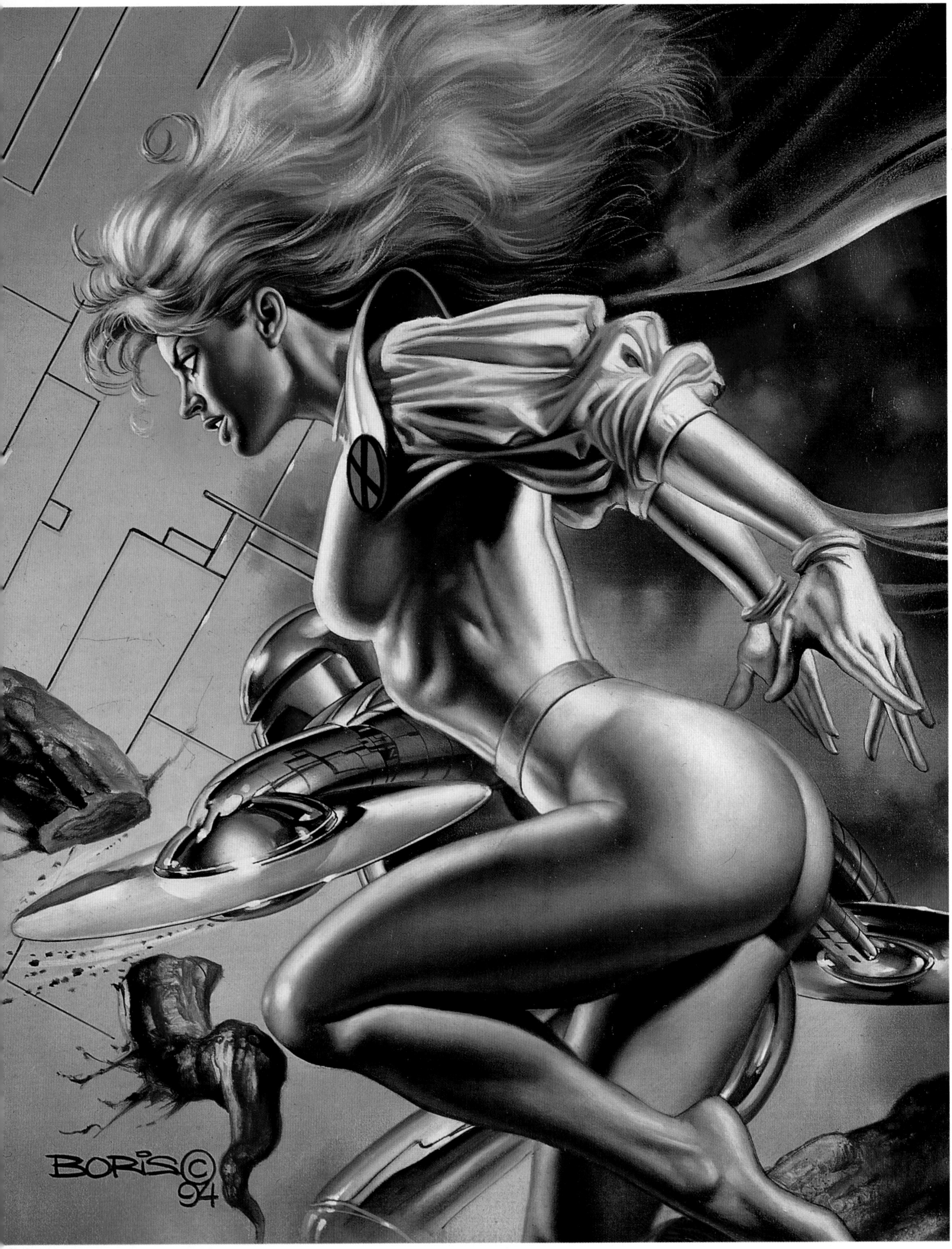
BORIS©
94

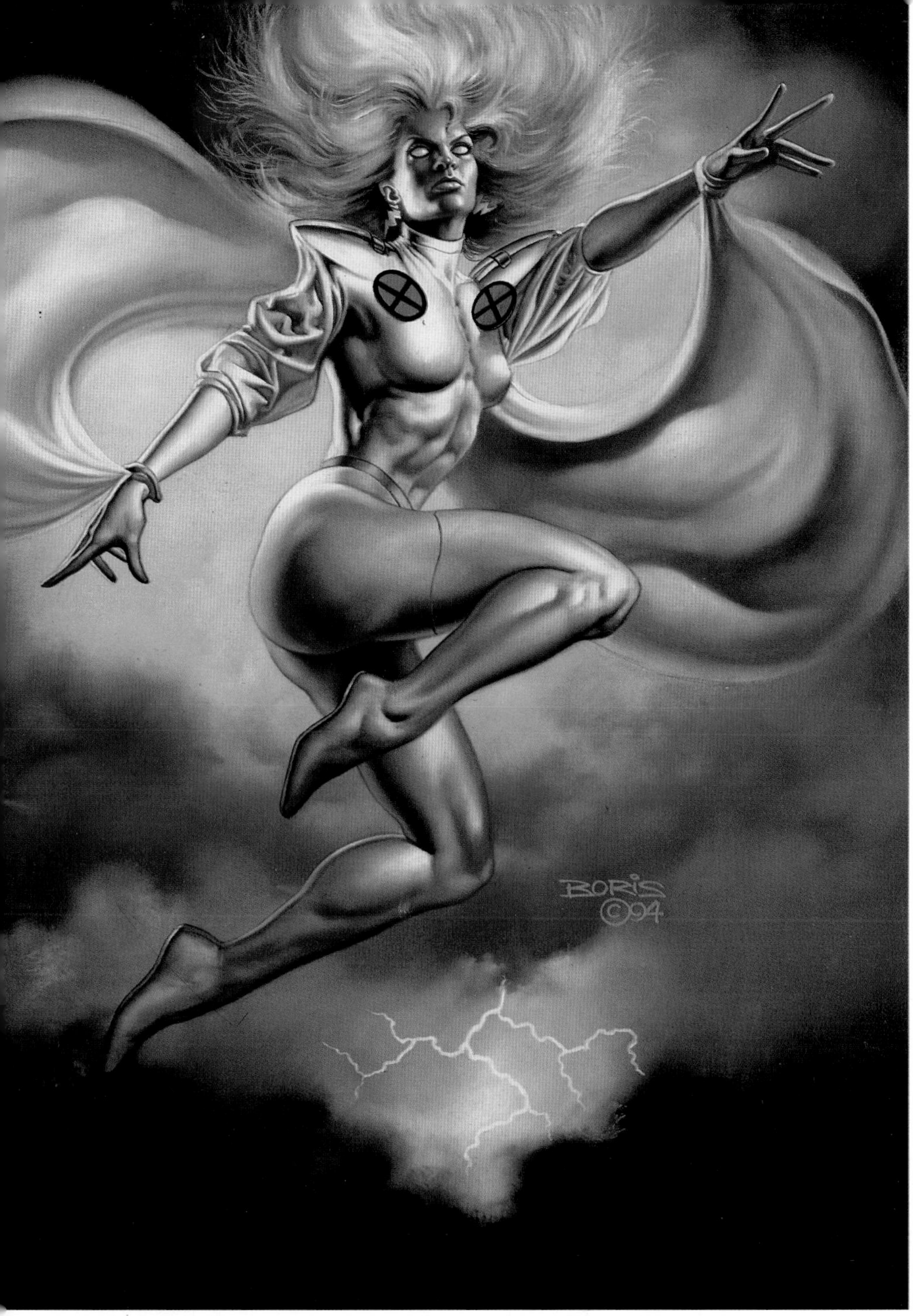
BORIS
©94

(far left)

STORM

1994, Boris

Trading Card. Fleer Publishing Co.

(left)

RIDING THE WIND

1994, Boris

Trading Card. Fleer Publishing Co.

(below)

STORM 3

1995, Boris

Trading Card. Fleer Publishing Co.

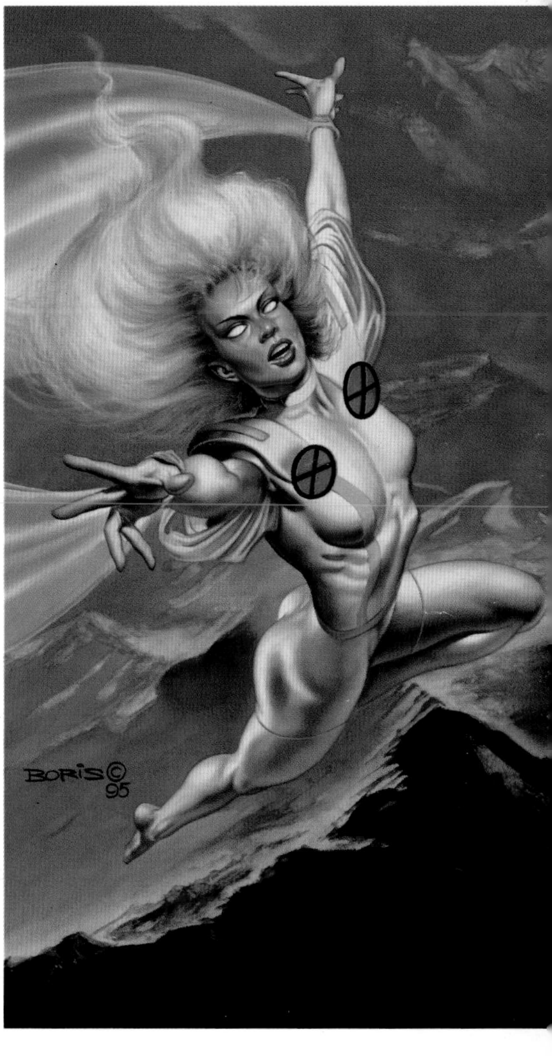
BORIS©
95

Storm (true name Ororo Munroe) comes from a rare line of Africans with blue eyes, white hair and grey skin. Her mother was a Kenyan princess who married a visiting American photographer, David Munroe, and returned with him to New York where Ororo was born. Later they moved to Egypt where her parents were killed by a bomb. The child survived but only after being buried in the rubble, which gave her lasting claustrophobia. Like Oliver Twist, the orphan fell into the hands of a thief who trained her as a master lock-pick, a skill which has been useful ever since.

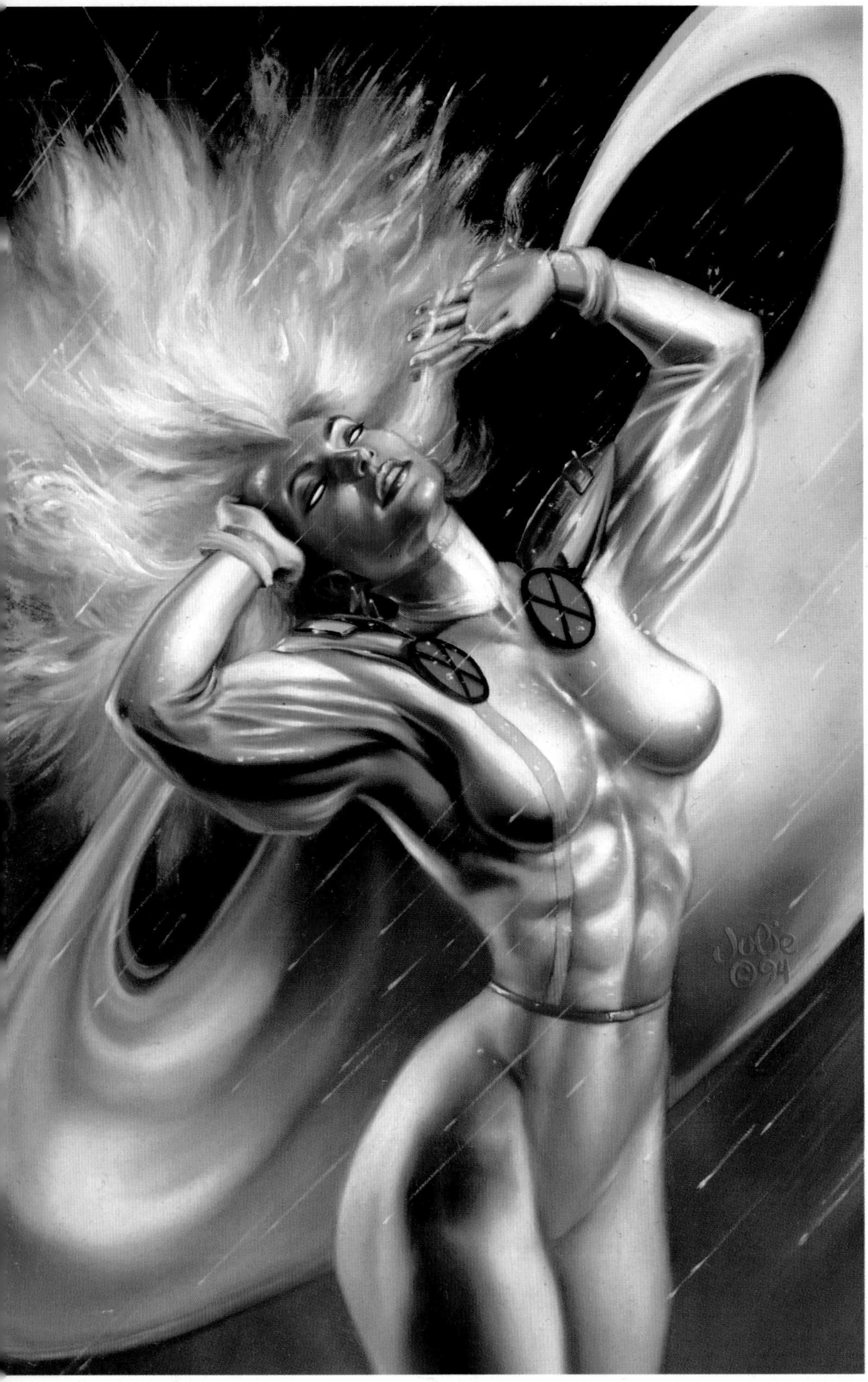
Julie
©94

(left)

RAINSTORM

1994, Julie

Trading Card. Fleer Publishing Co.

(right)

ELECTRICAL STORM

1994, Julie

Trading Card. Fleer Publishing Co.

(below)

LIGHTNING CONDUCTOR

1993, Julie

Trading Card. Fleer Publishing Co.

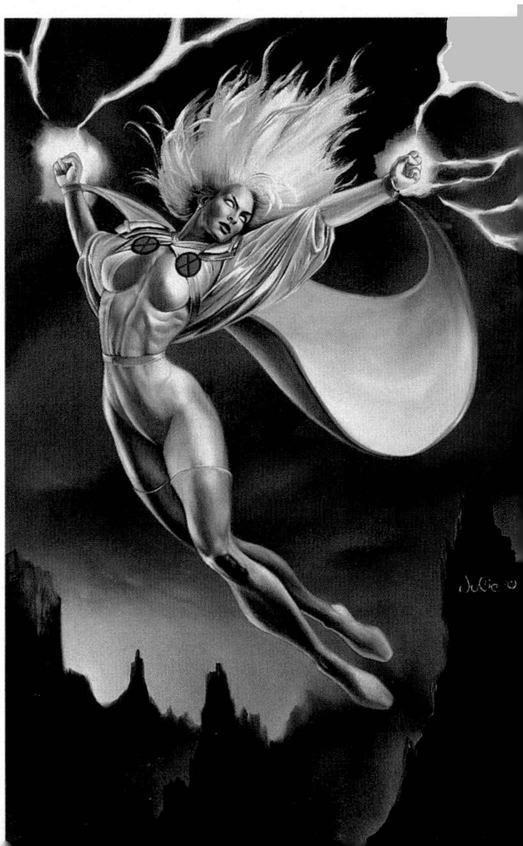

Storm's main talent is control of the weather, which she uses to carry her through the air. But her passing moods also affect the elements, so if she loses her temper everyone has to take cover. For a while she was revered as a rain-goddess in Africa, until Xavier recruited her for the X-Men.

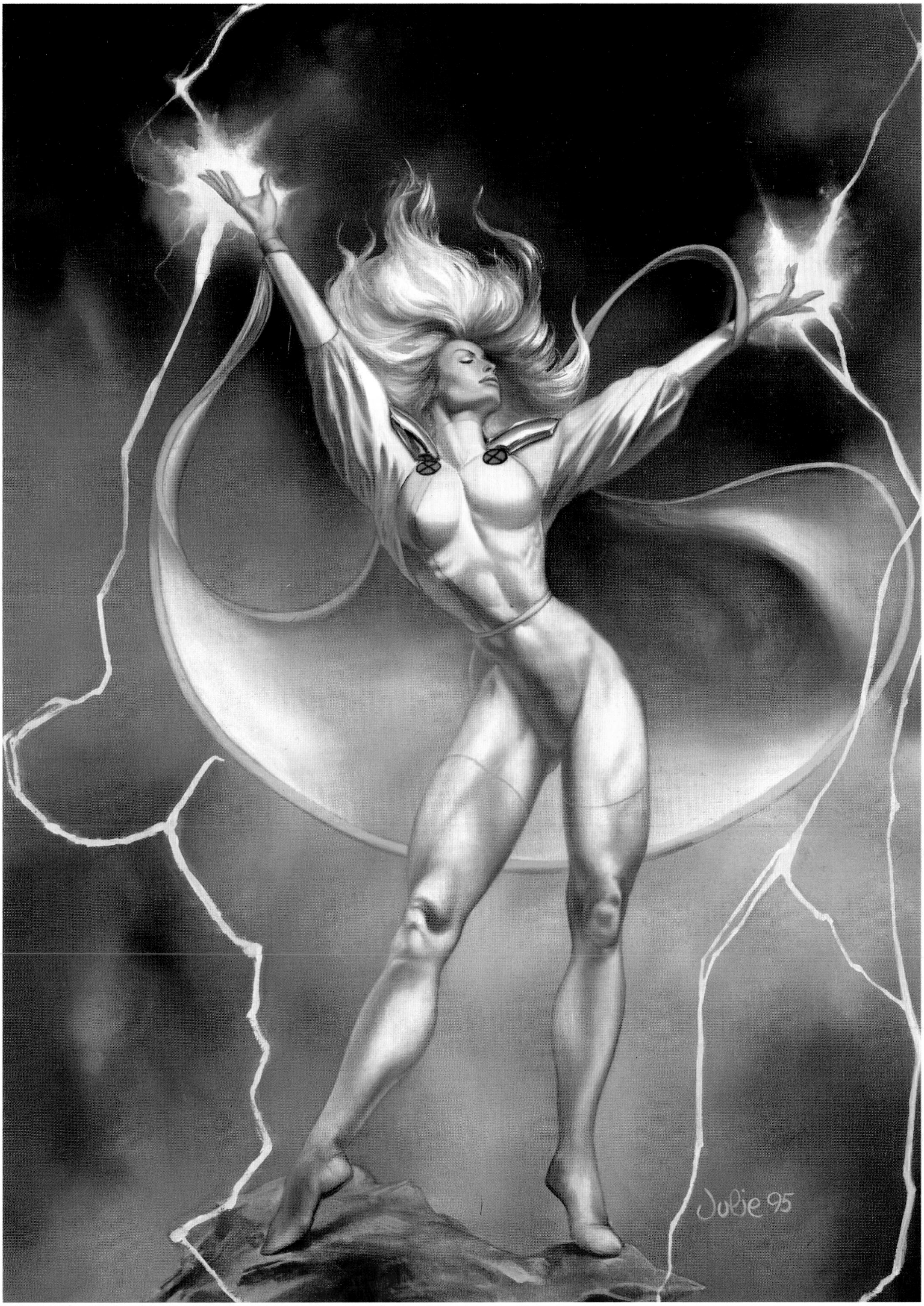
Julie 95

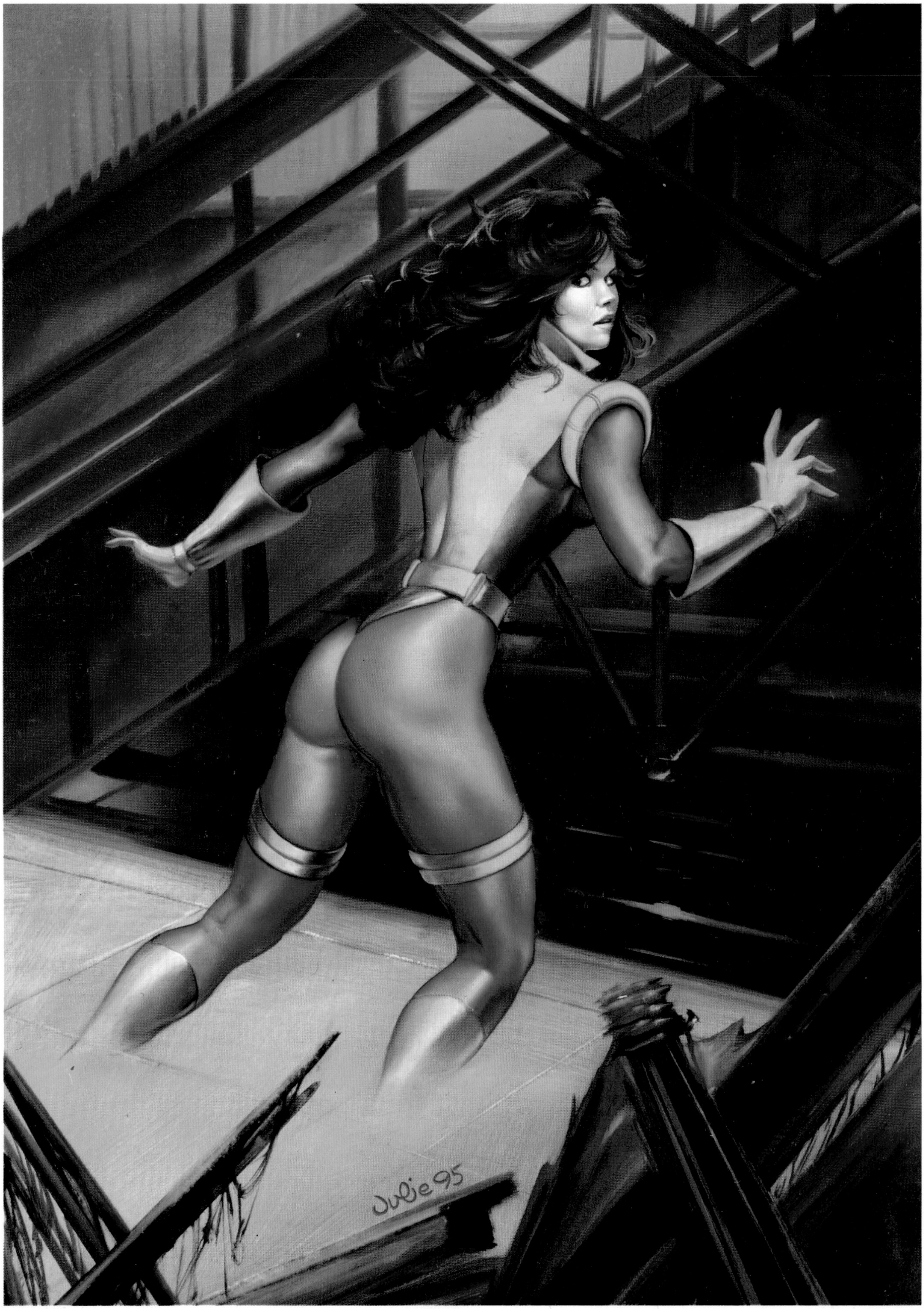
Julie 95

(left)

PSYLOCKE

1994, Boris

Trading Card. Fleer Publishing Co.

TM & © 1994 Marvel Characters, Inc.

All rights reserved.

Psylocke (Betsy Braddock) is the twin sister of the champion who became Captain Britain. Their father was in fact sent to earth by Merlin mainly to bring this about.

(below)

SWORD MISTRESS

1995, Boris

Trading Card. Fleer Publishing Co.

TM & © 1995 Marvel Characters, Inc.

All rights reserved.

(left)

SHADOWCAT

1995, Julie

Trading Card. Fleer Publishing Co.

TM & © 1995 Marvel Characters, Inc.

All rights reserved.

Shadowcat's talent is to pass through solid objects by 'phasing' her own atoms through the spaces between the objects' atoms. She can also phase any object or person she is in physical contact with. By reversing the process she can also walk on air, climbing up it as if on a stair.

(right)

FLYING LEAP

1999, Julie

Trading Card. Fleer Publishing Co.

(far right)

PSYLOCKE / REVANCHE

1995, Julie

Trading Card. Fleer Publishing Co.

For a while Betsy developed twin careers as a fashion model and psychic agent for the STRIKE agency. Then briefly she became Captain Britain herself when her brother Brian became disillusioned with the job. He returned to the role when she was almost killed by some of his old enemies. After a series of further adventures, Betsy was recruited into the X-Men, taking the name Psylocke. Later she was captured by a Japanese crimelord who swapped her mind into the body of his own lover, Kwannon. But there was also a certain intermingling so that Psylocke retained many of her new body's memories. So did Kwannon, who became the X-Man Revanche, but she later died. This relieved some confusion because many could not tell them apart.

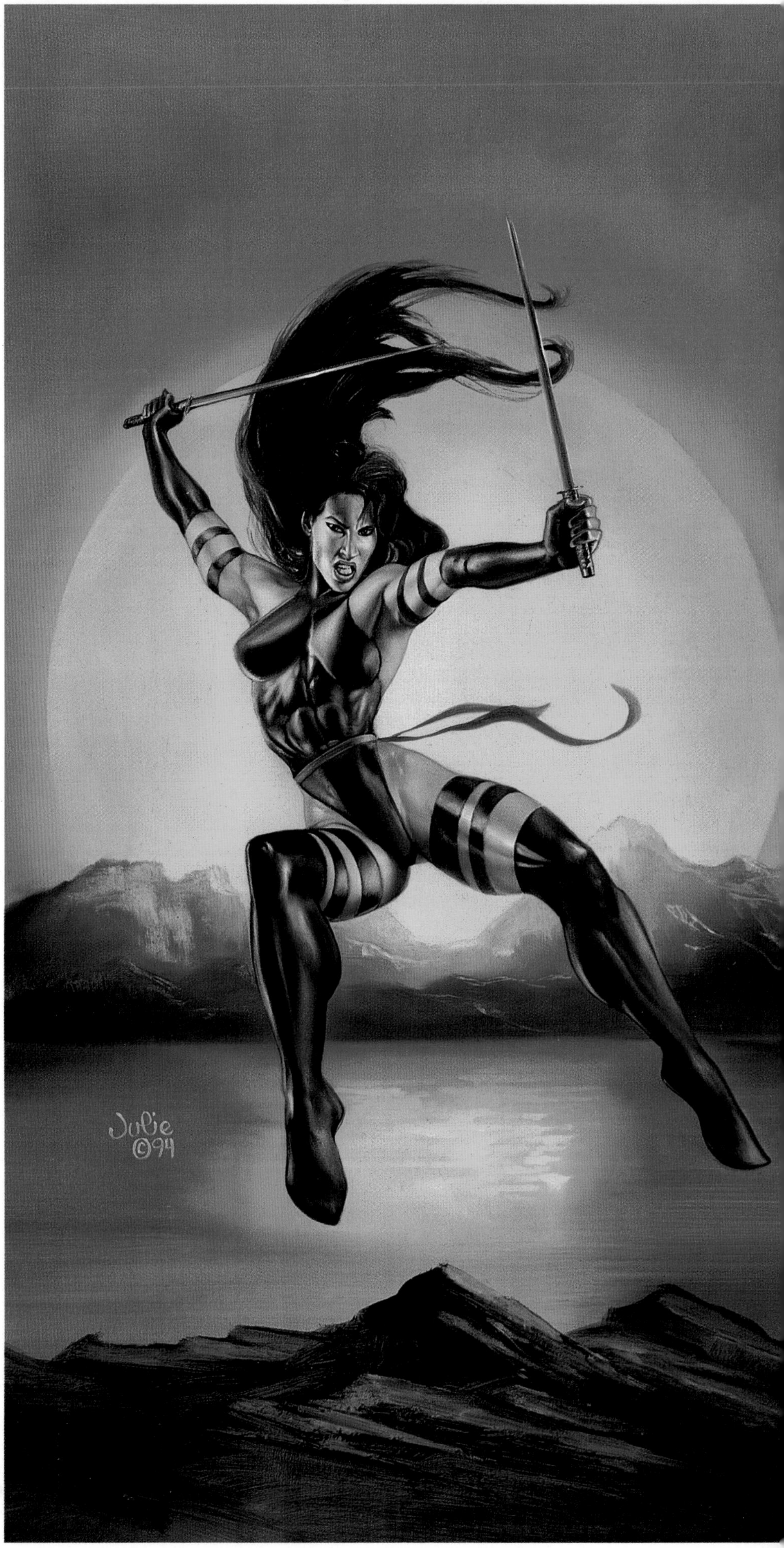
Julie
©94

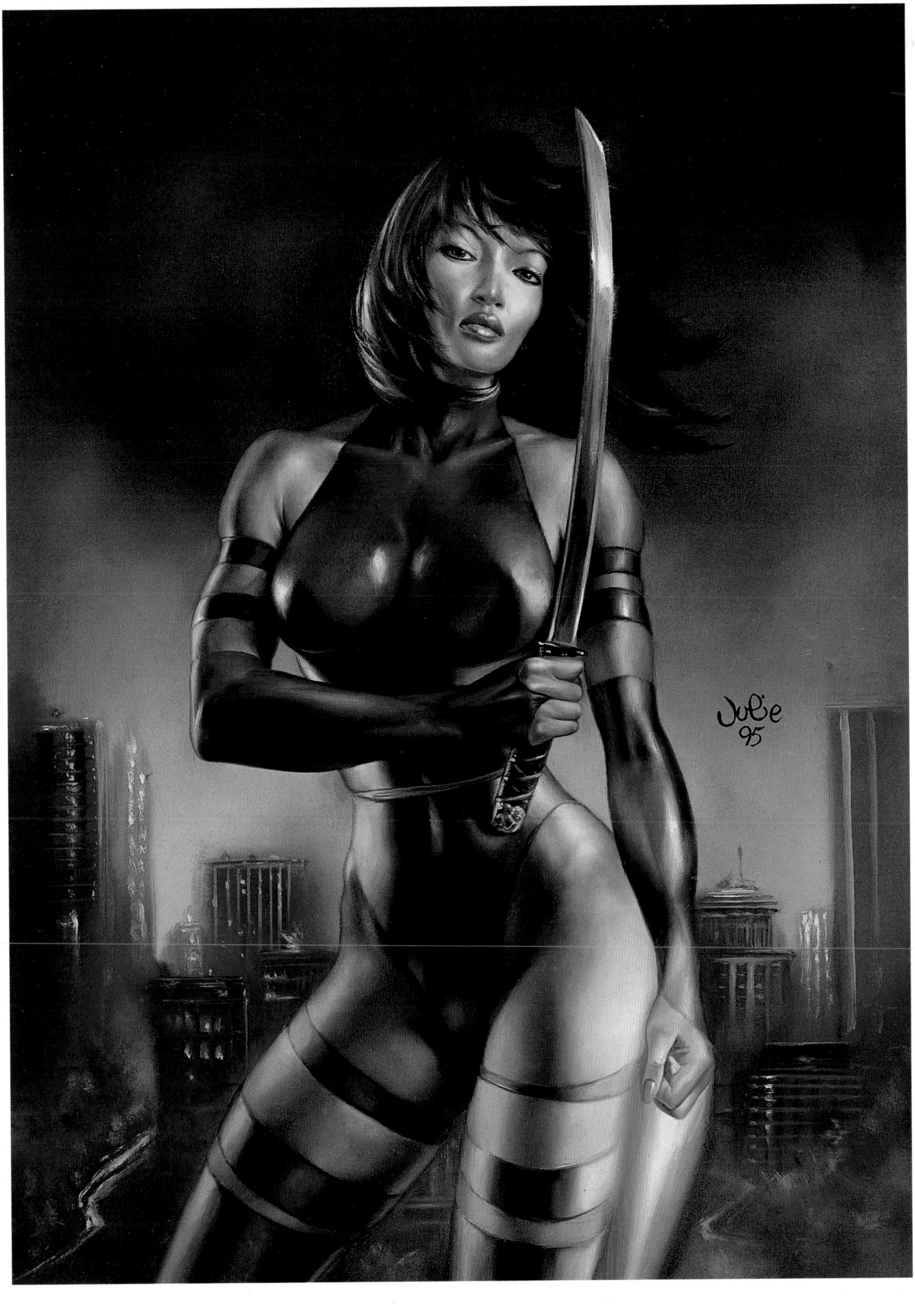
Julie
95

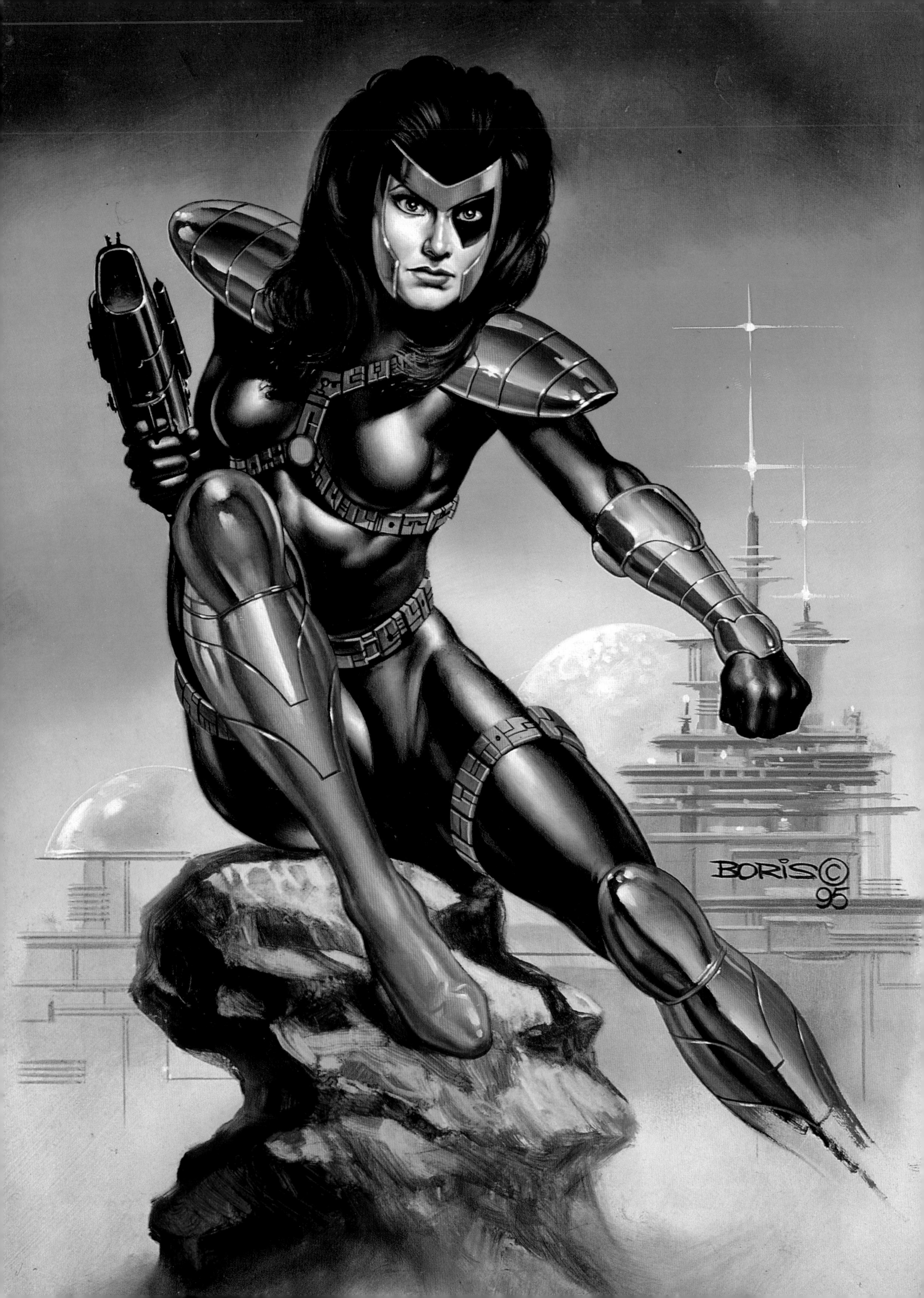
BORIS©
95

(left)

DOMINO

1995, Boris

Trading Card. Fleer Publishing Co.

(right)

REAR SHOT

1994, Julie

Trading Card. Fleer Publishing Co.

Domino chose her own name mainly because of her chalk-white skin and the black mark around her left eye, both of which are natural. But she does also have a certain unconscious talent for tilting the balance of luck in her own favour and against her opponents. She is a formidable marksman and also often uses a staff that discharges blasts of some undetermined form of energy. Not strictly speaking one of the X-Men, she is a leader instead of the X-Force, which many of them join when life gets too complicated elsewhere. The X-Force was founded by the original X-Men when the second wave of recruits joined. Some, like Cyclops, have since rejoined the team.

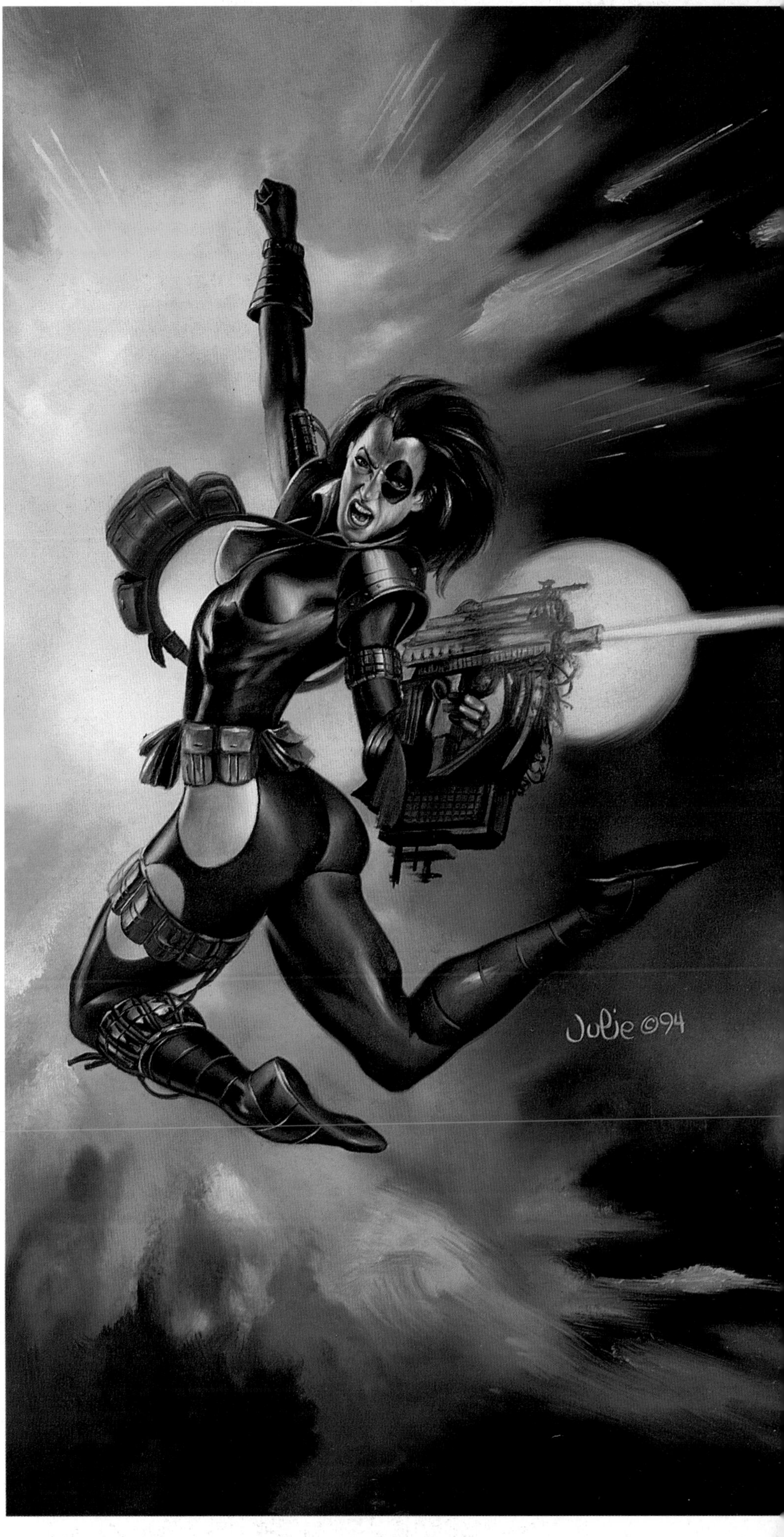
Julie ©94

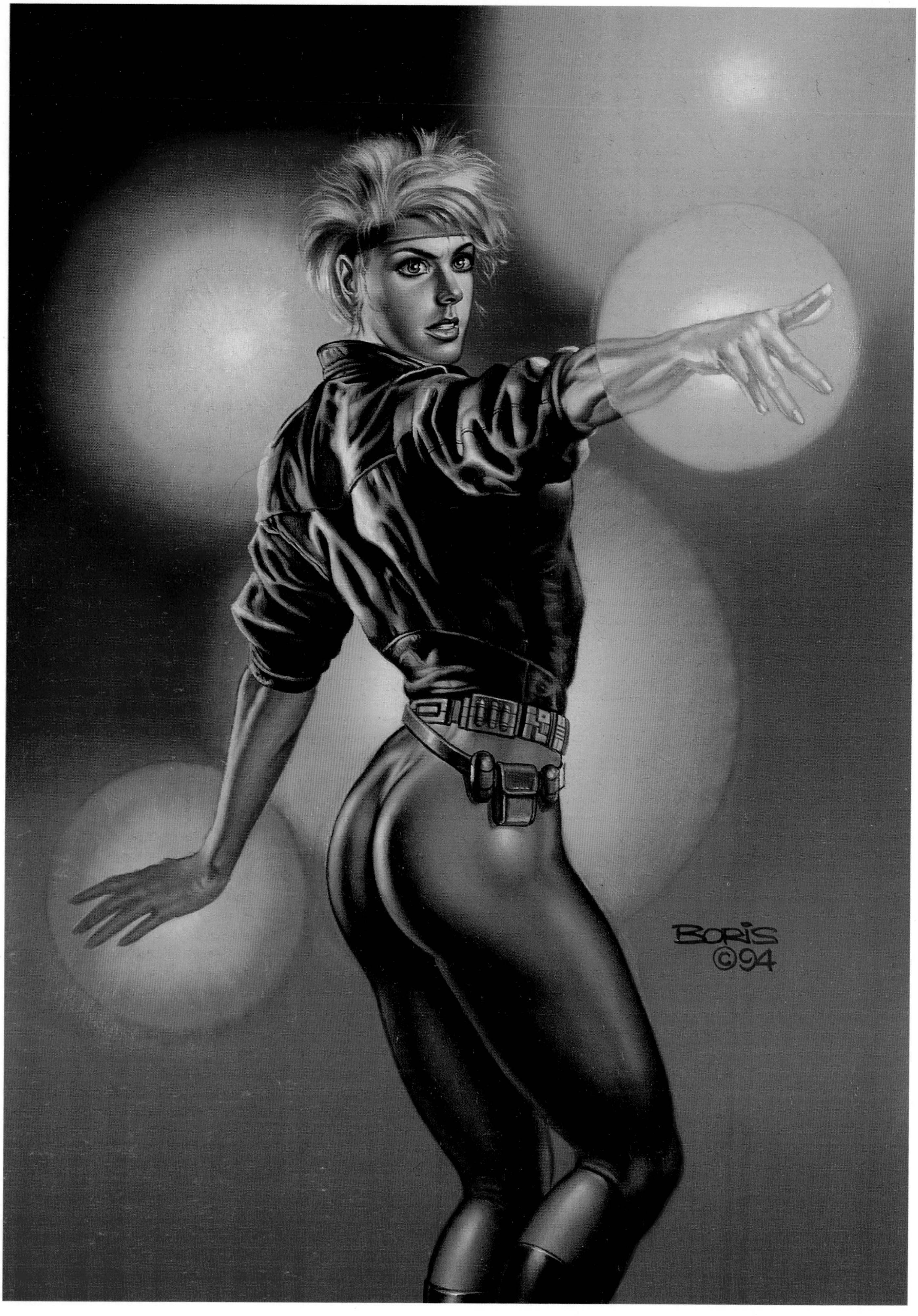
BORIS
©94

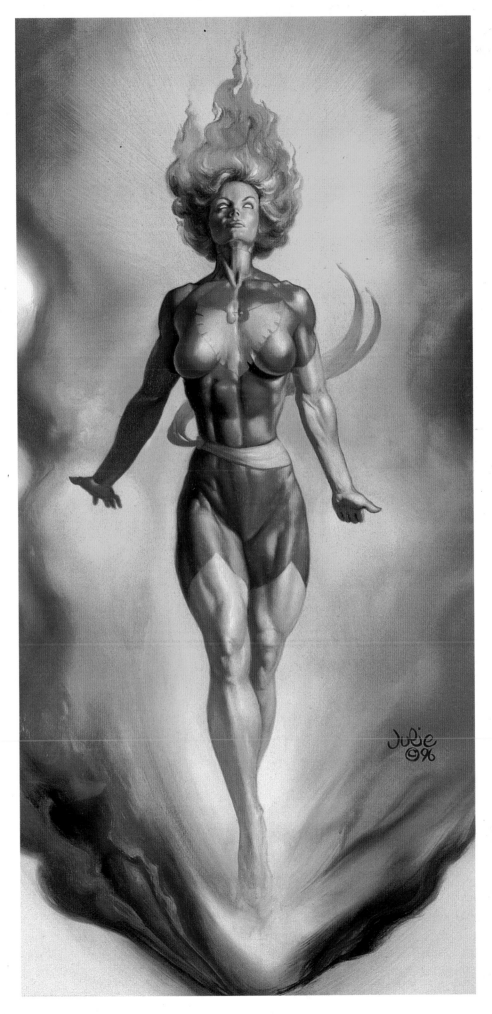

(far left)

DAZZLER

1994, Boris
Trading Card. Fleer Publishing Co.
TM & © 1994 Marvel Characters, Inc.
All rights reserved.
Dazzler, formerly known as Disco
Dazzler, was briefly a member of the X-
Men before going on to lead the Rebel
Underground in Mojoworld. Her talent
is converting sound into light.

(left)

PHOENIX II

1996, Julie
Trading Card. Fleer Publishing Co.
TM & © 1996 Marvel Characters, Inc.
All rights reserved.
Phoenix II, a.k.a. Rachel Summers, is the
daughter of Jean Grey and Scott
Summers in an alternate reality (where
in fact they both get killed, along with
most of the X-Men). Attempting to go
back in time to change history in her
own reality, she lands in the mainstream
Marvel universe at a point where Jean
Grey is believed dead, but is in fact only
in a coma. For reasons that are
fascinating but far too complex to go
into here, she adopts her 'mother's' X-
Men name and when Grey revives
Rachel becomes Phoenix II.

(right)

PHOENIX II VS MAGNETO

1996, Julie

Trading Cards. Fleer Publishing Co.

Rachel has formidable superpowers that she has still not fully explored. Being host to the impersonal Phoenix Force that saved Jean Grey, she is often surrounded by a bird-like aura and, in the right circumstances, can manipulate time, space, energy and matter to almost limitless extent. She can discharge bolts of vast energy and is a mistress of illusion. A worthy opponent for Magneto, whose powers also often seem almost limitless. Magneto's main talent is the manipulation of electromagnetic forces, by which he can also manipulate matter. He also has considerable psychic powers.

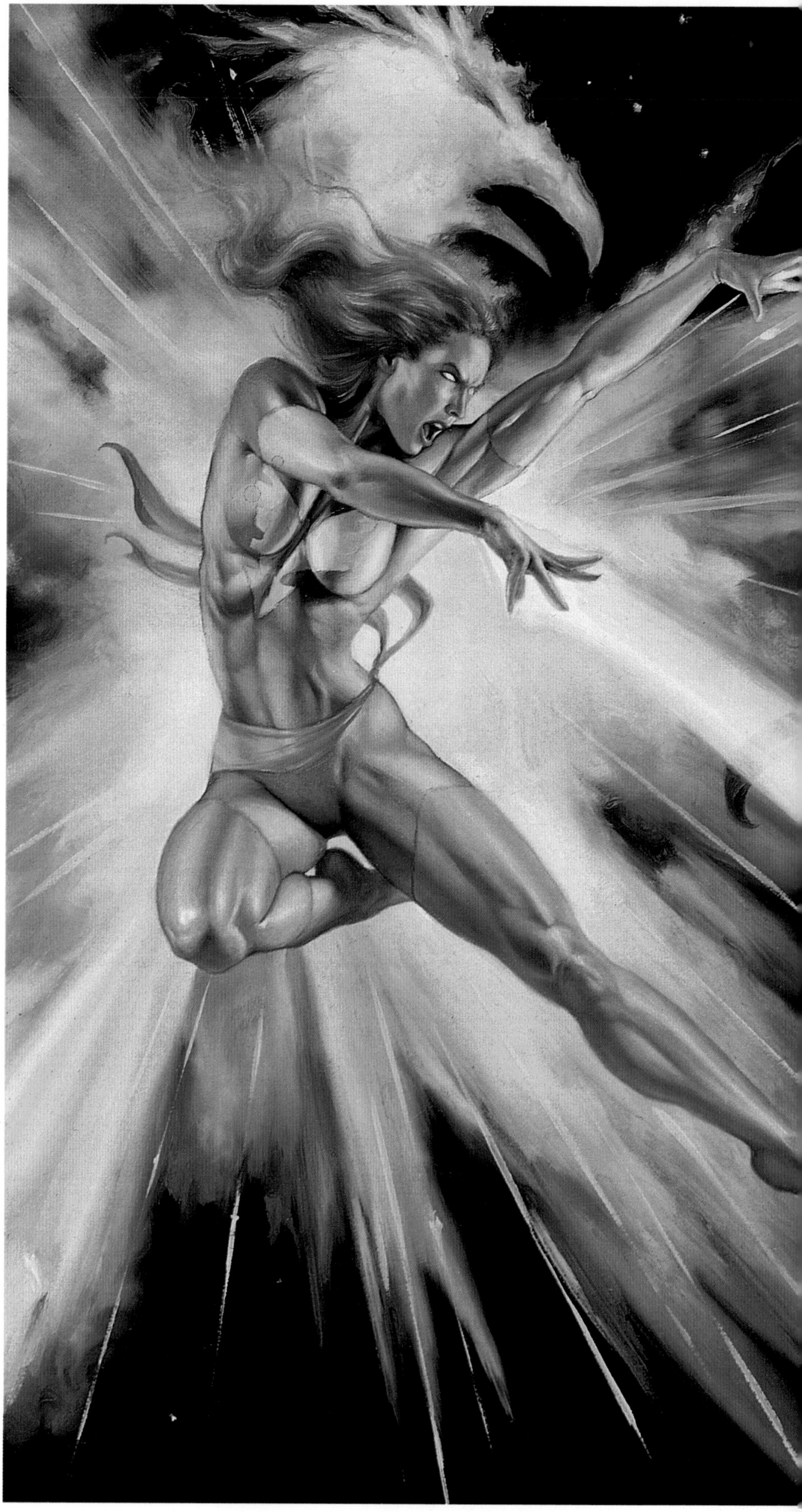

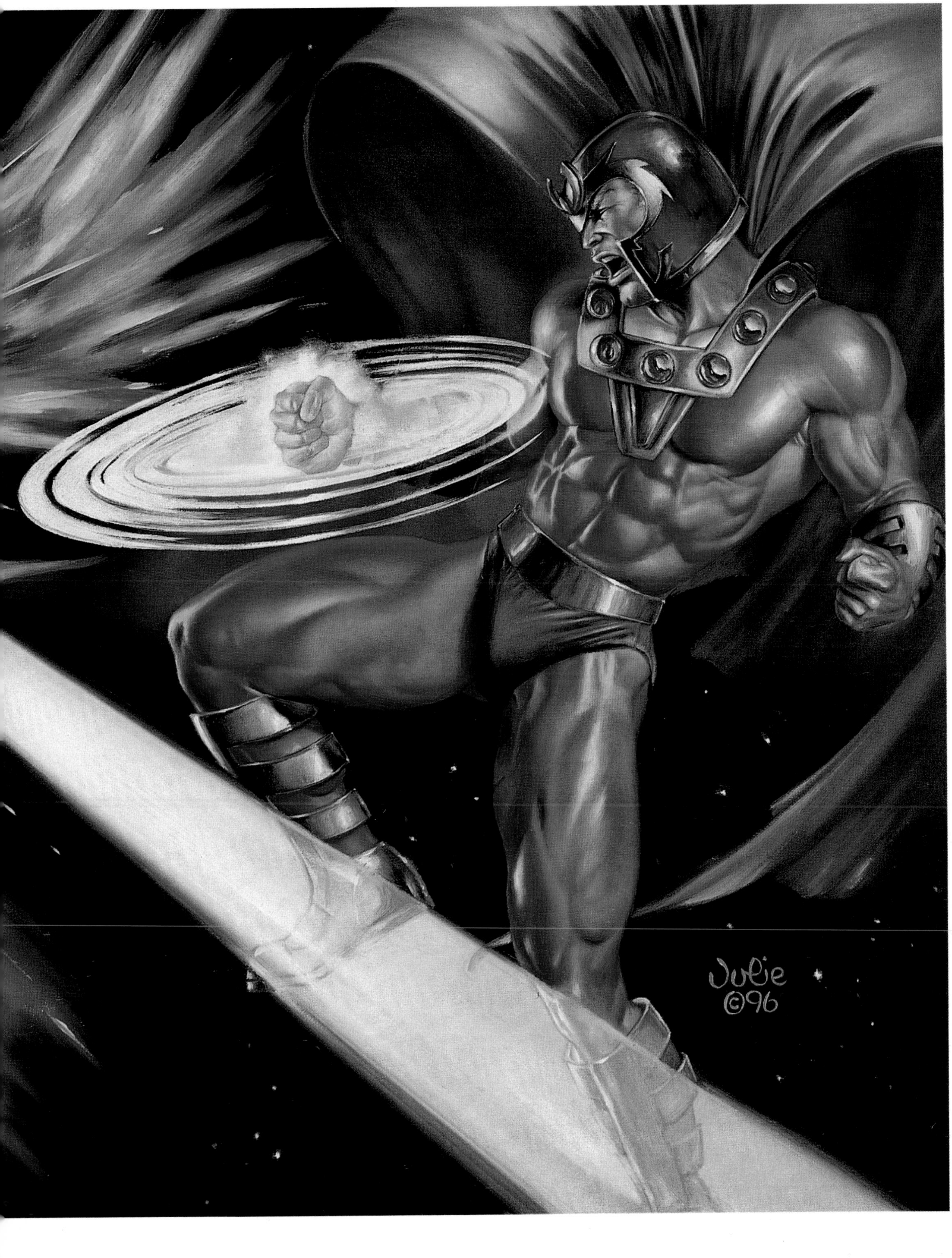
Julie
©96

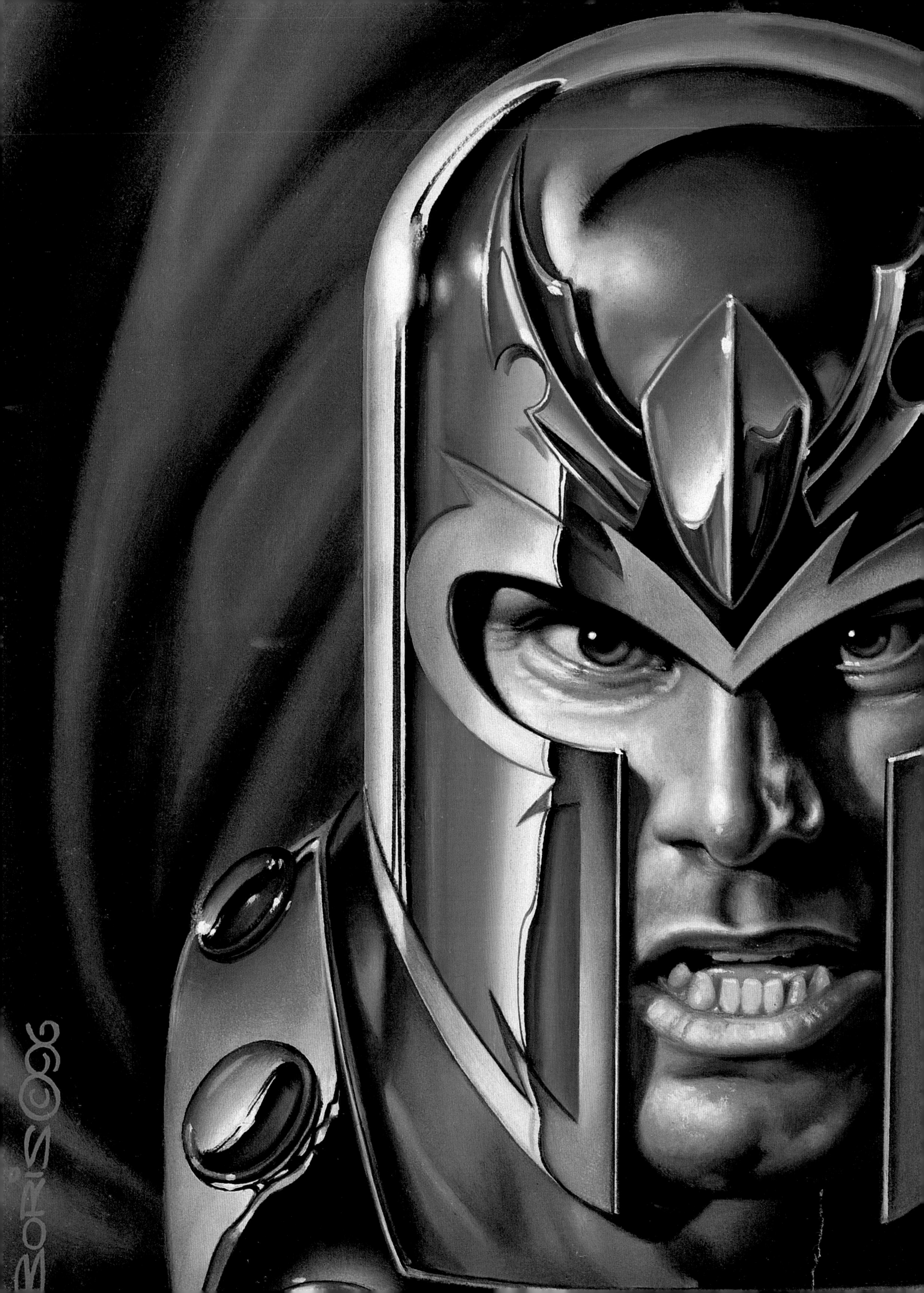
BORIS©96

X-MARAUDERS

(left)

MAGNETO

1996, Boris

Trading Card. Fleer Publishing Co.

Everyone loves a good villain, especially if there is a degree of ambivalence, which is definitely the case with Magneto. Mostly he is the X-Men's arch foe, but he has on occasion been their ally and began as a great friend of Professor X. They met in Israel after the Second World War and had heated debates about the problem of coexistence between humans and mutants. Having survived Auschwitz, Magneto (or Magnus as he was then known) had jaundiced views about likely human tolerance towards mutants, while Xavier dreamed of peaceful coexistence. They next met as enemies after Magneto declared war on all humans.

Boris and Julie live in Pennsylvania within easy reach of New York, which is useful for business and also pleasure, as it is the undisputed (well, by New Yorkers anyway) cultural capital of the United States. But they both came from very different environments, Texas and Peru. Do they have a dormant urge to move elsewhere sometime in the future? Perhaps even to another country?

Not really, it seems. They love the East Coast, and Pennsylvania in particular. They love the weather and the people, it really is their favourite place. Julie still loves to travel, to Arizona especially, where she often goes to refresh her spirit. She also enjoys revisiting Texas, but only for a change. Boris says he has become a very 'homey' person and doesn't really go for travel any more. Their house is fairly big but sometimes it feels cramped for space and could maybe do with extending, but that is about the size of his restlessness. If some reason came up that forced them to think of moving, he really wouldn't know what to say.

But basically as long as he is with Julie he is happy. Julie agrees, and adds that when they are travelling, it doesn't matter how small and unexciting the town they happen to find themselves in, they're happy as long as they're together.

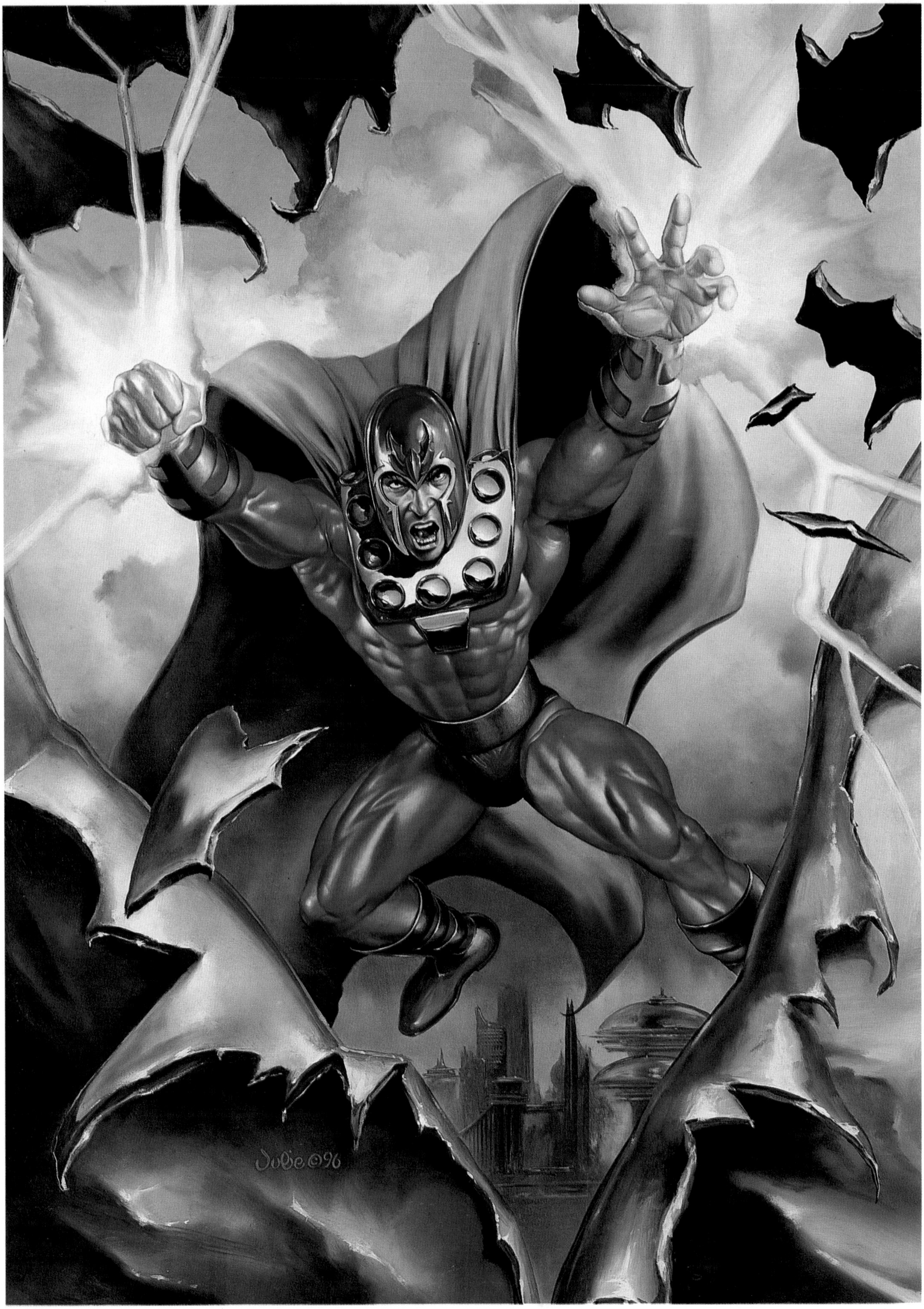
Julie ©96

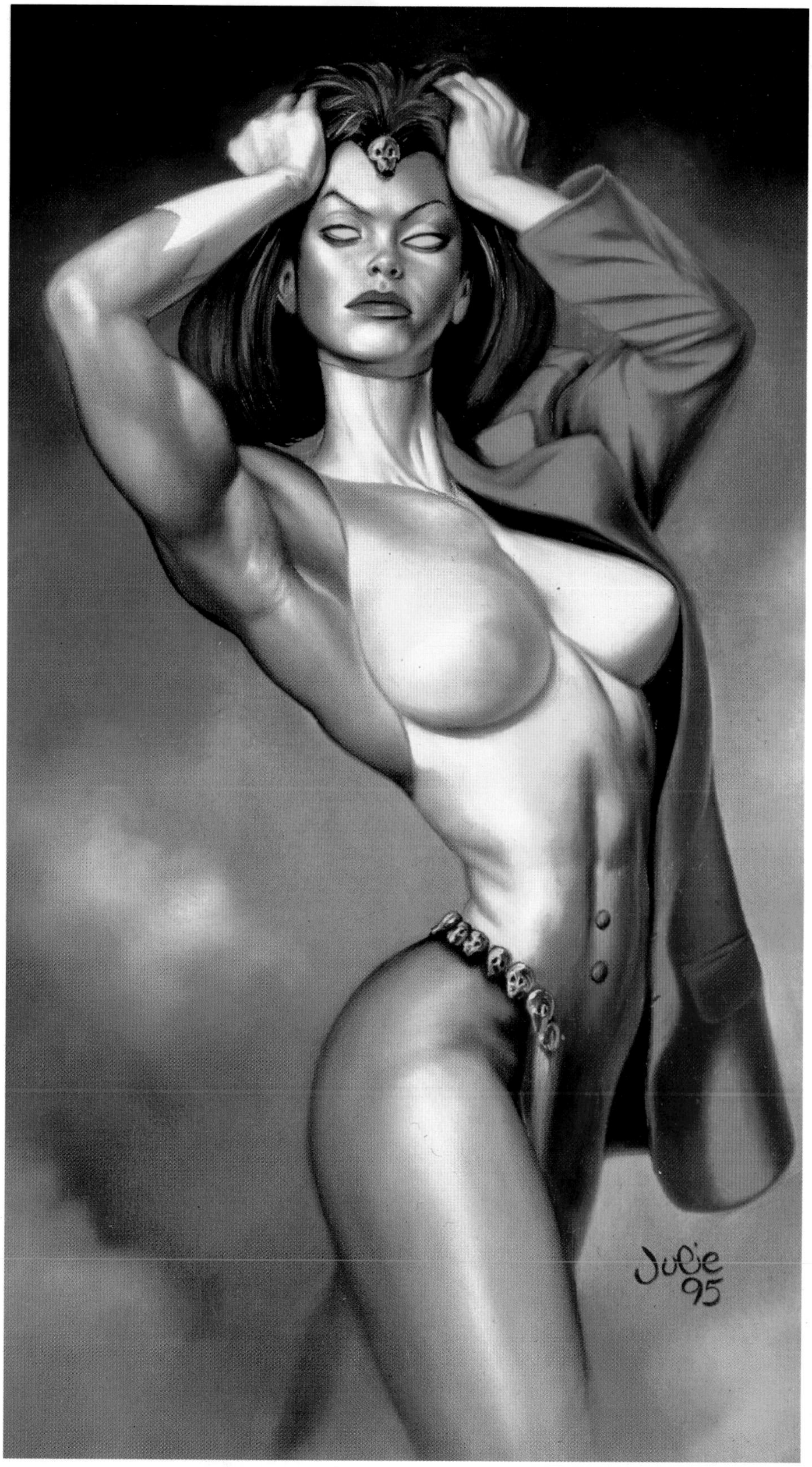
Julie
95

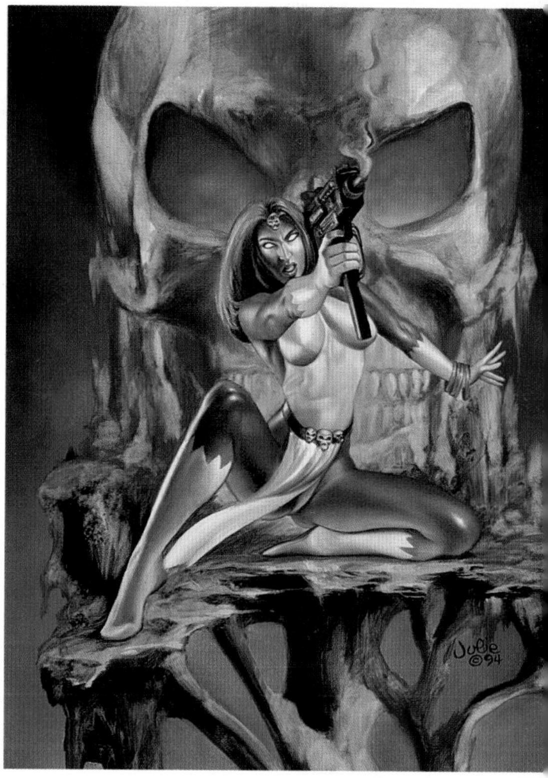
Julie
©94

(left)

MYSTIQUE

1995, Julie

Trading Card. Fleer Publishing Co.

Founder of the Third Brotherhood of Evil Mutants, Mystique (Raven Darkholme) is a shape-shifter who can exactly assume the form (and clothing) of any other humanoid. She thus maintains another identity as the respectable wife of a US senator, and yet another as deputy director of a US defence agency, which has helped her criminal activities no end. By delivering Magneto into US government hands she managed to make the Brotherhood outwardly respectable, changing its name to the Freedom Force.

(left)

MAGNETO 2

1995, Julie

Trading Card. Fleer Publishing Co.

Occasionally Magneto has had a change of heart and was even briefly put in charge of Xavier's School for Gifted Youngsters, but this is more commonly how the X-Men encounter him.

(above)

MYSTIQUE 2

1994, Julie

Trading Card. Fleer Publishing Co.

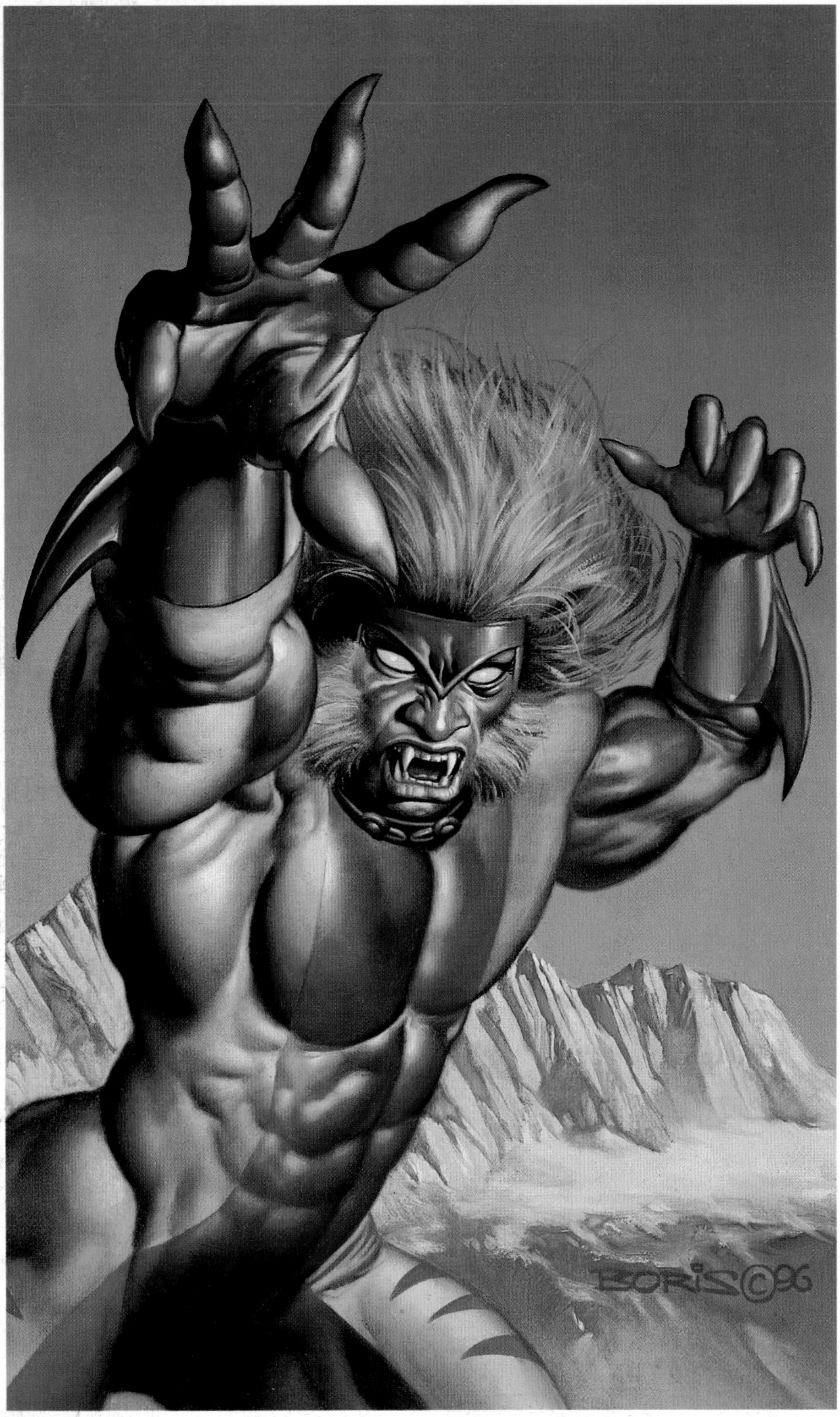
BORIS©96

(left)

SABRETOOTH

1996, Boris

Trading Card. Fleer Publishing Co.

A former ally and subsequent deadly enemy of Wolverine, Sabretooth is a psychotic killer gifted with heightened animal senses and a hyperfast ability to heal wounds. As the result of an affair with Mystique early in his life he fathered Gaydon Creed, an anti-mutant who ran for president of the US. As a member of the Marauders he took part in the massacre of the underground mutants known as Morlocks but has since operated independently.

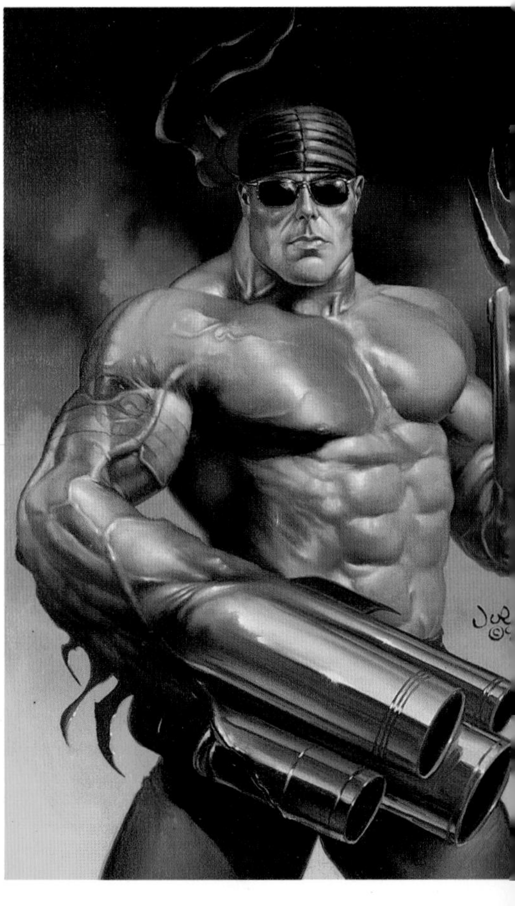

(right)

RANDOM

1996, Julie

Trading Card. Fleer Publishing Co.

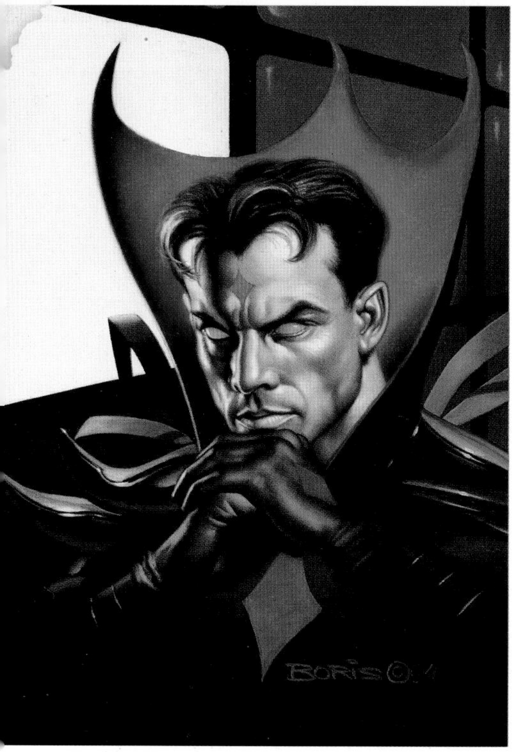

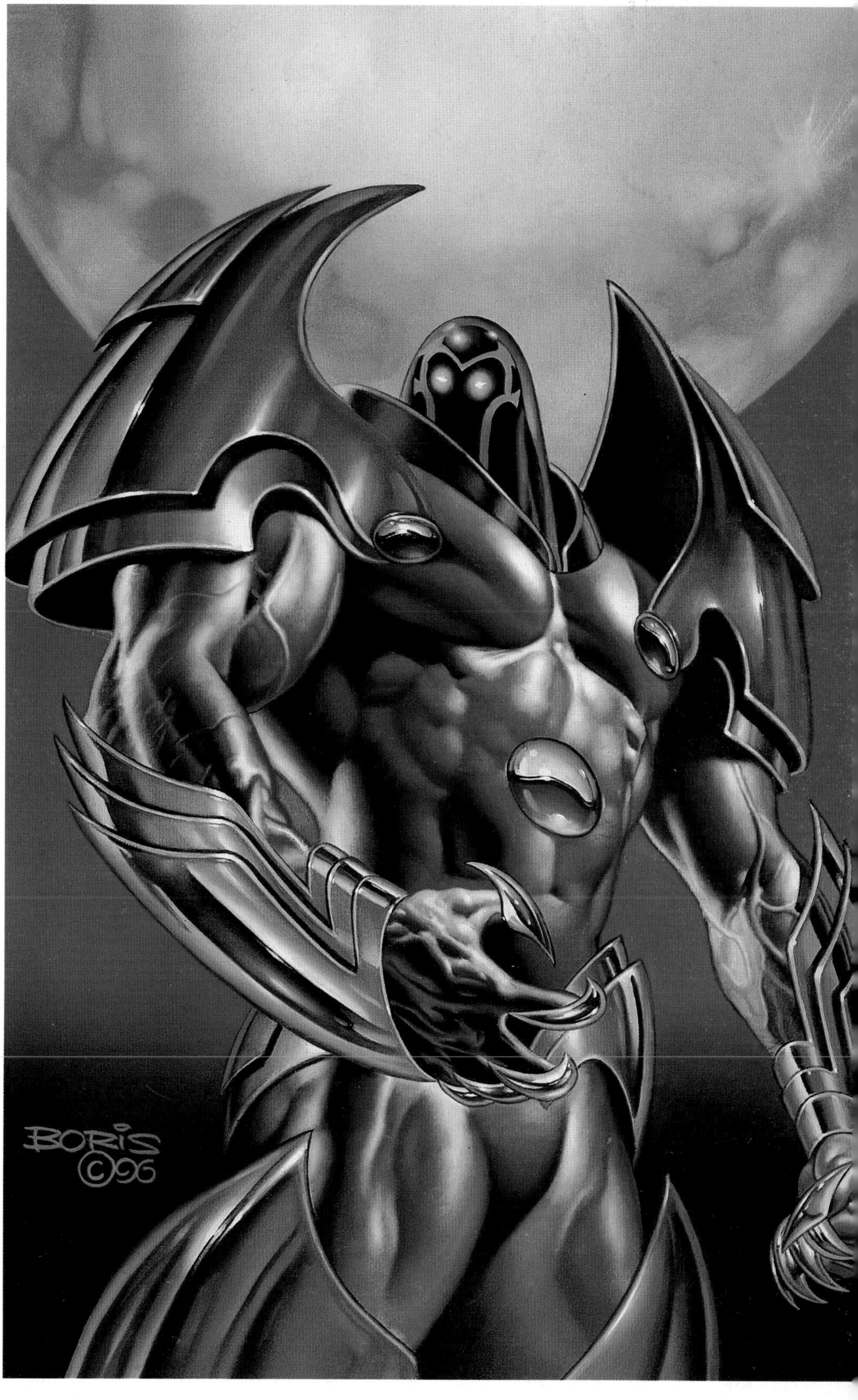

(above)

MISTER SINISTER

1994, Boris

Trading Card. Fleer Publishing Co.

Genetic engineer and founder of the Marauders assassins team, Sinister kept a record of their DNA so that whenever one was killed they could be replaced with a clone.

(right)

ONSLAUGHT

1995, Boris

Trading Card. Fleer Publishing Co.

Onslaught is an artificial being created from elements of the consciousness of Professor X and Magneto. During one battle Xavier used his telepathic powers to reach into Magneto's mind and shut it down. This worked but there was a backlash in which some of Magneto entered Xavier and latched onto his suppressed shadow self. From this mingling Onslaught emerged.

(right)

FITZROY

1993, Julie

Trading Card. Fleer Publishing Co.

TM & © 1993 Marvel Characters, Inc.

All rights reserved.

Like Bishop, who came to the mainstream Marvel timeline in pursuit of him, Fitzroy comes from the alternate future in which the X-Men are destroyed. A former Sentinel commander, he is now White Rook in the Hellfire Club.

(far right)

WAR MACHINE

1996, Julie

Trading Card. Fleer Publishing Co.

TM & © 1996 Marvel Characters, Inc.

All rights reserved.

War Machine is James Rhodes. Like Iron Man, his superpowers all come from his solar-powered armour and weaponry. Iron Man in fact created it for him so he could take his place during an absence. War Machine is not intentionally an enemy of the X-Men, quite the opposite in fact. He was a champion for WorldWatch International, a human rights group opposed to tyranny, but his extreme methods brought him into conflict with the X-Men and eventually Iron Man himself.

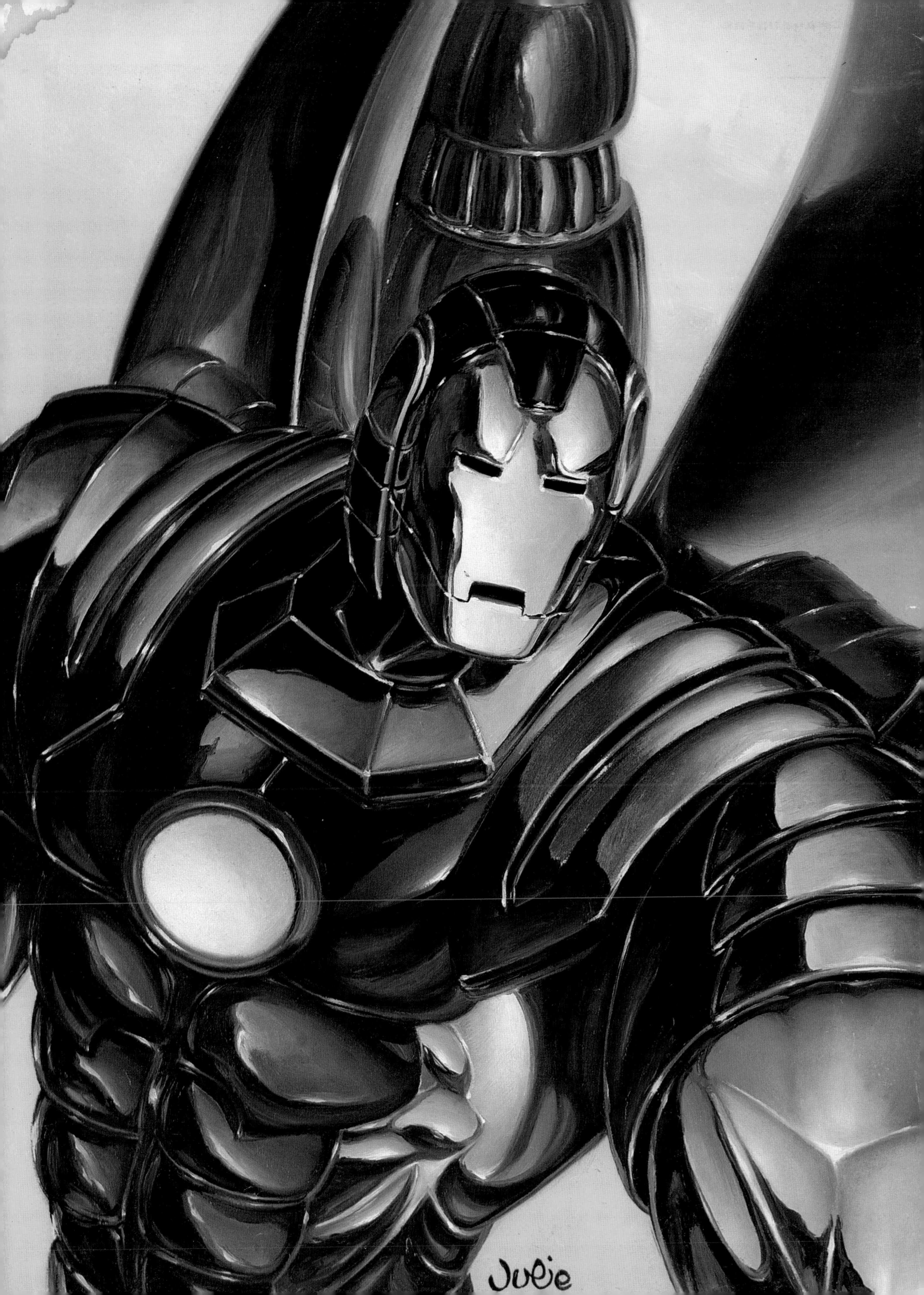
Julie

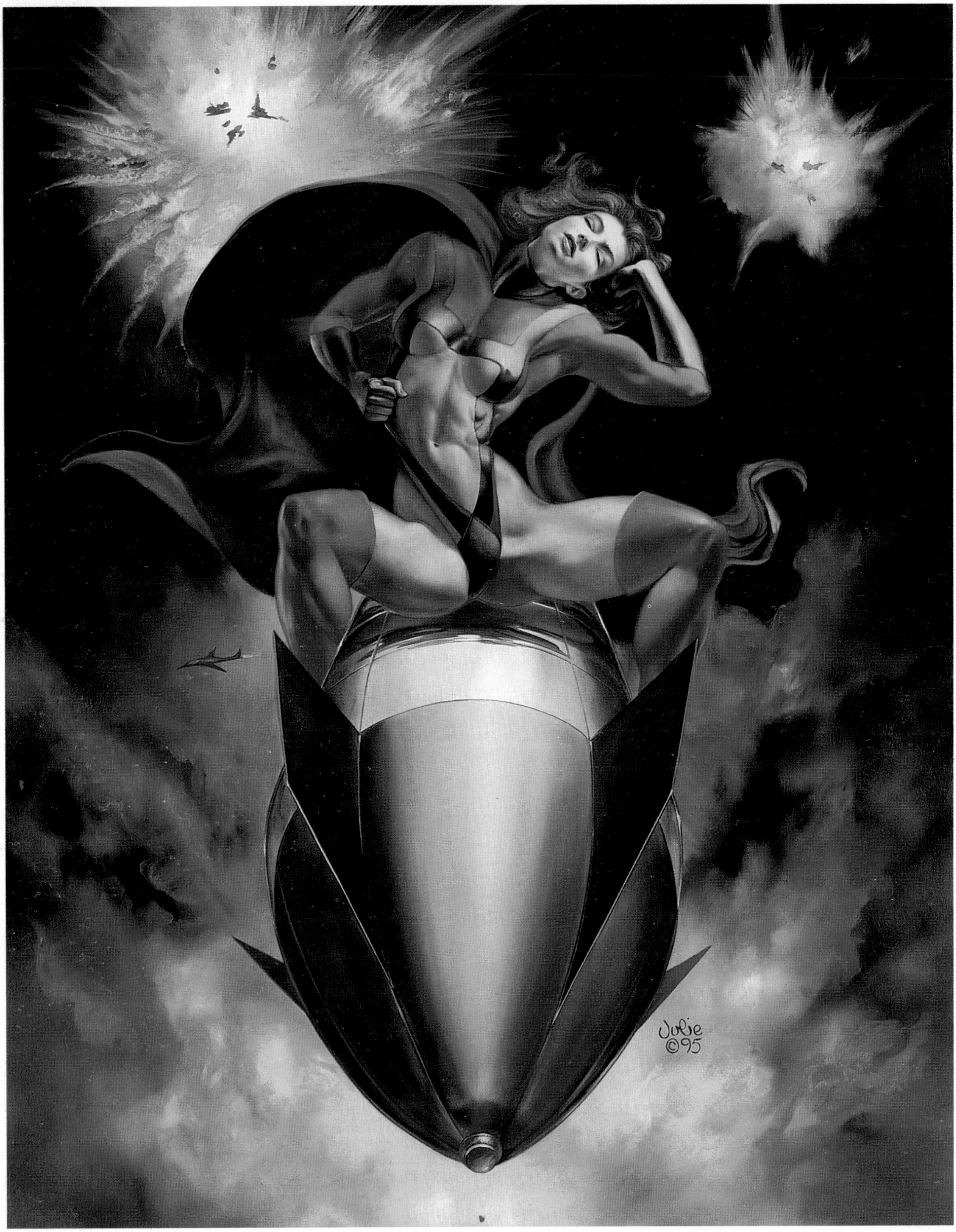
Julie
©95

HERICANE

1995, Julie

Cover. Penthouse Comix